HANDY GUIDE TO

VIRGINIA

WINERIES

—— 2018 Edition ——

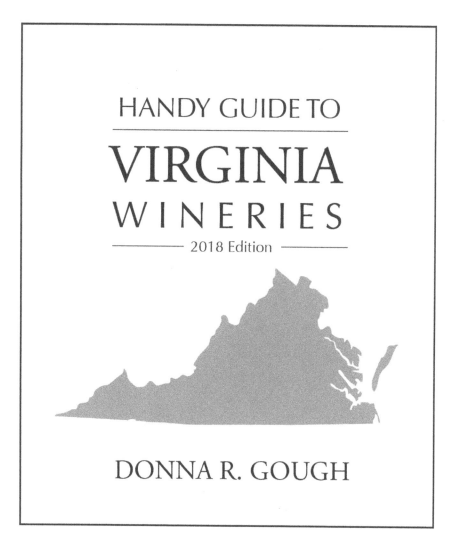

DONNA R. GOUGH

ISBN-10: 1974443787

ISBN-13: 978-1974443789

DEDICATION

To Amanda, in honor of her independence, personal strength, and unfailing dedication to and love for family and friends.

CONTENTS

MAPS

WINE BASICS

ACKNOWLEDGMENTS

For this 2018 edition, my thanks and appreciation continue to go out to the winery owners and employees who graciously shared their time and information with me. It has been a pleasure and an honor getting to know you and see how dedicated you all are to making Virginia wine great.

I also want to thank my fellow members of the Virginia Wine Mafia (especially Kurt Jensen, our unofficial leader) for their cheerful friendship, mutual support, and dedication to exploring Virginia wineries and wine.

And, of course, none of this would have been possible without the warm and continuous support of my family, who have all continued to join in exploring Virginia wineries with me, both revisiting familiar places and discovering new ones. Thank you!

All errors and inadvertent omissions in this book are mine alone.

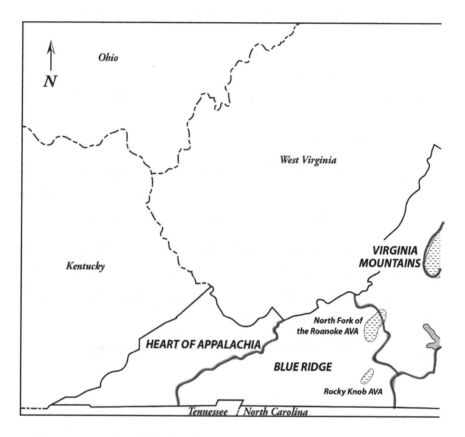

Map 1.1 Virginia Wine Regions & American Viticultural Areas (AVAs)

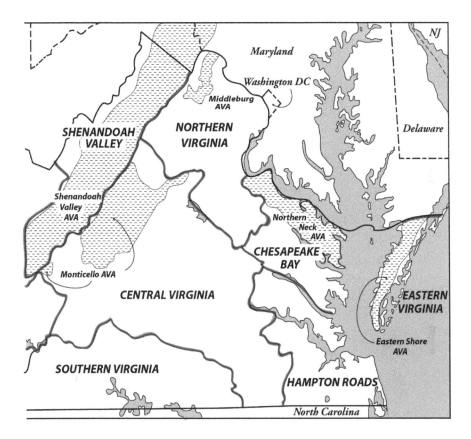

Map Legend

Roads and Road Symbols

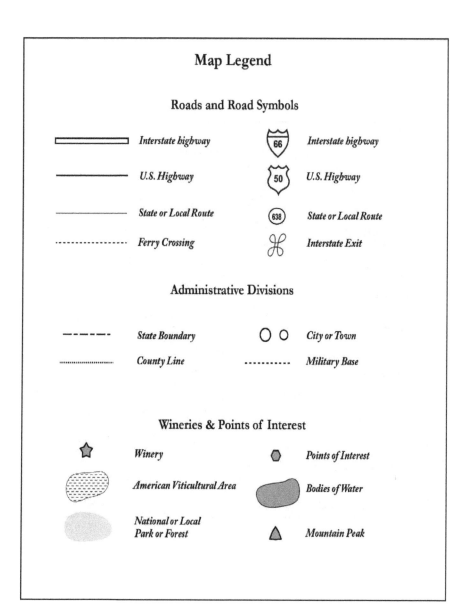

Interstate highway

Interstate highway

U.S. Highway

U.S. Highway

State or Local Route

State or Local Route

Ferry Crossing

Interstate Exit

Administrative Divisions

State Boundary

City or Town

County Line

Military Base

Wineries & Points of Interest

Winery

Points of Interest

American Viticultural Area

Bodies of Water

National or Local
Park or Forest

Mountain Peak

1. INTRODUCTION TO VIRGINIA WINERIES

Welcome to the world of Virginia wine! Virginia was the first American colony to grow grapes with the intent of making wine and is now the fifth largest wine producer in the country by number of wineries. Its diverse topography, geologic complexity, and numerous mesoclimates give rise to distinct differences in its wines, from dry to sweet, light to full-bodied. There are vineyards across the state, from the flat sandy soils on the Eastern Shore to the high slopes of the Blue Ridge and limestone basin of the Shenandoah.

Temperatures and precipitation vary not only from region to region but also from year to year, resulting in wide variations in vintages in a way that resembles France much more so than California. Summers in Virginia can alternate between cool and rainy or very hot and dry, seasonal differences that produce very different expressions of a wine's character and personality.

While Virginia's winemaking roots reach back to the first permanent English colony on America's shores, its modern wine industry is young, having blossomed only within the past forty years. And it is only even more recently that the reputation of Virginia wines has extended beyond state lines. To cite but one example, the Wine Enthusiast has extolled Virginia wine tourism and trails, with its online buying guide listing Virginia wines from around the state, with 21 receiving scores of "excellent" (90 or higher) and another 194 rated as "very good" (scores of 87 to 89). One personal anecdote: on a visit to Chicago, our daughter texted us a photo of a well-known restaurant's wine list that featured a Barboursville Chardonnay.

Updating the Handy Guide every year since March 2012 continues to be a great vantage point from which to spot trends in the Virginia wine industry that have emerged over that nearly four-year period. Here are some:

Numbers of wineries: This 2018 edition includes 224 wineries, a net increase of two over last year. The eight new (or newly opened to the public) wineries are: Eden Try, Quièvremont *(Northern Virginia)*; Brix and Columns, Marceline, Muse, Purple Wolf, Third Hill *(Shenandoah)*; Ashton Creek *(Central Virginia)*; and Iron Heart *(Blue Ridge)*. At the same time, seven either closed or now can be visited only by appointment: Athena, Belle Mount, Greenwood, Miller, and Seven Doors *(closed)* as well as Grey Horse and DelFosse (by appointment only). One winery, Hampton Roads, opened in 2016 but was inadvertently left out of the 2017 edition and has been added here.

Grape sources: The demand for Virginia-grown grapes continues to be high, which translates to more people planting new vineyards and expanding existing ones. While this will provide Virginia wineries with at least a steady source of grapes, it also means a growing, though still comparatively small, number of wineries that use out-of-state sources for their grapes, mainly from the West Coast. For winery visitors, that means it is always worth asking where the wines you are tasting are sourced.

Grape varieties: Virginia wineries produce varietals familiar to any wine drinker, such as Chardonnay, Cabernet Sauvignon, and Merlot. Over the years, the state's signature varietals are Cabernet Franc and Viognier, which is Virginia's official grape, although Petit Verdot and Chambourcin are growing in use and popularity. But several winery owners continue to experiment with other varieties, including Austria's Grüner Veltliner and Zweigelt (Ox-Eye), as well as Sauvignon Gris (Boxwood), a clonal mutation of Sauvignon Blanc found in limited quantities in France and Chile.

❖ ❖ ❖

This book starts with a brief review of the history of grape growing and winemaking in Virginia. Each of Virginia's ten wine regions has its own chapter that begins with an introduction along with a snapshot of things to see and do, including the various wine trails in the area. The wineries are grouped along those regional lines with a few exceptions. For the larger wine regions, wineries are further sorted into geographic clusters for ease of trip planning. Only those wineries with regular tasting room hours are included in this guide. All information is current as of September 15, 2017.

For each winery, the address and contact information is provided, as well as usual business hours and seasonal closings. However, always check the website to be sure as closing times may change, particularly if the winery can be rented for weddings or special events. A brief description of the facilities and features is offered, including a sampling of special events and festivals, whether the winery may be rented for special occasions, and, if known, whether children or pets may accompany visitors.

Wines: Each winery's wines are sorted by type, from sparkling to sweet. While the wines you find when you visit will vary as the year progresses, this list will provide a window into the styles and types of wines at a given winery to help tailor your visit according to your interests and preferences. Please be aware that even wines labeled as varietals may be a blend that includes up to 25 percent of another grape variety. While many Virginia wineries produce reserve wines, these are not listed separately as their availability will vary from year to year, depending on the quality of a given vintage. Similarly, library wines are not included, as their availability may vary considerably.

If you spot a specific varietal or blend that intrigues you, always call ahead to confirm if it is still available if that is one of the main goals of your visit. Many of Virginia's wineries are small producers and often run out of a given vintage. Advance research will help prevent disappointment.

Tastings: Most wineries charge a tasting fee that may vary depending on the number of wines or special vintages being sampled. In some cases, souvenir glasses convey with the tasting, particularly for groups. In addition, wineries occasionally offer a discount depending on the amount of wine purchased. If no tasting fee is specified, the tasting is complimentary. At small wineries, tastings are often handled informally, with guests paying for their tasting at the very end. However, many high-volume wineries require that a tasting ticket be purchased first.

Groups: Most wineries require advance reservations for groups, especially of six or more. Please note that some wineries limit the size of groups they will accept, and some do not permit van, bus, or limo tours at all. Check the winery listings for more details. If you are planning to tour wineries with friends or family, call at least one day in advance to confirm that the tasting room can accommodate your group. This is especially helpful for smaller wineries with limited space in their tasting rooms. Weekends have become very popular times for group tours, particularly in the northern Virginia and Charlottesville areas. Early reservations can make all the difference.

Hours: Call ahead to confirm closing times and last pours if you are planning to arrive late in the day. A number of Virginia wineries rent out their spaces for private parties, dinners, or weddings, and may close earlier than the posted hours to accommodate a special event.

Food: Cheese, crackers, and often cold cuts are available for purchase at many wineries, especially those that also offer tables either inside the tasting area or outside on patios and decks. Some wineries also allow guests to bring their own food for a picnic on the grounds. Always call or e-mail first to determine a particular winery's restrictions if you are planning to bring food.

Alcoholic Beverages: Most wineries sell their wine by the glass or bottle. Please note, however, that Virginia state law prohibits the consumption of any alcoholic beverage on winery property that was not produced by that winery itself. If you are planning to snack or picnic at a winery, be prepared either to bring water or soft drinks, or to purchase wine on-site to have with your food.

Pets: A number of wineries are pet-friendly and allow leashed, well-behaved dogs on the winery grounds, though Virginia law prohibits dogs in the tasting rooms. A few, such as Breaux Vineyards, even host Dog Days that are very popular with two- and four-legged visitors alike. Even pet-friendly wineries may not allow pets during special events and festivals. Check the events calendar for any restrictions, or call ahead to confirm that your pet will be able to join you on the grounds. Pet-friendly wineries will be identified as such in the winery description.

Children: Rules on children vary from winery to winery. Many welcome children and families while others restrict access to adults twenty-one and older. Wineries can be boring places for children, and bored children often are eager to let adults know just how unhappy they are. If you are planning a family excursion to Virginia's wine country, it's easy to map out an itinerary that focuses on wineries offering adequate indoor and outdoor spaces for children to amuse themselves. Child-friendly wineries will be identified as such in the winery description.

Purchasing: All Virginia wineries offer their products for sale in the tasting room, but not all offer telephone or e-mail ordering, and their ability to ship to out-of-state customers can vary significantly. If nothing is listed in the Purchasing section, the winery does not ship at this time but always check with the tasting room as restrictions can quickly change.

Directions: Basic driving directions to each winery are given from the closest major highway, either an interstate highway, U.S. highway, or major parkway. Please keep in mind that some winery addresses are not easily recognized by computer mapping sites or by GPS, particularly if the winery is located off the beaten track. Two good atlases to consider are the *Virginia State Road Atlas* (American Map) and the *Virginia Atlas and Gazetteer* (DeLorme). The *Virginia State Road Atlas* is easier to read and has more wineries marked; the *Gazetteer* is a topographic map that provides more details and a good sense of the terrain, but it is harder to decipher.

A Final Note: Wine tastings and tasting tours can be a fun and enjoyable way to spend a weekend afternoon. However, even small pours can add up to a considerable amount of alcohol when multiplied over numerous samplings. It is also worth noting that under Virginia law, all wineries have the right to refuse service to patrons who are noticeably intoxicated. Please be responsible and choose either a designated driver or use one of the many wine country tour groups now operating in the state.

As mentioned earlier, please keep in mind that Virginia's Department of Alcoholic Beverage Control (ABC) has ruled that the only alcoholic beverages permitted on winery grounds are wines produced by that winery itself. Please leave any other alcoholic beverages, including wines from other wineries, in your car, limo, or tour bus.

The guide also includes a bibliography, information on Virginia wine trails and Virginia wine blogs, a glossary of wine and wine-related terms (including the grape varieties used in Virginia wines), an alphabetical index of Virginia's wineries, and a general index at the very end.

For readers already familiar with Virginia wines, this guide may introduce you to wineries and wines you might not otherwise have tried. For visitors who are new to the state, it provides a broad overview of the vibrancy and diversity of all that Virginia has to offer. For everyone, may this guide help you discover something new about Virginia and its wines.

Cheers.

2. THE HISTORY OF WINEMAKING IN VIRGINIA

Virginia is credited with a number of "firsts" in American history: the first permanent English settlement in North America; the site of the first representative assembly in the American colonies; the birthplace of the first President of the United States. What is less well known is that Virginia can also be called the birthplace of winemaking in the United States, although its rise as a wine-producing state was long in coming and, until recent years, marked more often by failure than success.

But why would English colonists in early Virginia even try to cultivate grapes, much less to make wine from them? After all, England was never one of the great wine-producing countries in Europe. It has no long history of grape cultivation and no deeply rooted wine culture. In the seventeenth century, as now, England's alcoholic production and consumption centered around beer, ale, and hard cider, not wines—and certainly not fine wines.

The answer lies both in the natural resources the colonists found in Virginia when they arrived and in the governing structures and aims of the Jamestown colony in its early years.

A COLONY IN SEARCH OF A PRODUCT

In the late sixteenth century, England lagged far behind other European countries—especially its archrival, Spain—in wealth, power, and prestige, and English leaders were determined to catch up. Trade offered the best prospect for doing just that, and English merchants and investors launched numerous ventures aimed at either breaking into trade relationships in

Africa and the East or exploring new opportunities in lands across the Atlantic. Nearly all these initiatives were set up in England as joint stock companies, a structure that allowed investors to pool their resources and finance projects in the expectation of sharing in the profits.

In 1606, the London Virginia Company was established to finance and direct an exploratory venture in the general Chesapeake Bay area. The company's goal was to establish a small colony that would uncover a marketable commodity—gold, spices, or dyes, for instance—to serve as a foundation for trade between the native peoples and England, much as the French had successfully done in establishing a lucrative fur trade with native tribes in Quebec some years earlier. One result of their efforts was the English colony at Jamestown, founded the year after the Virginia Company was launched.

As Jamestown passed its tenth anniversary, however, the colony was still searching for products that would help it become self-sufficient and profitable. Colonists shipped various goods back to England—sassafras, clapboard, and pitch, among others—but their marketability was limited because of distance and cost. Officers in the London Virginia Company offered ideas as well, sending to the colony silkworms and silk experts, ironworkers and refiners, and glassblowers from Italy, but none of these projects panned out. Tobacco was growing in popularity and importance as colonists became more skilled at its cultivation and processing, but it had not yet become the breakthrough crop that would fuel Virginia's future growth.

From the colony's earliest days, Jamestown settlers also explored the production of another commodity: wine. The region was rich in native grapevines, and the colonists soon turned to producing a quickly made and highly alcoholic wine. The fact that wine was being produced was noted by several of Jamestown's early leaders—as was the fact that this wine was not high in quality. Upon being appointed Governor of Virginia in 1610, for instance, Lord Delaware sent a cask of Virginia wine to London, "sour as it is." About the same time, Colony Secretary William Strachey wrote that he had tasted wine in Jamestown made by a Doctor Bohoune, Virginia's first named winemaker, describing it as "strong and heady."

By 1619, Sir Edwin Sandys had assumed the leadership of the Virginia Company. That year was known for three pivotal events: the first slaves brought from Africa; the granting of land to male settlers; and the creation of the Virginia Assembly, the first representative governmental body in America. During the Assembly's initial session, delegates enacted measures on land distribution, tobacco prices, mulberry cultivation for silkworms, and hemp production to help improve the colony's economic health.

Delegates also passed "Acte 12," a measure that required every house-holder to "yearly plante and maintaine ten vines, untill they have attained to the arte and experience of dressing a Vineyard, either by their owne indus-try, or by the Instruction of some Vigneron." The Virginia Company also arranged for eight French vignerons, or vineyardists, to go to Jamestown to help kick-start the effort. In 1621, King James I gave an extra push to the fledgling industry by ordering that translations of a French manual on cultivating vines be sent to the colonists.

All these efforts ultimately fizzled out, as the colonists increasingly turned to the much more lucrative tobacco as their cash crop of choice.

For roughly the next 50 years, Virginia's leaders continued to gently prod colonists toward vine cultivation, including dispatching more vineyard experts, importing European grape stock, even establishing a prize for any-one who could produce "two tunne of wine out of a vineyard made in this colony." Ultimately all their efforts proved unsuccessful. Some colonists dutifully planted vines and cultivated vineyards, but fungus and mildew—as well as the still unknown phylloxera louse—took their toll on the imported vines, while the profitability of the tobacco leaf lured others away.

Despite the frustrations and ultimate failures, however, the seeds of Virginia's future wine industry had been planted.

GENTLEMEN FARMERS AND THEIR VINES

In the decades that followed, records both public and private are largely silent about grape cultivation and wine production in Virginia. Judging from the occasional references to Virginia wine, some vineyards of native root-stock did exist and some wine was indeed produced. But ordinary farmers would not have been engaged in winemaking, since cultivating and tending to tobacco, the main cash crop of the colony, was a labor-intensive endeavor that demanded constant attention and time in the fields. They simply had no time to spare to indulge in an effort that had little to do with the hard business of eking out a living.

Instead, what winemaking occurred in Virginia during this period was done by the well-to-do, particularly members of Virginia's "First Families," a network of wealthy landowners often related by intermarriage. Only they would have had the time and financial resources to invest in planting a vineyard and attempting to make wine. As plantation owners whose fortunes rose and fell with the value of tobacco, these gentlemen farmers would also have had an economic interest in developing an alternative crop for export, such as wine.

One such individual was Robert Beverley, a large landowner and author of the first history of Virginia. In 1709, Beverly planted a three-acre vineyard of native grapes in King and Queen County to the north of what is now Richmond. Six years later, the Irish diarist John Fontaine visited Beverley's home and reported that his vineyard had produced about four hundred gallons of wine, adding that they "were verry merry with the wine of his own making and drunk prosperity to his vineyard."

By 1722, Beverley was producing roughly 750 gallons a year of wine, which was described by a local pastor as being similar in taste to claret and as strong as port, suggesting it had been fortified with additional alcohol. Beverley died that same year, however, and his heirs proved less interested in viticulture than he had been.

About that same time, Beverley's brother-in-law, William Byrd, became intrigued with the idea of grape cultivation. In the 1720s, he planted a vineyard of about twenty native grape varieties at his Westover Plantation on the James River. Byrd was an astute businessman, and his initial successes helped persuade some of his neighbors to consider planting their own vines as well. Within ten years, however, his vineyards fell victim to harsh frosts and insect infestations, and his efforts at grape cultivation ended.

In the late 1750s, Charles Carter—another First Family member—also began cultivating grapes at his Cleve plantation in King George County. By 1762, Carter had planted around 1,800 vines and sent twelve bottles of wines made from a native American grape and from what he described as a "white Portugal summer grape" to the London Society for the Encouragement of the Arts to demonstrate the quality of his product.

Grape cultivation and wine production was not solely the purview of wealthy landowners, however. In 1769 Frenchman André Estave persuaded the Virginia House of Burgesses to provide him with land, money, and labor to establish a vineyard of both native and European grapes near Williamsburg. The endeavor ultimately collapsed when the European vines failed due to disease and pests, and Estave himself proved to be a failure at managing an estate.

By contrast, Colonel Robert Bolling from Buckingham County believed Virginia's wine potential lay with European, not native American, varieties. Bolling wrote an unpublished treatise on grape cultivation in the middle colonies, one of the earliest studies on the subject written by an American. Unfortunately, his efforts to promote the cultivation of southern European grapes in Virginia were cut short by his sudden death in 1775.

THOMAS JEFFERSON

Perhaps the most well-known "gentleman farmer" involved in early Virginia viticulture was Thomas Jefferson, who has become emblematic of Virginia wine even though he met with no success during his lifetime. In 1773, Jefferson met Philip Mazzei, a Florentine exporter who arrived in America in the hope of establishing commercial vineyards and olive farms in Virginia's back country. Captivated by the idea, Jefferson gave Mazzei two thousand acres near Monticello to build a house and establish a vineyard.

Mazzei brought in workers and rootstock from Italy and planted the vineyard with both European and native grape varieties. The European vines successfully fruited and produced flavorful grapes, but they soon withered on the vine. The vineyard fell into near-total neglect after Mazzei left for Europe in 1779 to raise funds for the American government during the Revolutionary War. He returned only once—briefly—and then spent the remainder of his days in Europe.

After leaving the White House in 1809, Jefferson revived his efforts to cultivate vines, corresponding frequently with John Adlum, often called the Father of American Viticulture. Adlum had succeeded in producing wine from both European and native grapes from his Georgetown vineyard in what is now the District of Columbia and provided Jefferson cuttings of various vines on several occasions. Jefferson's efforts invariably ended in frustration and failure, however, although he never lost interest and faith in the ultimate success of American viticulture.

POST-CIVIL WAR RISE AND DEMISE

In the nineteenth century, the American wine industry as a whole took root and expanded significantly, including in Virginia. The first commercially successful American winemaker was Nicholas Longworth, a wealthy Cincinnati businessman. Longworth's sparkling pink Catawba became wildly popular in the United States, and by the 1850s his winery was producing 100,000 bottles a year.

Although Longworth's vineyards had fallen victim to disease and withered by the time of his death in 1863, his success inspired potential American winemakers across the country, who began to try their hand at growing grapes and producing wine. In Virginia as well, farmers began considering their options for diversifying away from the labor-intensive tobacco. The most notable successes came from German immigrants who moved to Virginia after the Civil War.

The first of these vineyards was planted by William Hotopp, a Hanover native who had come to America around 1852. After establishing a successful business in New Jersey, Hotopp moved to Charlottesville in 1866 and purchased the Pen Park estate (the modern-day Pen Park and Meadow Creek Golf Course). Four years later, he began producing both red and white wines from his own vineyard in a winery he built to process his grapes.

In 1873, several other German grape growers led by Oscar Reierson founded the Monticello Wine Company, Virginia's first large-scale commercial winery. Their four-story winery located in the middle of what is now Perry Drive and McIntire Road in Charlottesville could process up to 200,000 gallons of wine, all from native American vines, including Virginia's own Norton grape, first cultivated in 1822.

Their success spurred others to follow suit in planting grapes, and by 1888, there were at least three thousand acres of vineyards in Albemarle County alone. By 1890, Virginia's wine industry ranked fifth in the United States, with a total production that year of 461,000 gallons.

Within two decades, however, wine production in the Commonwealth had all but disappeared. The Panic of 1893—second only to the Great Depression in its severity—struck Virginia hard, particularly its agricultural sector. Plant diseases also took their toll on the vineyards.

But it was the emerging temperance movement that ultimately played the greatest role in extinguishing Virginia's wine industry. The Anti-Saloon League was formed in Virginia in 1901 with the expressed purpose of banning the sale of alcoholic beverages. The League made rapid progress: by 1905, only thirty of the state's one hundred counties still allowed alcohol to be sold. And in September 1914, the Virginia legislature passed a state-wide prohibition law that made Virginia one of the earliest states to go "dry."

Five years later, the entire country followed suit with the ratification of the 19th Amendment, commonly termed Prohibition. Although Prohibition did not ban all commercial wine production—wine could still be produced commercially for sacramental and medicinal purposes—the net effect was the closure of most small wineries. States with mostly small wineries, such as Virginia, were particularly hard hit.

The ratification of the Twenty-First Amendment in December 1933 finally brought an end to Prohibition. Former wine-producing states throughout the country had to start almost from scratch to rebuild their wine industries. In Virginia, this rebuilding process was long in coming. From the end of Prohibition to the 1960s, Virginia regulators issued a grand total of twenty-two winery licenses, and all but four of these twenty-two wineries had closed their doors by 1970.

VIRGINIA VITICULTURE REBORN

In the early 1970s, Virginia's wine industry began to stir again. In 1973, Treville Lawrence helped found the Vinifera Wine Growers Association, which actively promoted the cultivation of European *Vitis vinifera* vines in Virginia and elsewhere on the East Coast. By 1980, half a dozen new wineries had opened, including several that are still in operation: Barboursville, Ingleside, Mountain Cove, Shenandoah, and Willowcroft.

The government of Virginia began to take an active interest in promoting the development of the state's wine industry. In 1980 the Virginia legislature passed a farm winery bill that required such wineries to have a producing vineyard in Virginia with facilities for bottling wine on the premises. The bill allowed sales at both the wholesale and retail levels, including on-site tasting rooms. Farm wineries were also permitted to buy grapes from other vineyards, as long as 75 percent of the grapes used in their wines were grown in Virginia.

This legislation allowed Virginia's wine industry to blossom. In 1980, Virginia had 286 acres under vine, a figure that grew nearly tenfold by 2011, reaching over 2,600 acres. Virginia vineyardists cultivate more than seventy different varieties of grapes, led especially by Dennis Horton, founder of Horton Winery and a pioneer in bringing Viognier to the United States, a varietal that is now one of Virginia's signature wines. Horton and Jennifer McCloud of Chrysalis Vineyards also have actively cultivated the Norton grape, restoring it to greater prominence in its state of origin.

Virginia winemakers themselves come from across the country and even the world. Whether from Canada, France, Germany, Greece, Italy, Lebanon, Portugal, South Africa, or Turkey, all are drawn to a winemaking community that is characterized by the same energy, determination, and vision that marked the state's earliest efforts. This wide variety in background, training, and experience is contributing additional vitality to a wine industry that is vibrant and ever-growing.

From fine wines that can compete on an equal basis with Europe's classic varieties to more homegrown wines that have long been part of America's wine production, there is truly something for all wine tastes and preferences in Virginia.

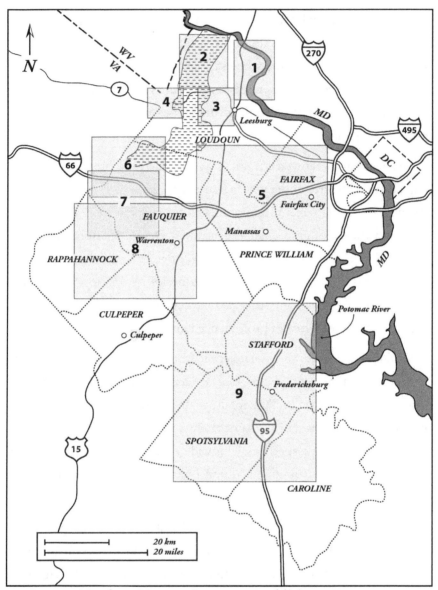

Map 3.1. Northern Virginia Region & Middleburg AVA:
(1) Leesburg North; (2) Northwest Loudoun; (3) Leesburg West;
(4) Bluemont; (5) Middleburg-Fairfax; (6) Delaplane;
(7) Northern Blue Ridge; (8) Warrenton; (9) Fredericksburg

3. NORTHERN VIRGINIA REGION & MIDDLEBURG AVA

The Northern Virginia wine region stretches from busy suburbs to small towns much calmer in pace and personality. Less than an hour's drive from our nation's capital are historic villages with deep colonial roots, working farms owned by the same families for generations, and winding country lanes that quickly go from paved to gravel.

Northern Virginia is home to about 80 wineries with regular tasting room hours, from small boutique operations that produce only a few hundred cases per year to larger wineries whose annual production is in the thousands. Given the region's proximity to Washington D.C. and its suburbs, wineries in this region can be crowded places on weekends, especially in summer months, with peak visiting hours from noon to 3:00 p.m.

The region's topography, soils, and climate are quite diverse. The crest of the northern Blue Ridge tops out at over 3,000 feet in elevation, sloping rapidly to the east in a sequence of rolling hills and broad basins. This pattern of mountains, hills, and valleys gives rise to numerous mesoclimates which help produce a rich variety of wines.

The Northern Virginia is also home to Virginia's newest American Viticultural Area, or AVA. The Middleburg AVA, approved in mid-2012, stretches from Loudoun County's border with Maryland down into Fauquier County at Little Cobbler Mountain.

❖ ❖ ❖

<u>Things to See and Do</u>: There are numerous activities and sites available for visitors in the Northern Virginia region. Historic town centers, such as Old Town Alexandria and downtown Fredericksburg, are filled with Colonial- and Civil War-era homes along with numerous restaurants and cafes. George Washington's Mount Vernon, just south of Alexandria, gives visitors a thorough introduction to our nation's first president and his home.

Northern Virginia also is dotted with many small villages that allow visitors a glimpse of life in early rural Virginia. Among others, these include Waterford, founded in 1733 by Quakers; Hillsborough, the birthplace of Susan Koehner Wright, mother of aviation pioneers Orville and Wilbur Wright; and "little" Washington, whose town grid was surveyed by George Washington in 1749.

The region includes several Heritage Trails that take visitors through sites of historic significance. The Journey Through Hallowed Ground (www.hallowedground.org), for instance, is a scenic 180-mile driving route from Charlottesville, Virginia to Gettysburg, Pennsylvania, featuring over 10,000 sites, including presidential homes, African American and Native American historical sites, and battlefields from the French and Indian War, Revolutionary War, and War of 1812.

The Trail to Freedom (http://www.trailtofreedomva.com) begins in Fredericksburg and is a combination walking-driving tour retracing the steps of an estimated 10,000 slaves who crossed the Rappahannock River beginning in May 1862 to put themselves under the protection of the Union Army that occupied the northern bank opposite that city.

Those interested in the Civil War can choose from a number of driving trails that explore the military history of that four-year war which touched Virginia more than any other state. Key battlefields in the Northern Virginia Region include Bull Run near Manassas, where two major battles were fought; Brandy Station, the war's largest cavalry battle; and the Fredericksburg area, including battlefields at Spotsylvania, Chancellorsville, and the Wilderness, where General Ulysses Grant began his pursuit of General Robert E. Lee that finally brought the war to an end. Self-guided tour maps and guides can be downloaded from Virginia's Civil War Trails website (www.civilwartraveler.com/EAST/VA/).

Nature lovers can choose from among several state parks and nature preserves that offer hiking, horseback riding, camping, and boating. These include Lake Anna, Mason Neck, and Sky Meadows State Parks; more information about these can be accessed at http://www.dcr.virginia.gov/state-parks/find-a-park. Hikers can follow the Appalachian Trail which crosses into Virginia at Clarke County and meanders south and west along the crest of the Blue Ridge Mountains. And the Shenandoah River is a popular rafting site, with several outfitters that will arrange a complete rafting trip for visitors.

❖ ❖ ❖

Wine Trails: Over a dozen Virginia wine trails include at least one winery in the Northern Virginia region. Trails that focus primarily on Northern Virginia wineries include the Blue Ridge Whiskey Wine Loop, the Blue Ridge Wine Way, Fauquier County Wine Trail, Loudoun Wine Country, and Vintage Piedmont. See Appendix 1 for more details on these and other wine trails.

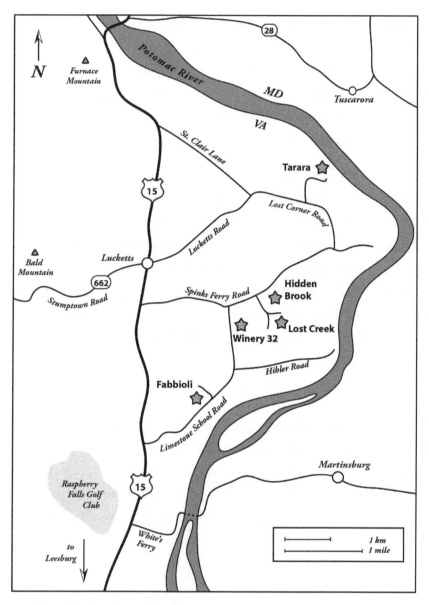

Map 3.2. Leesburg North

LEESBURG NORTH

Fabbioli Cellars
15669 Limestone School Road
Leesburg VA 20176

Hours: Daily 11:00–5:00
Closed New Year's, Thanksgiving, Christmas

703-771-1197
www.fabbioliwines.com
E-mail: info@fabbioliwines.com

Owner-winemaker Doug Fabbioli has been in the wine business in one way or another for thirty years, beginning with his studies at the University of California, Davis. After returning to the East Coast, Doug and wife Colleen Berg founded Fabbioli Cellars in 2000. The winery's tasting room offers several tasting stations for visitors. Be sure to check in first at the cash register to purchase your tasting ticket. Bread and cheeses are available for purchase and enjoyment indoors or on the outdoor patio area, which overlooks part of the Fabbioli vineyards. Fabbioli also sponsors a range of events, including a home winemaking class, an annual customer harvesting day, and occasional charity benefits. Pets are welcome.

Fruit Wines: Una Pera *(pear)*.

White Wines: Chardonnay, Something White, Viognier.

Rosé Wines: Rosa Luna *(Sangiovese)*.

Red Wines: Cabernet Franc, Chambourcin, Paco Rojo, Petit Verdot, Sangiovese, Tannat, Tre Sorelle *(Bordeaux-style blend)*, Zinfandel.

Sweet/Dessert Wines: Raspberry Merlot.

Fortified Wines: Aperitif Pear Wine, Rosa Nera (raspberry), Royalty *(port-style)*.

Price Range: $18–$45

Tastings: $15 per person (with food pairings).

Groups: Reservations required for any groups arriving by limo or bus.

Purchasing: Online ordering to most states available through the website.

Directions: From U.S. Route 15, turn onto Limestone School Road (Route 661) (portions unpaved) to the winery, 1.3 miles on the left.

❖ ❖ ❖

Hidden Brook Winery
43301 Spinks Ferry Road
Leesburg VA 20176

Hours: Sa–Su 11:00–5:00 (6:00 in summer); M, Th–F 12:00–5:00   703-737-3935
Closed New Year's, Thanksgiving, Christmas   www.hiddenbrookwinery.com
E-mail: info@hiddenbrookwine.com

Eric and Deborah Hauck established Hidden Brook in 1999, literally next door to Eric's parents, Bob and Carol Hauck, who founded Lost Creek Winery. The rustic tasting room seats 48 and provides a calm atmosphere for visitors to relax, both indoors next to the fireplace or on the covered porch and deck under the trees. Hidden Brook sponsors a range of events, including live music on summer weekends, special brunches, and charity fundraisers, such as the Toast for Hope in support of the Susan G. Komen Race for the Cure. The winery's gift shop offers light fare for purchase, as well as gifts and works by local artists. Children and pets are welcome.

White Wines: Chardonnay, Reserve White, Vidal Blanc.

Rosé Wines: Rosé *(Chambourcin, Vidal Blanc)*.

Red Wines: Cabernet Sauvignon, Chambourcin, Merlot, Reserve Red.

Sweet/Dessert Wines: Late Harvest *(Vidal Blanc)*, Sweet Amber *(Chambourcin)*.

Price Range: $22–$30

Tastings: $8 per person, $12 for reserve flight.

Groups: Reservations required for groups of 10 or more; $10 per person.

Directions: From Leesburg, drive north on U.S. Route 15 for about 7 miles. Turn right onto Spinks Ferry Road (Route 657) (portions unpaved). Continue 2 miles to the winery entrance on right.

❖ ❖ ❖

Lost Creek Winery & Vineyards
43277 Spinks Ferry Road
Leesburg VA 20176

Hours: M, Th–F, 12:00–5:00, Sa–Su 11:00–5:00   703-443-9836
(Sa 7:00, Su 6:00 in summer)   www.lostcreekwinery.com
Closed New Year's, Thanksgiving,   E-mail: winery@lostcreekwinery.com
Christmas Eve & Day

Founded in 1995 by Bob and Carol Hauck, parents of the owners of nearby Hidden Brook, Lost Creek has been owned by Todd and Aimee Henkle since early 2013. The tasting room includes a large fireplace and a number of tables in addition to the tasting bar where the winery's mostly estate-grown production can be sampled. Visitors can purchase a glass or bottle of wine and snacks to enjoy either indoors or outside on the two patios. Lost Creek sponsors live music on select weekends. The winery can be rented for private events and weddings, and has a caterer's kitchen that can be used for special events. Children and leashed pets are welcome.

White Wines: Chardonnay, Serenity, Vidal Blanc.

Rosé Wines: Rosé.

Red Wines: Cabernet Franc, Cabernet Sauvignon, Genesis *(Bordeaux-style blend)*, Merlot.

Price Range: $22–$36

Tastings: $12 per person; $20 per person (truffles & wine).

Groups: No buses or groups over 6.

Purchasing: Phone and online ordering for DC, FL, MD, and VA residents.

Directions: From Leesburg, drive north on U.S. Route 15 for about 7 miles. Turn right onto Spinks Ferry Road (Route 657) (portions unpaved). Continue 2 miles to the winery entrance on right, next to Hidden Brook Winery; continue another ½ mile to the Lost Creek parking lot.

❖ ❖ ❖

Tarara Winery
13648 Tarara Lane
Leesburg VA 20176

Hours: M–Th 11:00–5:00, F–Su 11:00–6:00 (May–Dec)   703-771-7100
M, Th 11:00–5:00, F–Su 11:00–6:00 (Jan–Apr)   www.tarara.com
Closed New Year's, Easter,   E-mail: bryan.winfrey@tarara.com
Thanksgiving, Christmas

Carved into a bluff on the Potomac River, Tarara Winery was built in 1985 by Whitie and Margaret Hubert and produced its first wines four years later. Tarara's 475 acres currently include 60 acres of vineyards, orchards, and 6 miles of hiking trails. Winemaker Jordan Harris, who hails from Canada, has overseen Tarara's wine operations since 2007, focusing on classic French varietals using mostly Virginia fruit as well as grapes from

Washington state for wines under the Killer Cluster label. After sampling wines, visitors can enjoy a light picnic at the tables and benches on the two patios that overlook the river and the Maryland hills beyond. A self-guided tour of the wine cave is also available. Be sure to purchase your tasting tickets at the cash register at the entrance to the tasting room.

White Wines: Albariño, Chardonnay, Charval, Muscat, Nevaeh White, Riesling, #SocialSecretWhite, Viognier.

Rosé Wines: Rosé.

Red Wines: Cabernet Sauvignon, Long Bomb *(Bordeaux-style blend)*, Merlot, Nevaeh Red, #SocialSecretRed, Syrah, Tranquility.

Sweet/Dessert Wines: Late Harvest Petit Manseng.

Price Range: $20–$45

Tastings: $10 for 6 wines; $20 for premier tasting (75 minutes, with cheese plate, reservations requested).

Groups: Reservations required for groups of 10 or more on weekends; $35 per person fee.

Purchasing: Online or telephone purchases are available for AK, CA, CO, DC, FL, GA, LA, MD, MN, MO, NV, NH, NY, NC, ND, OR, VT, VA, WA, and WV.

Directions: From U.S. Route 15, turn onto Lucketts Road (Route 662) and continue 3 miles to the ¼-mile-long winery driveway on left.

❖ ❖ ❖

Winery 32
15066 Limestone School Road
Leesburg VA 20176

Hours: F–Su 11:00–5:00 (Sa to 6:00 in summer) 240-687-1989
Closed New Year's, Christmas www.winery32.com
E-mail: info@winery32.com

Opened in 2014 by Michael and Roxanne Moosher, Winery 32 sits on 32 acres at the end of a drive lined with 32 peach trees. While their own vineyards mature, the Mooshers are using all Virginia-grown grapes for their production. Visitors may purchase light snacks or enjoy the special dishes that Michael prepares, such as lasagna, pulled pork barbecue, or eggplant parmesan. The tasting room offers seating indoors on two levels while tables on the spacious wrap-around deck and winery grounds provide a lovely view of the winery pond and vines. Leashed pets and well-behaved children are welcome.

Fruit Wines: Gloria's Sunshine *(peach)*.

White Wines: Being Koi *(Vidal Blanc, Traminette)*, Chardonnay.

Red Wines: Cabernet Franc, Cabernet Sauvignon, Chambourcin, Merlot, Syrah, Thoroughbred Blend.

Sweet/Dessert Wines: Gloria *(peach)*.

Price Range: $16–$28

Tastings: $8 per person.

Groups: Reservations requested for groups of 8 or more; $12 per person.

Directions: From U.S. Route 15, turn onto Limestone School Road (Route 661) (portions unpaved) to the winery, 2.3 miles on the right.

☙❧

WINE ORIGINS

The *Oxford Companion to Wine* defines wine as the fermented juice of fruits or berries, a broad category that excludes ales, beers, and distilled liquors but includes fermented products flavored from flowers or herbs. Most frequently, wine refers specifically to the fermented beverage made from the juice of grapes.

The earliest archeological evidence of grape cultivation for the express purpose of winemaking was found in the southern Caucasus, the region between the Black Sea and the Caspian Sea in the areas of modern-day Georgia, Armenia, and Azerbaijan, according to Hugh Johnson in *Vintage: The Story of Wine.*

By 500 BC, vines were being cultivated and wine made throughout the eastern Mediterranean region. Tomb paintings from ancient Egypt include depictions of grape cultivation and winemaking, and ancient Greek historians such as Herodotus and Thucydides have left references to viticulture in their writings.

With the rise of the Roman Empire, winemaking began to expand to the areas of modern-day France, Spain, and Germany. Even in areas not as suitable for grape cultivation, such as modern-day Britain, wine was a much-prized commodity.

All of these wines would have been made from the *Vitis vinifera* species of grapevine (sometimes abbreviated as *V. vinifera* or simply *vinifera*). Widely adaptable to a broad range of climates and regions, *V. vinifera* includes over five thousand different varieties and accounts for the vast majority of wines made around the world today.

☙❧

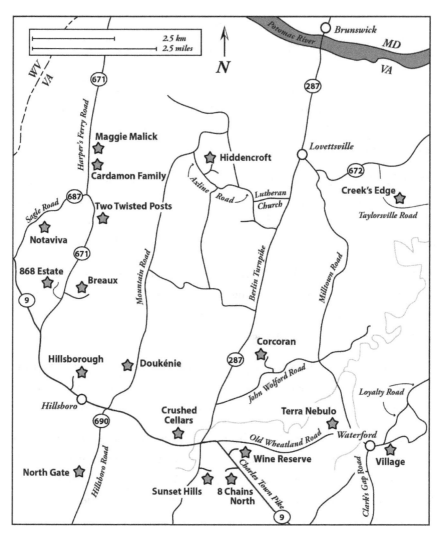

Map 3.3. Northwest Loudoun

NORTHWEST LOUDOUN

8 Chains North

38593 Daymont Lane

Waterford VA 20197

Hours: M, Th, F 12:00–6:00 (8:00 in summer), Sa–Su 11:00–6:00

Closed New Year's, Thanksgiving, Christmas

571-439-2255

www.8chainsnorth.com

E-mail: info@8chainsnorth.com

Owner-winemaker Ben and Connie Renshaw opened 8 Chains North Winery to the public in 2010, housing their tasting room in a restored barn with seating indoors and out. Wines are sources from Loudoun County as well as from the Pacific Northwest (NW label). Visitors may purchase a glass or bottle to enjoy either inside or on the patio overlooking the winery's vineyards. Vineyard tours are offered by reservation only on certain summer weekends. The winery features live music on Friday evenings in summer. Children and leashed pets are welcome.

White Wines: Chardonnay, LoCo Vino, Sauvignon Blanc.

Rosé Wines: Pink Link.

Red Wines: Cabernet Sauvignon, Furnace Mountain Red *(Bordeaux-style blend)*, Malbec, Merlot, Petit Verdot.

Price Range: $22–$30

Tastings: $8 per person, $15 per person for groups of 8 or more.

Wheelchair accessible.

Purchasing: Available through the website for select states.

Directions: From Leesburg, take Route 7 West and drive 2 miles. Merge onto Route 9 West (Charles Town Pike). Drive 4 miles and turn left onto Daymont Lane (portions unpaved). The winery is on the left after ¼ mile.

❖ ❖ ❖

868 Estate Vineyards
14001 Harpers Ferry Road
Purcellville VA 20132

Hours: W, Th 11:00–5:00, Fr 12:00–7:00,   540-668-7008
Sa 11:00–7:00 , Su 11:00–6:00   www.868estatevineyards.com
Closed New Year's, Thanksgiving, Christmas   E-mail: info@868estatevineyards.com

Carl DiManno, Peter Deliso, and Wendy Charron opened 868 Estate Vineyards in May 2012 after working in the Maryland wine industry. The winery's name comes from the elevation of the property's highest point. Guests can sample 868's wines from the tasting room or, in warmer weather, the spacious outdoor patio. The winery often features live music on weekends and may be rented for special events. The Grandale Restaurant, located on the property, is open for reservations Wednesday through Sunday. Children and leashed dogs are welcome.

White Wines: Chardonnay, Riesling.

Red Wines: Altezza, Cabernet Franc, Cabernet Sauvignon, Meritage, Merlot, Nebbiolo, Petit Verdot.

Price Range: $21–$26

Tastings: $8 per person.

Groups: Reservations required for groups of 6 or more, $15 per person.

Wheelchair accessible.

Purchasing: Online to AK, CA, DC, FL, MD, MN, and VA, or via Vino-Shipper to AL, AZ, CO, GA, HI, IA, ID, IL, IN, KS, LA, MA, ME, MO, NC, ND, NE, NH, NM, NV, NY, OH, OR, PA, SC, TN, TX, WA, WI, WV, and WY.

Directions: From Route 7, merge onto Route 9 West (Charles Town Pike). Drive 9.8 miles and turn right onto Harper's Ferry Road (Route 671). Continue 0.8 mile to the winery entrance on left.

❖ ❖ ❖

Breaux Estate Vineyards
36888 Breaux Vineyards Lane
Purcellville VA 20132

Hours: Daily 11:00–6:00 (Apr–mid-Oct), 11:00–5:00 (mid-Oct–Mar)   1-800-492-9961
Closed New Year's, Easter,   www.breauxvineyards.com
Thanksgiving, Christmas   E-mail: info@BreauxVineyards.com

Breaux [pronounced *bro*] Vineyards is located on a 404-acre estate with over one hundred fifteen acres of vineyards planted to seventeen different grape varieties. All their wines are from estate-grown grapes. The tasting room's patios offer visitors panoramic views of the vines, the valley, and nearby mountains. Tours are given daily when permitted by winery operations with a three-dollar per person fee. For tastings, last pours begin thirty minutes before closing. Gourmet snacks and breads are available for purchase. Breaux sponsors several festivals, including a Key West Festival, a Cajun Festival, and Dog Days. The winery can be rented for private events and weddings. Children and pets are welcome.

White Wines: Chère Marie *(Vidal Blanc)*, Jennifer's Jambalaya, Jolie Blonde, Madeleine's Chardonnay, Sauvignon Blanc, Viognier.

Rosé Wines: Rosé.

Red Wines: Cabernet Franc, Cabernet Sauvignon, Equation, Marquis de Lafayette *(Cabernet Franc)*, Meritage, Merlot, Nebbiolo.

Sweet/Dessert Wines: Nebbiolo Ice Late Harvest.

Price Range: $18–$38

Tastings: $10 per person.

Groups: Reservations required for groups of 8 or more, $15 per person fee.

Wheelchair accessible.

Restrictions: Dogs are not permitted on the grounds during special events or festivals with the exception of Dog Day, when dogs are the stars.

Purchasing: Online or phone purchases for CA, DC, FL, LA, MD, NC, TX, and VA.

Directions: From Route 7, merge onto Route 9 West (Charles Town Pike). Drive 9.8 miles and turn right onto Harper's Ferry Road (Route 671). Continue 1 mile to the winery entrance on right.

❖ ❖ ❖

Cardamon Family Vineyards
12226 Harpers Ferry Road
Purcellville VA 20132

Hours: Sa–Su 11:00–5:00 (April–Dec)　　　　540-668-9018
Closed Christmas, Jan–Mar　　　www.cardamonfamilyvineyards.com
E-mail: winemaker@cardamonfamilyvineyards.com

Cardamon Family Vineyards was founded by Chuck and Ana Cardamon in May 2013. The Cardamons pair their Virginia-grown wines with gourmet salsas created and prepared by Chuck, who attended the California Culinary Institute in San Francisco after retiring from his career as a Navy SEAL. Salsas and snacks are available for purchase and enjoyment on the outdoor deck overlooking the vines or indoors.

Fruit Wines: Vino de Mele *(apple)*.

White Wines: Duesili, Macha, Ofdil, Rkatz *(Rkatsiteli).*

Rosé Wines: Emilia.

Red Wines: Amico, Batoria, Donald J, Peter Pie.

Price Range: $12–$25

Tastings: $5 per person.

Groups: Reservations requested for groups of 6 or more.

Directions: From Route 7, merge onto Route 9 West (Charles Town Pike). Drive 9.8 miles and turn right onto Harper's Ferry Road (Route 671). Continue 4.5 miles to the winery entrance on right.

❖ ❖ ❖

Corcoran Vineyards & Cidery
14635 Corkys Farm Lane
Waterford VA 20197

Hours: Sa–Su 12:00–5:00
Closed New Year's, Easter, Christmas

540-882-9073
www.corcorancider.com
E-mail: info@corcorancider.com

Jim and Lori Corcoran opened their winery just outside Waterford in 2002. Winemaker Lori focuses on producing high-quality wine using both her own estate-grown grapes and fruit from two neighboring vineyards. She has now added ciders to her lineup, made from Virginia apples. The tasting room includes indoors seating as well as outdoor tables and chairs with a view of the nearby hills and pond. Corcoran offers free Wi-Fi, as well as occasional wine-tasting classes.

Ciders: Hard Cider, Knot Head, Popo Peach, Sinful.

Fruit Wines: Apple.

White Wines: Chardonnay, Riesling, Seyval Blanc, Traminette, Vidal Blanc.

Rosé Wines: Rosé.

Red Wines: Cabernet Franc, Chambourcin, Petit Verdot, Pinot Noir, Tannat.

Sweet/Dessert Wines: BlackJack, Cello, RAZ.

Fortified Wines: USB *(port-style)*, Waterford *(white port-style)*.

Price Range: $16–$20

Tastings: $7 per person.

Price Range: $16–$20

Tastings: $7 per person.

Groups: Reservations required for groups of 6 or more; $10 per person fee.

Wheelchair accessible.

Directions: From Leesburg, drive west on Route 7 and merge onto Route 9 West (Charles Town Pike). Drive 5.7 miles and turn north onto Berlin Turnpike (Route 287). After 1 mile, turn right onto John Wolford Road (portions unpaved). Continue 1.5 miles. Turn left onto Corkys Farm Lane (portions unpaved); the winery's gravel driveway will be ⅓ mile on the left.

❖ ❖ ❖

Creek's Edge
41255 Anna's Lane
Lovettsville VA 20180

Hours: M , Th 12:00–8:00, F–Sa 12:00–9:00, Su 12:00–8:00
Closed New Year's, Thanksgiving, Christmas

540-822-3825
www.creeksedgewinery.com
E-mail: info@creeksedgewinery.com

Opened by Todd Durden in 2014, Creek's Edge is located on the banks of Catoctin Creek in the hamlet of Taylorstown. The winery offers indoor seating in its spacious tasting room as well as on the decks overlooking the lawn and 11-acre vineyard. The tasting bar is carved from hickory trees that were cleared from the property. Light fare is available for purchase. The winery can be rented for special events and weddings, and features a beautiful barrel-shaped circular stairwell leading to a private room upstairs. Children are welcome.

White Wines: Chardonnay, Pinot Gris, Riesling, Vidal Blanc.

Red Wines: Cabernet Franc, Cabernet Sauvignon, Chambourcin, Merlot.

Price Range: $18–$35

Tastings: $8 per person.

Groups: Reservations required for groups of 6 or more, $12 per person fee.

Directions: From Route 9 (Charles Town Pike), drive north on Route 287 (Berlin Turnpike) for 6.6 miles to the town of Lovettsville. Turn right onto East Broad Way (VA 673). After ½ mile, turn left onto Lovettsville Road (VA 672) and drive 3.1 miles. Turn right onto Taylorstown Road (VA 668). After crossing Catoctin Creek, make an immediate left onto Anna's Lane.

❖ ❖ ❖

Crushed Cellars
37938 Charles Town Pike
Purcellville VA 20132

Hours: Sa, Su 12:00–5:00
Closed New Year's, Christmas

571-374-9463 (WINE)
www.crushedcellars.com
E-mail: info@crushedcellars.com

Bob Kalok opened Crushed Cellars in 2011 on the grounds of his family farm. Indeed, visitors may well spot a chicken or two strolling about the property, as well as one of the winery cats sunning itself on the porch. The family is currently using grapes from other Virginia vineyards while their own vines mature. The winery offers cheeses, spreads, and bread for purchase and enjoyment on the front porch or grounds. The two-story winery tasting room is available for small parties. Children are welcome.

White Wines: Chardonnay, Seyval Blanc, Vidal Blanc.

Red Wines: Cabernet Sauvignon, Meritage.

Price Range: $19–$25

Tastings: $8 per person.

Restrictions: No groups over 6.

Directions: From Route 7, merge onto Route 9 West (Charles Town Pike). Drive 5.8 miles to the winery's gravel driveway on the right.

❖ ❖ ❖

Doukénie Winery
14727 Mountain Road
Purcellville VA 20132

Hours: Daily 10:00–6:00 (F to 9:00, Sa to 8:00, summer only) Closed Thanksgiving, Christmas

540-668-6464
www.doukeniewinery.com
E-mail: info@DoukenieWinery.com

Doukénie Winery was founded by George and Nicki Bazaco and is named in honor of George's grandmother, Doukénie Bacos who arrived in the United States from Greece in 1920. Located on five hundred acres near the Blue Ridge Mountains, Doukénie offers scenic views of the surrounding hills, the vineyards, and winery pond from its tasting room and veranda. The winery hosts frequent events, including Taste of Greece and Taste of Italy festivals, barrel and harvest tastings, and cooking classes. Children and pets are welcome on the winery patio and grounds.

Fruit Wines: Hope's Legacy Raspberry Wine.

White Wines: Chardonnay, Mandolin, Pinot Grigio, Riesling, Sauvignon Blanc, Viognier.

Red Wines: Cabernet Franc, Cabernet Sauvignon, Cabernet/Syrah, Merlot, Petit Verdot, Sangiovese, Syrah, Vintner's Reserve *(Bordeaux-style blend)*, Zeus.

Price Range: $20–$38

Tastings: $10 per person.

Groups: Reservations required for groups of 8 or more, $15 per person.

Restrictions: Limos and buses by appointment only.

Purchasing: Phone orders for all states *except* AL, DE, KY, MS, OK, PA, SD, and UT..

Directions: From Route 7, merge onto Route 9 West (Charles Town Pike). Drive 7.3 miles and turn right onto Mountain Road (Route 690 North). Continue 1 mile to the winery entrance on the left.

❖ ❖ ❖

Hiddencroft Vineyards
12202 Axline Road
Lovettsville VA 20180

Hours: Th–M 12:00–6:00 (Sa to 8:00, May–Oct)   540-535-5367
Closed New Year's, Thanksgiving, Christmas   www.hiddencroftvineyards.com
E-mail: winery@hiddencroftvineyards.com

The northernmost winery in Virginia, Hiddencroft is a family-run operation owned by Terry and Clyde Housel; Clyde also serves as winemaker. The Housels have been cultivating grapes on six acres of their sixteen-acre property since 2001; they also produce several fruit wines from their own harvests. The tasting room is an 1830s-era farmhouse with a deck featuring tables and umbrellas. The farmhouse's original laundry and smokehouse outbuildings provide a scenic backdrop for photos. While no outside food is permitted, Hiddencroft offers snacks for purchase and enjoyment over a glass of wine on its patio. Children and leashed pets are welcome.

Fruit Wines: Blackberry, Grandma's Love Potion *(blueberry)*, Persephone's Punch *(pomegranate)*, Sweet Cherry, Vitis Rubus *(raspberry, Chambourcin)*.

White Wines: Chardonnay, Traminette, Vidal Blanc.

Rosé Wines: Chambourcin Rosé.

Red Wines: Cabernet Franc, Chambourcin, Dutchman's Creek, Petit Verdot, Tannat, Tranquility.

Fortified Wines: Cackling Crow.

Price Range: $18–$40

Tastings: $8 per person.

Groups: Reservations required for groups of 9 to 25; $10 per person fee.

Restrictions: No groups over 25.

Purchasing: Online via VinoShipper to AK, AL, AZ, CA, CO, DC, FL, GA, HI, IA, ID, IL, IN, KS, LA, MA, MD, ME, MN, MO, NC, ND, NE, NH, NM, NV, NY, OH, OR, PA, SC, TN, TX, VA, WA, WI, WV, and WY.

Directions: From Route 7, merge onto Route 9 West (Charles Town Pike). Drive 5.7 miles and turn right onto the Berlin Turnpike (Route 287) toward Lovettsville. Continue 5 miles and turn left at Lutheran Church Road (unpaved). At the end of the road, turn right onto Axline Road (Route 680) (portions unpaved). Drive 1.6 miles and turn right into the winery drive (unpaved). Bear left at the large red barn to the winery parking lot entrance on the right.

❖ ❖ ❖

Hillsborough Vineyards
36716 Charles Town Pike
Purcellville VA 20132

Hours: Daily 11:00–6:00 (Apr–Dec),
F-M 11:00–5:00 (Jan–Mar)
Closed Easter, Thanksgiving, Christmas

540-668-6216
www.hillsboroughwine.com
E-mail: info@hillsboroughwine.com

A family-owned farm winery, Hillsborough Vineyards was founded by Bora and Zeynep Baki who moved to the Washington, D.C., area from their native Turkey in 1979 and purchased the property in 2001. Their son Kerem serves as winemaker. Many of Hillsborough's mostly estate-grown wines bear the name of a gemstone, such as two named after Bora and Zeynep's mothers. The tasting room is in a restored pre-Civil War barn, with two stone patios that offer a splendid view of the mountains and adjoining valley. Hillsborough hosts numerous events, including an annual Caribbean Nights festival, and is available for private parties and weddings.

White Wines: Carnelian *(Roussanne)*, Chardonnay, Opal *(Petit Manseng)*.

Rosé Wines: Serefina *(Viognier, Tannat)*, White Merlot.

Red Wines: Bloodstone, Cabernet Sauvignon, Garnet *(Bordeaux-style blend)*, Onyx *(Tannat)*, Petit Verdot, Ruby.

Sweet/Dessert Wines: Moonstone *(late-harvest Viognier)*.

Price Range: $22–$38

Tastings: $10 per person.

Groups: Reservations required for groups of 8 or more, $12 per person.

Wheelchair accessible.

Purchasing: Phone orders for all states *except* AL, DE, KY, MS, and UT.

Directions: From Route 7, merge onto Route 9 West (Charles Town Pike) and drive 8 miles. The winery entrance will be on the right about ½ mile past the town of Hillsboro.

❖ ❖ ❖

Maggie Malick Wine Caves
12138 Harpers Ferry Road
Purcellville VA 20132

Hours: M–Th, 11:00–5:00, F–Su 11:00–6:00 (summer only)   540-905-2921
Th–F, M 11:00–5:00, Sa–Su 11:00–6:00   www.maggiemalickwinecaves.com
Closed New Year's, Thanksgiving, Christmas   E-mail: info@maggiemalickwinecaves.com

Maggie Malick opened her winery in 2013, twelve years after she and husband Mark planted their first vineyard on their 215-acre property. The tasting room is a concrete cave, dug into a hillside and built by the Malicks themselves. After sampling the all estate-grown wines, visitors can stay and enjoy the view of the vines over a glass or bottle of wine on the patio just outside the wine cave. Light fare is available for purchase at the winery.

White Wines: Albariño, Chardonnay, Mélange Blanc, Petit Manseng, Viognier.

Rosé Wines: Rosé.

Red Wines: Cabernet Franc, Cabernet Sauvignon, Garnacha, Mélange Rouge, Meritage, Merlot, Petit Verdot, Tannat.

Price Range: $12–$26

Tastings: $8 per person.

Groups: Reservations required for groups of 8 or more, $15 per person fee.

Directions: From Route 7, merge onto Route 9 West (Charles Town Pike). Drive 9.8 miles and turn right onto Harper's Ferry Road (Route 671). Continue 4.6 miles to the winery entrance on right.

❖ ❖ ❖

North Gate Vineyard
16031 Hillsboro Road
Purcellville VA 20132

Hours: Th–M 11:00–6:00 (F to 8:00 in summer) 540-668-6248
Closed Thanksgiving, Christmas, New Year's www.northgatevineyard.com
E-mail: info@northgatevineyard.com;

Owner/vintners Mark and Vicki Fedor purchased their North Gate farm in 1997 and became interested in winemaking after discovering grape vines on the property. Their LEED-certified tasting room opened in 2011 and includes both indoor and outdoor seating. The winery sponsors live music on weekends. All the wines are from grapes grown either from North Gate's own vineyards or from other Loudoun County vineyards. The winery may be rented for private events. North Gate often participates in the annual Grapehound Wine Tour, a benefit for greyhound adoption.

Fruit Wines: Apple *(proceeds go to Blue Ridge Greyhound Adoption)*

White Wines: Chardonnay, Rkatsiteli, Viognier.

Rosé Wines: Rosé of Chambourcin.

Red Wines: Cabernet Franc, Meritage, Merlot, Petit Verdot.

Price Range: $14–$28

Tastings: $7 per person.

Groups: Reservations required for groups of 8 or more, $12 per person fee.

Restrictions: No smoking permitted; no groups on Saturdays.

Purchasing: Shipping to DC, FL, IA, MN, NM, and VA.

Directions: From Route 7, merge west onto Route 9 (Charles Town Pike). Drive 7.6 miles and turn left onto Hillsboro Road (Route 690). The winery will be on the right in 1.7 miles.

❖ ❖ ❖

Notaviva Vineyards
13274 Sagle Drive
Purcellville VA 20132

Hours: Th–F, Su, holiday M11:00–5:00, Sa to 6:00 (Apr–Dec)   540-668-6756
Th–Su 11:00–5:00 (Jan–Mar)   www.notavivavineyards.com
Closed New Year's, Thanksgiving, Christmas   E-mail: info@notavivavineyards.com

Stephen and Shannon Mackey established Notaviva Vineyards in 2004 in the secluded northwest corner of Loudoun County. The winery's two-story tasting room offers a scenic view of the winery pond and nearby hills; the grounds also include a number of benches and picnic tables for guests to use. Both Mackeys have backgrounds as musicians, and their winery frequently sponsors live musical performances on weekends. Notaviva has launched a co-working initiative; see the website for details. Children and leashed pets are welcome.

White Wines: Calor Chardonnay, Ottantotto Viognier, Verano Vidal Blanc, Vincerò Viognier.

Red Wines: Cantabile Cabernet Franc, Celtico Chambourcin, Excelsis Petit Verdot, Ode to Joy Meritage, Vierzig Blaufränkisch.

Dessert Wines: Gitano Chambourcin.

Price Range: $17–$28

Tastings: $8 per person.

Groups: Reservations required for groups of 8 or more; $12 per person fee.

Wheelchair accessible (some limitations).

Purchasing: Online ordering is available for VA and FL.

Directions: From Route 7, take Route 9 West (Charles Town Pike) for 11.6 miles. Turn right onto Sagle Road (Route 687) (portions unpaved). The winery will be on the right after 1 mile.

❖ ❖ ❖

Sunset Hills Vineyard
38295 Fremont Overlook Lane
Purcellville VA 20132

Hours: M–Th 12:00–5:00, F 12:00–6:00, Sa–Su 11:00–6:00   540-882-4560
Closed New Year's, Thanksgiving, Christmas   www.sunsethillsvineyard.com
E-mail: tastingroom@sunsethillsvineyard.com

Located on a rise overlooking the Loudoun Valley and Blue Ridge Mountains, Sunset Hills Vineyard was established by Mike and Diane Canney who now have over 160 acres under vine in the Monticello and Shenandoah AVAs. The spacious two-story tasting room is in a 130-year-old barn that was carefully restored by Amish carpenters; solar energy powers both the tasting room and production facility in the largest solar installation in the county. The winery offers breads, artisanal cheeses, and spreads for purchase, as well as live music on weekends, charity events such as the Loudoun Therapeutic Riding fundraiser, and an annual wine harvest tasting series in the fall. The facilities may be rented for private functions or weddings. Children and pets are welcome.

Sparkling Wines: Dawn.

White Wines: Chardonnay, Petit Manseng, Sunset White, Viognier.

Rosé Wines: Sunset Rosé.

Red Wines: Cabernet Franc, Cabernet Sauvignon, Merlot, Mosaic, Nebbiolo, Petit Verdot, Sunset Red.

Dessert Wines: Nettare di Tramonto.

Fortified Wines: Dusk *(port-style)*.

Price Range: $22–$50

Tastings: $10 per person.

Groups: Reservations required for groups of 8 or more, $15 per person fee.

Purchasing: Shipping to AK, CA, DC, FL, MD, MN, NC, NY, and VA.

Directions: From Route 7, merge onto Route 9 West (Charles Town Pike). Drive 5.7 miles to the Berlin Turnpike (Route 287). Turn left and drive 2.6 miles. Turn left into Fremont Overlook Lane (portions unpaved) to the winery parking lot on the right.

❖ ❖ ❖

Terra Nebulo
39892 Old Wheatland Road
Waterford VA 20197

Hours: Sa–Su 11:00–6:00   540-882-3800
Closed New Year's, Christmas   www.terranebulo.com
                                              E-mail: info@terranebulo.com

Michael and Cheryl Morrison opened their winery in August 2015 on a hill just outside the historic Quaker village of Waterford. The two-story tasting and production facility is housed in an Amish-built replica of a nineteenth-century barn in Maryland and offers a large stone fireplace on the upper level. The wines are made by Randy Phillips (Cave Ridge) and are sourced from a vineyard in the Shenandoah Valley. Supervised children are welcome.

White Wines: Chardonnay, Riesling, Traminette, Viognier.

Red Wines: Blended Red *(Bordeaux-style blend)*, Cabernet Franc, Chambourcin.

Fortified Wines: Chambourcin *(port-style)*.

Price Range: $17–$33

Tastings: $5 per person.

Groups: Reservations required for groups of 8 or more.

Directions: From Leesburg, take Route 7 and merge onto Route 9 West (Charles Town Pike). Drive ½ mile, then turn right onto Clarks Gap Road. In the village of Waterford, turn left onto Water Street, which quickly merges into Main Street. Make a slight left onto Old Wheatland Road and continue 0.4 miles to the winery entrance on the right.

❖ ❖ ❖

Two Twisted Posts
12944 Harpers Ferry Road
Purcellville VA 20132

Hours: Sa 11:00–6:00, Su 11:00–5:00   540-668-6540
Closed New Year's, Christmas   www.twotwistedposts.com
E-mail: contact@twotwistedposts.com

Two Twisted Posts was founded by Theresa and Brad Robertson, who planted their vineyard in 2008 on their scenic property at the base of the Short Hills. They named the winery after the Two Twisted Posts Tavern in Theresa's native town of Colchester, England. The tasting room and production facilities are housed in a large red barn that offers seating for guests both indoors and out. Light snacks are available for purchase on site. Future plans include adding walking trails around the property and winery pond, as well as a putting green behind the barn.

White Wines: Chardonnay, Sweet Life, Vidal Blanc.

Red Wines: Cabernet Franc, Cabernet Sauvignon, Petit Verdot.

Price Range: $17–$33

Tastings: $5 per person.

Groups: Reservations required for groups of 8 or more.

Directions: From Route 7, merge onto Route 9 West (Charles Town Pike). Drive 9.8 miles and turn right onto Harper's Ferry Road (Route 671). Continue 3.1 miles to the winery entrance on right.

❖ ❖ ❖

Village Winery
40405 Browns Lane
Waterford VA 20197

Hours: Sa 11:00–6:00, Su 12:00–5:00
Closed New Year's, Christmas

540-882-3780
www.villagewineryandvineyards.com
E-mail: info@villagewineryandvineyards.com

The Village Winery is a small family-owned farm winery located on a working farm in the historic village of Waterford. Kent and Karen Marrs opened the winery in 2005 and grow Cabernet Franc, Merlot, and Petit Verdot on their ten-acre vineyard. Winemaker Kent crafts his wines entirely by hand, using no mechanical pumps during the process. The tasting room is located in a small restored farm building on the property, with standing room at the tasting bar for about ten visitors; limited additional seating is available outside. Village Winery also offers several elderberry products for sale. Children are welcome.

Fruit Wines: Apple, Elderberry, Elderberry-Apple, Raspberry-Apple.

White Wines: Viognier.

Red Wines: Cabernet Franc, Merlot, Merlot-Cabernet Franc, Petit Verdot.

Price Range: $15–$22

Groups: Reservations requested for groups of 6 or more.

Directions: From Leesburg, take Route 7 and merge onto Route 9 West (Charles Town Pike). Drive ½ mile, then turn right onto Clarks Gap Road. Continue 3 miles through Waterford and bear right onto Loyalty Road. Take the second right onto Browns Lane and turn into the first drive on the right.

❖ ❖ ❖

The Wine Reserve At Waterford
38516 Charles Town Pike
Waterford VA 20197

Hours: Th 3:00–7:00, F 2:00–8:00,
Sa 11:00–6:00, Su 12:00–6:00 (summer)
Th 3:00–6:00, F 2:00–6:00,
Sa 11:00–6:00, Su 12:00–6:00 (fall, spring)
Closed New Year's, Easter, Thanksgiving, Christmas

540-692-9463
www.waterfordwinereserve.com
E-mail: contact@waterfordwinereserve.com

Jon and Cori Phillips purchased the former Loudoun Valley Vineyards, one of the oldest vineyards in Loudoun County, re-opening it as The Wine Reserve at Waterford in late 2016. They are using Virginia-grown grapes while their own vineyard matures and are featuring wines from elsewhere in the state and the world as part of their tasting flights. The tasting room offers scenic views of the surrounding valley and nearby Blue Ridge Mountains from the windows and outdoor decks. The Wine Reserve often sponsors live music on weekends and offers cheese plates for purchase on-site. The facilities may be rented for weddings and private events. Supervised children and leashed pets are welcome.

White Wines: Chardonnay.

Red Wines: Meritage.

Tastings: $12 per person

Groups: Reservations required for groups of 8 or more.

Directions: From Route 7, merge onto Route 9 West (Charles Town Pike). Drive 5 miles to the winery's gravel drive on the right.

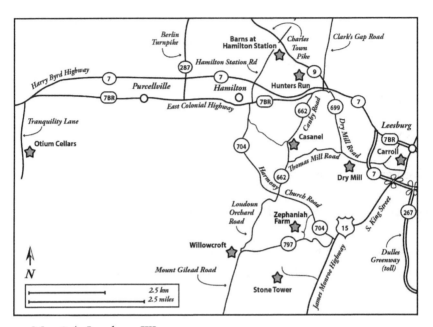

Map 3.4. Leesburg West

LEESBURG WEST

The Barns at Hamilton Stations
16804 Hamilton Station Road
Hamilton, VA 20158

Hours: Th 11:00–5:30, F 12:00–8:00, Sa–Su, holiday M 11:00–5:30   540-338-5309
Closed New Year's Eve & Day, Easter,   www.thebarnsathamiltonstation.com
Thanksgiving, Christmas Eve & Day   E-mail: thebarns.hamilton@gmail.com

The Barns at Hamilton Station is under the ownership of Andrew and Marianne Fialdini, with Michael Shaps as winemaker. Located on an old dairy farm, the winery's tasting room is in a restored barn that can be rented for weddings and parties. Wines are made from their own vineyards and from a leased vineyard near Charlottesville. The Barns features live music on select Friday evenings and offers a range of cheeses, spreads, and meats for purchase in the tasting room.

White Wines: Bank Barn White, Bliss, Chardonnay, Viognier.

Red Wines: Bank Barn Red, Cabernet Franc, Cabernet Sauvignon, Harmony (*Meritage*), Malbec, Merlot, Petit Verdot.

Price Range: $24–$38

Tastings: $8 per person for regular, $15 for extended.

Groups: Reservations required for groups of 8 or more; $13 per person fee.

Restrictions: No limo or bus parking on site.

Wheelchair accessible.

Purchasing: Online through VinoShipper to AK, AL, CA, DC, FL, ID, IL, LA, MN, MO, ND, NE, NH, NM, NV, OH, OR, WV, and WY.

Directions: From Leesburg, take Route 7 West and drive 7 miles. Turn right at the Hamilton exit and then left onto VA Route 704. Drive 0.7 miles to the winery entrance on the right.

❖ ❖ ❖

Carroll Vineyard
29 South King Street
Leesburg VA 20175

Hours: Tu-Sa 10:00–6:00, Su 12:00–5:00
Closed Thanksgiving, New Year's, Christmas

703-777-3322
www.leesburg-vintner.com
E-mail: leevinmike@aol.com

Mike Carroll opened his tasting room in the Leesburg Vintner, a wine store in historic downtown Leesburg that he has owned and operated for over twenty years. Lori Corcoran serves as winemaker using grapes from Corcoran and Carroll Vineyards. Visitors can also purchase a wide range of wines from other Virginia wineries at the Vintner.

Fruit Wines: Apple.

White Wines: Chardonnay, Traminette, Viognier.

Red Wines: Cabernet Franc, Chambourcin, Merlot, Petit Verdot.

Price Range: $14–$20

Tastings: $5 per person.

Directions: From Market Street in downtown Leesburg, go south on King Street one block to the corner of King and Loudoun Streets.

❖ ❖ ❖

Casanel Vineyards
17956 Canby Road
Leesburg VA 20175

Hours: Th 2:00–6:00, F–M 11:00–6:00 (Apr–Nov) 540-751-1776
F–M 12:00–6:00 (Dec–Mar) www.casanelvineyards.com
Closed New Year's, Easter, July 4ᵗʰ, E-mail: info@casanelvineyards.com
Thanksgiving, mid-Dec to mid-Jan

Casey and Nelson DeSouza opened Casanel Vineyards to the public in 2008, several years after Nelson, a native of Brazil, retired as head of DeSouza Construction, which he had founded in the 1980s. Casanel is on forty scenic acres with a winery pond and tranquil picnic area overlooking the vines. Casanel also sponsors special events, including live music on summer weekends. Light picnic snacks are available for purchase and enjoyment inside the spacious tasting room or outdoors on the patio. Children and pets are welcome. Please note that last pours are thirty minutes before closing. Military service personnel receive a 10% discount.

White Wines: Chardonnay, Elleana, Patricia Marie.

Rosé Wines: José Rosé.

Red Wines: Cabernet Sauvignon, K2, Petit Verdot, Red Blend.

Fortified Wines: The Full Nelson (*port-style*).

Price Range: $20–$55

Tastings: $7 per person, $10 per person for groups.

Groups: Reservations required for groups over 7, no groups after 2:00.

Wheelchair accessible.

Purchasing: Online via VinoShipper to AL, AK, AZ, CA, CO, DC, FL, GA, HI, IA, ID, IL, IN, KS, LA, MA, MD, ME, MN, MO, NC, ND, NE, NH, NM, NV, NY, OH, OR, PA, SC, TN, TX, VA, WA, WI, WV, and WY.

Directions: From Leesburg, drive on Route 7 West and take the Route 9 exit (Charles Town Pike). Turn left at the bottom of the exit ramp onto Route 9 East. At the stop sign, turn right onto East Colonial Highway (Business Route 7). Drive ½ mile and turn left onto Canby Road (portions unpaved). The winery will be 1.4 miles on the left.

❖ ❖ ❖

Dry Mill Vineyards & Winery
18195 Dry Mill Road
Leesburg VA 20175

Hours: Tu–Th 12:00–5:00 (6:00 in summer); F 12:00–8:00;   703-737-3930
Sa 11:00–6:00 (7:00 in summer), Su 11:00–5:00 (6:00 in summer)   www.drymillwine.com
Closed New Year's, Easter, Thanksgiving, Christmas   E-mail: info@drymillwine.com

Dry Mill Vineyards & Winery, located just outside Leesburg, opened its doors in early 2009 in the renovated stable and barn of the former Loudoun Hunt Club. Owners Dean and Nancy Vanhuss source their wines from the Vanhuss's Short Hill Vineyards near Lovettsville, and winemaker Karen Reed is gradually increasing the varietals under production. The tasting room offers visitors a pleasant setting in which to enjoy Dry Mill's wines, including a fireplace, verandas overlooking the grounds, and a patio that seats up to 30 for wine tastings. Light fare is available for purchase. The winery offers live music on weekends. Children are welcome.

White Wines: Chardonnay, Traminette.

Rosé Wines: Chambourcin Rosé.

Red Wines: Cabernet Franc, Cabernet Sauvignon, Chambourcin, Merlot, Norton, Petit Verdot.

Sweet/Dessert Wines: Sweet Stallion.

Price Range: $18–$25

Tastings: $7 per person; $10 per person for groups of 8 or more.

Groups: Reservations required for groups of 8 or more.

Wheelchair accessible.

Directions: From Leesburg, drive south on U.S. Route 15 (King Street) and turn west onto Catoctin Circle SE. Drive about ½ mile and turn left onto Dry Mill Road SW. The winery entrance will be two miles on the left.

◈ ◈ ◈

Hunters Run Wine Barn
40325 Charles Town Pike
Hamilton VA 20158

Hours: Sa–Su 12:00–5:00
Closed New Year's, Christmas

703-926-4183
www.huntersrunwinebarn.com
E-mail: geri@huntersrunwinebarn.com

Geri Gleeson Nolan launched her winery eight years after planting a vineyard in the Shenandoah Valley. A native of County Limerick, Ireland, Geri has infused the tasting room with a welcoming atmosphere. All the wines are estate-grown, with Randy Phillips (Cave Ridge Vineyard) as winemaker. Visitors can linger at one of the tables in the main tasting area or at one of the side nooks. The winery features live music on many weekends. Children and leashed pets are welcome. Last pours are thirty minutes before closing.

White Wines: Chardonnay, Riesling, Traminette, Viognier.

Rosé Wines: Bridie's Rosé.

Red Wines: Cabernet Franc, Chambourcin, Gypsy Red, Wine Barn Red.

Fortified Wines: Todd's *(port-style)*.

Price Range: $26–$29

Tastings: $11 per person.

Groups: Reservations required for groups of 8 or more; no groups after 1:00 on Saturday or 1:30 on Sunday.

Directions: From Route 7, merge onto Route 9 West (Charles Town Pike) and drive 1.2 miles to the winery entrance on the left.

❖ ❖ ❖

Otium Cellars at Goose Creek Farms
18050 Tranquility Lane
Purcellville VA 20132

Hours: M, Th 11:00–5:00, F 11:00–8:00; 540-338-2027
Sa–Su 11:00–6:00 www.otiumcellars.com
Closed New Year's, Thanksgiving, Christmas E-mail: tara@otiumcellars.com

Gerhard Bauer opened Otium Cellars in May 2012 on the grounds of his family's Goose Creek Farms, where the family breeds Hanoverian show horses. Gerhard serves as winemaker, working closely with Ben Renshaw of nearby 8 Chains North. The two-story tasting room, by the stables, offers seating both indoors and out, and includes a two-sided wood stove that adds a cozy touch on chilly days. The pavilion next to the tasting room may be rented for parties or special events. Children and dogs are welcome.

White Wines: Chardonnay, Grüner Veltliner, Pinot Gris.

Red Wines: Blaufränkisch, Cabernet Sauvignon, Dornfelder, Malbec, Merlot.

Price Range: $20–$36

Tastings: $12 per person.

Groups: Reservations recommended for groups of 6 or more.

Wheelchair accessible (some limitations).

Directions: From Route 7, take the Route 7 Business exit at Round Hill. Drive east for 1.3 miles toward Purcellville and turn right at Tranquility Road (portions unpaved). Drive 1.8 miles to the winery entrance on the left.

❖ ❖ ❖

Stone Tower Winery
19925 Hogback Mountain Road
Leesburg VA 20175

Hours: Th–M 11:00–6:00
Closed Easter, Thanksgiving, Christmas

703-777-2797
www.stonetowerwinery.com
E-mail: info@stonetowerwinery.com

Stone Tower is on 300 scenic acres owned by Michael and Kristi Huber, who opened their winery in 2013. The winery has an expansive events building as well as a two-story tasting room that are both popular weekend destinations for wine lovers who may purchase a range of light snacks and food. The tasting room opens onto a sloping lawn with a beautiful view of the winery's vineyards. The winery may be rented for weddings or private events. Children and leashed pets are welcome in designated areas.

Sparkling Wines: Rosé Cuvée, Wild Boar Blanc de Blanc.

White Wines: Chardonnay, Sauvignon Blanc.

Rosé Wines: Rosé.

Red Wines: Cabernet Franc, Cabernet Sauvignon, Hogback Mountain, Petit Verdot, Wind Swept Hill.

Price Range: $24–$69

Tastings: $15 per person.

Groups: Reservations required for groups of 8 or more.

Purchasing: Shipping to many states; see website for details.

Directions: From Leesburg, drive south on Route 15 for 4.5 miles. Turn right onto Hogback Mountain Road and continue 1.1 miles to the winery on the left.

❖ ❖ ❖

Willowcroft Farm Vineyards
38906 Mount Gilead Road
Leesburg VA 20175

Hours: Th–Su 11:00–5:30
Closed New Year's, Thanksgiving, Christmas

703-777-8161
www.willowcroftwine.com
E-mail: info@willowcroftwine.com

Willowcroft, the oldest winery in Loudoun County, was founded in 1979 by owner-winemaker Lew Parker. The tasting room is in a weathered barn that predates the Civil War; light food is available for purchase. The winery grounds include picnic tables and a one-mile walking trail with good views of Loudoun Valley. Willowcroft offers a range of events, including turkey chili weekends and an annual Oktoberfest. Supplies and seminars for home winemakers are also available. Children and pets are welcome.

Fruit Wines: Applause.

White Wines: Albariño, Chardonnay, Petit Manseng, Riesling-Muscat, Seyval Blanc, Traminette, Vidal Blanc.

Rosé Wines: Rose of Sharon.

Red Wines: Assemblage, Cabernet Franc, Cabernet Sauvignon, Chambourcin, Fitzrada's Reward *(Bordeaux-style blend)*, Merlot, Petit Verdot.

Sweet/Dessert Wines: Claire *(Petit Manseng)*.

Price Range: $18–$42

Tastings: $10 per person.

Groups: Reservations required for groups of 6–9 or more, $15 per person fee; groups of 10 or more, $15 per person plus $50 per hour. No groups after 2:00 p.m.

Purchasing: Online via VinoShipper to AL, AK, CA, DC, FL, ID, IL, LA, MN, MO, NC, ND, NE, NH, NM, NV, OH, OR, VA, WV, and WY.

Directions: Take U.S. Route 15 South from Leesburg for 3 miles. Turn right onto Harmony Church Road (Route 704) and drive 2.3 miles. Turn left on Loudoun Orchard Road (portions unpaved) and drive another 2.3 miles. Turn right onto Mt. Gilead Road and the winery on the right.

❖ ❖ ❖

Zephaniah Farm Vineyard
19381 Dunlop Mill Road
Leesburg VA 20175

Hours: F–Su 12:00–5:30 (Apr to mid-Dec)
Closed mid-Dec to early Mar

703-431-2016
http://zephwine.com/Z
E-mail: bonnie@zephwine.com

Zephaniah Farm Vineyard is on a 376-acre working farm that has been in the Hatch family for three generations. Owners Bill and Bonnie Hatch planted their first vines in 2002 and produced their first vintage six years later; Bill and son Tremaine are the winemakers. Zephaniah's main weekend tasting room is on the first floor of the family's historic manor house that was constructed by the builder of President James Monroe's Oak Hill. In addition, Friday tastings are held in the adjacent barn, which offers indoor seating as well as a shaded back porch.

White Wines: Adeline, Chardonnay, Steamship White, Viognier.

Rosé Wines: Rosé.

Red Wines: Cabernet Franc, Cabernet Sauvignon, Chambourcin, Three Captains Red.

Price Range: $20–$27

Tastings: $10 per person.

Groups: Reservations required for groups of 6 or more; no groups after 2:00 p.m..

Directions: Take U.S. Route 15 South from Leesburg for 3 miles. Turn right onto Harmony Church Road (Route 704). After one mile, turn left onto Dunlop Mill Road (portions unpaved) and the winery ½ mile on the right.

PHYLLOXERA

While Europe's grapes are from *Vitis vinifera*, native American grapevines are members of different *Vitis* species, including *Vitis labrusca*, *Vitis aestivalis*, or *Vitis riparia*. Many American grape varieties excel at producing table grapes or grape juice, but not all are well-suited for wine. Many have strong flavors, and some have a smell that professional wine tasters refer to as "foxiness," a colorful and self-explanatory term.

Native American rootstocks proved to be the salvation of *V. vinifera*—although it must be acknowledged that those same native rootstocks were at the origin of Europe's greatest vineyard crisis.

The mid-nineteenth century was a time of expanding interest in science, including botany, and wealthy Europeans brought back samples of American rootstocks for gardens and greenhouses. Unfortunately, those rootstocks also brought with them the almost microscopic phylloxera louse, which was (and still is) endemic to much of the United States. American grapevines had built up a resistance to phylloxera, but *V. vinifera* is highly vulnerable to phylloxera infestation. Europe's vineyards soon began dying off in an agricultural disaster second only to the Irish potato blight in terms of its impact.

In the 1870s, an American and a French scientist together found a solution. French scientist Jules Planchon was the first to identify the tiny phylloxera louse as the cause of the devastation spreading throughout European vineyards. Missouri state entomologist Charles Riley then uncovered a vital link by identifying the French louse as identical to the American one. Planchon came to Missouri in 1873 to study under Riley's guidance, and the two developed a new approach of grafting *vinifera* vines onto American rootstocks.

Today, roughly 85 percent of *vinifera* vines have been grafted onto native American rootstocks. Because phylloxera finds very dry and/or sandy soils inhospitable, however, ungrafted vines are still cultivated in such regions as South Australia, New Zealand, and Chile.

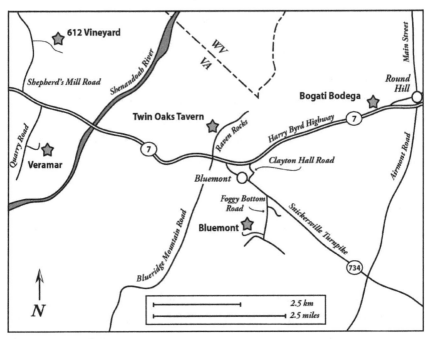

Map 3.5. Bluemont

BLUEMONT

612 Vineyard
864 Shepherds Mill Road
Berryville VA 22611

Hours: W–F 3:00–8:00 (summer & early fall only),
Sa–Su 12:00–6:00
Closed New Year's, Thanksgiving, Christmas

540-535-6689
www.612vineyard.com
E-mail: info@612vineyard.com

Lisa Clarke opened her Clarke County winery and tasting room near the Shenandoah River in 2014, naming it after the route number of her street. 612 Vineyard's wines are from all Virginia-grown grapes sourced in the Shenandoah and made by Randy Phillips of Cave Ridge Vineyards. Guests can linger indoors over wine and light fare at one of the tables near the long tasting bar or outside on the stone patio, which offers a scenic view of the hills surrounding the winery. 612 Vineyard offers live music on weekends. Most leashed dogs are welcome; see the website for breed restrictions. The winery may be rented for weddings

White Wines: Chardonnay, Riesling, Traminette, Viognier.

Red Wines: Always n'Forever, Cabernet Franc, Chambourcin, My Sweet Rouge *(Cabernet Franc)*.

Sweet/Dessert Wines: My Sweet White *(Viognier)*.

Fortified Wines: Sultry N'Red *(port-style)*.

Price Range: $25–$32

Tastings: $5 per person for basic, $10 for full.

Groups: Reservations required for groups of 6 or more.

Directions: From Leesburg, take Route 7 West for 22.5 miles. Once across the Shenandoah River, turn right onto Shepherds Mill Road (VA Route 612) and continue 0.9 mile to the winery entrance and driveway (portions unpaved) on the right.

❖ ❖ ❖

Bluemont Vineyard
18755 Foggy Bottom Road
Bluemont VA 20135

Hours: Daily 11:00–6:00 (F to 8:00) (Mar–Oct)   540-554-8439
Th–Su 11:00–5:00 (Nov–Feb)   www.bluemontvineyard.com
Closed New Year's, Thanksgiving, Christmas   E-mail: 951@bluemontvineyard.com

Bluemont Vineyard is Loudoun's highest winery, located on the eastern side of the Blue Ridge Mountains at 951 feet above sea level. The winery sources its wines both from its own vines and from other vineyards in the area. The main tasting area is upstairs in the two-story tasting room and features a wide deck with panoramic views of the valley toward Leesburg and Washington, D.C. The winery offers gourmet snacks as well as fare from food trucks on weekends for purchase; outside food is not permitted. Children and leashed pets are welcome.

Fruit Wines: Blackberry *(with red wine)*, Peach *(with Vidal Blanc)*, Strawberry *(with red wine)*.

White Wines: Albariño, Chardonnay, Farm Table White, Petit Manseng, Vidal Blanc, Viognier.

Rosé Wines: Rosé.

Red Wines: Cabernet Franc, Cabernet Sauvignon, Chambourcin, Epicurience, Farm Table Red, Meritage, Merlot, Norton.

Sweet/Dessert Wines: Petit Manseng.

Price Range: $22–$25

Tastings: $10 per person.

Groups: Reservations required for groups over 7, $12 per person fee.

Restrictions: No full-sized buses permitted; no outside food.

Directions: From Route 7, turn onto Clayton Hall Road (Route 760 South) toward the town of Bluemont. Take the first left onto Snickersville Turnpike and then turn at the first right onto Foggy Bottom Road to the winery driveway, ½ mile on the right. Continue up the hill to the parking lot.

❖ ❖ ❖

Bogati Winery
35246 Harry Byrd Highway
Round Hill VA 20142

Hours: M–Th 1:00–5:00; F noon–8:00, Sa to 7:00, Su to 6:00   540-338-1144
Closed New Year's, Thanksgiving, Christmas   www.bogatibodega.com
E-mail: info@bogatiwinery.com

Bogati Winery was opened to the public in 2010 by the Bogaty family, which also owns Veramar and James Charles. Justin Bogaty serves as winemaker for all three, using grapes grown at Veramar for production. The Bogatys opened this winery after a family trip to Argentina, and many of the winery's events and tastings reflect the inspiration of that wine-producing country. Bogati Winery also offers food and wine paired tastings

($25) as well as periodic wine and food pairing menus ($45). The tasting room is available for rental for parties and special events.

White Wines: B-Thin *(Seyval Blanc)*, Pinot Grigio, Seyval Blanc, Tango Blu, Viognier.

Red Wines: Collection I *(Bordeaux-style blend)*, Fat*ss Red, JB Merlot, Malbec.

Price Range: $20–$35

Tastings: $10 per person for classic; $8–$10 for self-guided flights.

Groups: Reservations required for groups of 8 or more, $15 per person.

Wheelchair accessible.

Purchasing: Online purchasing available to AK, CA, DC, FL, and VA.

Directions: From Leesburg, take Route 7 West for 15 miles. The winery will be on the right at the Hill High Orchard Building, about 3/4 mile past Airmont Road/Main Street in the village of Round Hill.

❖ ❖ ❖

Twin Oaks Tavern Winery
18035 Raven Rocks Road
Bluemont VA 20135

Hours: Th–M 12:00–6:00, (F–Sa til 7:00 in summer)   202-255-5009, 540-554-4547
Closed New Year's, Thanksgiving, Christmas   www.twinoakstavernwinery.com
                                                        E-mail: info@twinoakstavernwinery.com

Twin Oaks Tavern Winery is housed in a restored 100-year-old stone tavern of the same name at the northern edge of the Blue Ridge. Owner

Donna Evers and her late husband Bob first planted their vineyard in 1999, ultimately opening to the public in 2008 and expanding their production since. The tasting room is in a small restored outbuilding next to a comfortable deck where visitors can enjoy wine and food over a magnificent view of the Shenandoah Valley below. Events include live music on Saturday afternoons. The property is available for rental for small private events and weddings. Children and pets are welcome.

Fruit Wines: Peach, Raspberry.

White Wines: Chardonnay, Vidal Blanc, White Nights.

Red Wines: Cabernet Sauvignon, Norton, Raven Rocks Red (*Bordeaux-style blend*).

Price Range: $22–$25

Tastings: $12 per person.

Groups: Reservations required for groups over 6.

Directions: From Leesburg, drive west on Route 7 about 15 miles. Just past the village of Bluemont, turn right onto Raven Rocks Road to the winery, ⅓ mile on the left.

❖ ❖ ❖

Veramar Vineyard
905 Quarry Road
Berryville VA 22611

Hours: Daily 12:00–5:00 (Sa to 7:00) 540-955-5510
Closed New Year's, Thanksgiving, Christmas www.veramar.com
E-mail: info@veramar.com

Jim and Della Bogaty opened Veramar Vineyard in 2001 on one hundred acres that border the Shenandoah River. Veramar's estate-grown wines are produced under the supervision of son Justin Bogaty. The tasting room opens onto a covered deck overlooking a pond and the hills beyond. The winery is named after the Vera-Mar Steakhouse in North Carolina, where Jim and Della celebrated their honeymoon; their framed wedding photo and wedding dinner receipt are proudly displayed on the tasting room wall. Veramar hosts a number of special events, including Friday evening "Wine Downs," Elvis weekends, Dog Day afternoons in August, movie nights, and an annual Taste of Tuscany. Jim Bogaty also offers a wine camp workshop on viticulture, tastings, and wine blending. Breads, cheeses, and other snacks are available for purchase. The facilities are available for weddings and private events. Children and pets are welcome.

White Wines: Chardonnay, Riesling-Vidal Blanc, Seyval Blanc, Viognier.

Rosé Wines: Pink Chicken.

Red Wines: Cabernet Franc, Cabernet Sauvignon, Merlot, Rooster Red *(Bordeaux-style blend)*.

Sweet/Dessert Wines: D'Oro *(Vidal Blanc)*.

Price Range: $22–$30

Tastings: $10 per person; $15 for reserve tasting with food pairings (first Saturday of each month only, reservations requested).

Groups: Reservations and prepayment required for groups of 10 or more; $18 per person fee.

Purchasing: Online purchasing available for AK, CA, DC, FL, IN, KS, MO, NV, and VA.

Directions: From Leesburg, take Route 7 West for 22 miles. Once across the Shenandoah River, turn left onto Quarry Road (Route 612) and continue one mile to the winery entrance and driveway (portions unpaved) on the left.

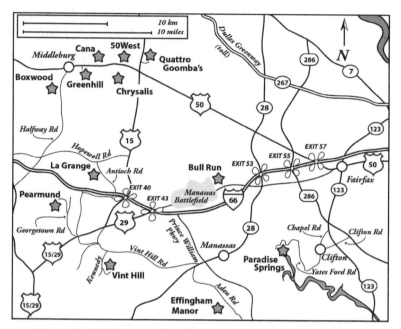

Map 3.6. Middleburg-Fairfax

MIDDLEBURG-FAIRFAX

50 West Vineyards
39060 John Mosby Highway
Middleburg VA 20117

Hours: Th 12:00–5:00, F 1:00–8:00,
Sa–Su 11:00–6:30
Closed New Year's, Christmas

571-367-4760
www.50westvineyards.com
E-mail: information@50westvineyards.com

Mike and Diane Canney, owners of Sunset Hills, opened 50 West Vine-yards in August 2015 on the slopes of a hill just east of Middleburg. The tasting room is in a tastefully renovated two-story stable, called the Tack Room, with seating and tasting bars on both levels; the downstairs opens onto a broad patio with tables overlooking the vineyards and Bull Run Hills beyond. Light fare is offered for purchase at the winery. Children and leashed dogs are welcome.

White Wines: Sauvignon Blanc, Vidal Blanc.

Rosé Wines: Rosé of Sangiovese.

Red Wines: Aldie Heights Cuvée, Chambourcin.

Price Range: $25–$36

Tastings: $10 per person.

Groups: Reservations required for groups of 8–20, $15 per person; no groups over 20.

Directions: From I-66 West, take Exit 57B onto U.S. Route 50 West toward Fair Oaks/Winchester. Continue on U.S. Route 50 for almost 20 miles and turn right into the winery driveway.

❖ ❖ ❖

Boxwood Winery
2042 Burrland Road
Middleburg VA 20118

Hours: Th–Su 11:00–6:00 (summer only)   540-687-8778
F–Su 11:00–6:00 (fall–spring)   www.boxwoodwinery.com
Closed New Year's, Thanksgiving, Christmas   E-mail: contact@boxwoodwinery.com

Boxwood Winery was founded by John Kent Cooke at the historic Boxwood Estate, one of the earliest farms established in the Middleburg area. Boxwood's wines are all Bordeaux-style reds made with grapes from its 19-acre vineyard; its first white, a Sauvignon Blanc, was introduced in 2017. Tastings are held either inside the small tasting room or outdoors on the patio. Cheese plates and bottled water are available for purchase. Boxwood wines are also available at the winery's satellite tasting rooms in Reston Town Center (1816 Library Street, Reston, VA) and the National Harbor (137 Waterfront Street, Oxon Hill, MD).

White Wines: Sauvignon Blanc.

Rosé Wines: Rosé.

Red Wines: Boxwood, Topiary, Trellis.

Price Range: $18–$25

Tastings: $10 per person.

Groups: Reservations required for groups of 10 or more, $20 per person.

Restrictions: No tour buses permitted; no smoking on the grounds.

Purchasing: Online for residents of CA, CO, DC, FL, MD, NC, and VA.

Directions: From I-66, take Exit 40 onto U.S. Route 15 North. Drive about 10 miles and turn onto U.S. Route 50 West. Continue 5 miles into Middleburg and turn left onto Loudoun Road, which will become Halfway Road. Drive about 1 mile to the winery entrance on the right.

❖ ❖ ❖

Cana Vineyards & Winery
38600 John Mosby Highway
Middleburg VA 20117

Hours: Th–F, Su–M 12:00–6:00 (F til 9:00 in summer)   703-348-2458
Sa 11:00–6:00 (til 8:00 in summer)   www.canavineyards.com
Closed Easter, Thanksgiving, Christmas   E-mail: info@canavineyards.com

The Bell family opened Cana Vineyards on the grounds of an old farm property just outside of Middleburg. The tasting room is sited on a hill, offering a nice view and cooling breezes from the porch and decks; the wines, made from Virginia and out-of-state grapes, are produced on-site. Visitors may bring their own picnic lunches to enjoy on the grounds or purchase snacks in the tasting room. The winery sponsors live music on Saturday and Sunday afternoon year-round. The facilities are available for weddings and private parties. Children and leashed dogs are welcome.

Sparkling Wines: Sparkling White.

Fruit Wines: Apple, Blueberry-Apple, Raspberry-Apple.

White Wines: Riesling, Rkatsiteli, Seyval Blanc, Tinaja Roja, Traminette, Vidal Blanc, Viognier.

Rosé Wines: Rosé.

Red Wines: Cabernet Franc, Casamento Reserve, Chambourcin, Merlot, Le Mariage, Tempranillo, Touriga.

Sweet/Dessert Wines: Petit Manseng.

Price Range: $16–$31

Tastings: $10 per person with souvenir glass.

Groups: Reservations required for groups of 8 or more; group tastings are held before 2:00.

Purchasing: Online ordering is available to CA, DC, FL, MD, NY, and VA.

Directions: From I-66 West, take Exit 57B onto U.S. Route 50 West toward Fair Oaks/Winchester. Continue on U.S. Route 50 for 20 miles and turn right into the winery driveway.

❖ ❖ ❖

Chrysalis Vineyards
39025 John Mosby Highway
Middleburg VA 20117

Hours: M–Th 10:00–6:00, F–Su 10:00–7:00 (Apr–Oct); 540-687-8222
Daily 10:00–5:00 (Nov–Mar) www.chrysaliswine.com
Closed New Year's, Thanksgiving, Christmas E-mail: info@ChrysalisWine.com

Founded in 1998 by Jennifer McCloud, Chrysalis has over seventy acres of vineyards with plantings in over twenty varieties; most of its wines are estate-grown. McCloud has long had a special interest in the Norton grape and actively works to promote a greater appreciation of this native American variety; indeed, Chrysalis has the largest planting of Norton in the country. Tastings are held outdoors at five covered stations or indoors. Chrysalis offers several indoor and outdoor spaces that may be rented for private events. Visitors may purchase cheese and sausage platters, sandwiches, and salads to enjoy at the winery; menus are available online for advance orders. Last tastings begin thirty minutes before closing.

White Wines: Albariño, Albariño Verde, Sarah's Patio White, Viognier.

Rosé Wines: Mariposa, Sarah's Patio Red *(Norton).*

Red Wines: Norton, Papillon, Petit Verdot, Rubiana, Tannat.

Sweet/Dessert Wines: Petit Manseng.

Fortified Wines: Borboleta *(port-style Norton).*

Price Range: $17–$48

Tastings: $15 per person.

Groups: Reservations required for groups of 8 or more; group tastings are held before 12:00; $15 per person for groups of 10–19, $25 per person for groups of 20–29.

Restrictions: Reservations required for tour buses.

Wheelchair accessible.

Directions: From I-66 West, take Exit 57B onto U.S. Route 50 West toward Fair Oaks/Winchester. Continue on U.S. Route 50 for almost 20 miles and turn left into the winery's gravel driveway. Cross the ford and drive up the hill to the tasting room.

❖ ❖ ❖

Effingham Manor
14337 Trotters Ridge Place
Nokesville VA 20181

Hours: Daily 11:00–7:00 (summer), Daily 11:00-6:00 (fall–spring)　　　703-594-2300
Closed New Year's, Thanksgiving, Christmas　　　www.effinghammanor.com

Chris Pearmund officially opened Effingham Manor in September 2017 on the grounds of a historic 1767-era manor house. Winemaking is under the seasoned guidance of Ashton Lough who also serves as winemaker at Pearmund Cellars and Winery at Bull Run. The tasting room offers a variety of seating options where guests may stay over cheese and crackers their tastings. The property may be rented for weddings and private events.

White Wines: Chardonnay, Traminette, Viognier.

Rosé Wines: Rosé.

Red Wines: King's Ransom (*Bordeaux-style blend*), Meritage, Merlot, Norton, Tannat.

Price Range: $25–$39

Tastings: $10 or $12 per person, depending on flight chosen.

Directions: From Manassas and the Prince William Parkway, take Route 28 South for 2.8 miles. Turn left onto Aden Road (VA 646). Continue to follow Route 646 for 6.5 miles in all. Turn right onto Trotters Ridge Place. The winery entrance will be 0.5 miles on the left.

❖ ❖ ❖

Greenhill Vineyard
23595 Winery Lane
Middleburg VA 20117

Hours: Daily, noon until sunset

Closed New Year's, Thanksgiving, Christmas

540-687-6968

www.greenhillvineyard.com

E-mail: info@greenhillvineyard.com

David Greenhill purchased the historic 128-acre Valley View Estate, home to the former Swedenburg Estate Winery, and opened to the public in mid-2013. Sébastien Marquet serves as the winemaker. The tasting room offers seating both indoors and out, with cheeses, cold cuts, and crackers available for purchase. The outdoor tables offer splendid views of the vineyards as well as of the original manor house that now serves as a space for wine club members only. Leashed dogs are welcome outdoors.

Sparkling Wines: Blanc de Blancs.

White Wines: Chardonnay, Intention, Riesling, Viognier.

Red Wines: Eternity, Mythology.

Price Range: $36–$45

Tastings: $14 per person.

Groups: Reservations required for groups of 10 or more; reservations also required for buses and limousines at least 48 hours in advance.

Purchasing: Online for all states *except* AL, AR, KY, ME, MO, MT, OK, PA, and SD.

Directions: From I-66, take Exit 57B onto U.S. Route 50 West and drive 21 miles to the winery on left.

❖ ❖ ❖

Paradise Springs Winery & Vineyard
13219 Yates Ford Road
Clifton VA 20124

Hours: W–Su 11:00–7:00 (F to 9:00, Apr–Dec only)　　　　703-830-9463
F–Su 11:00–6:00 (Jan–Mar)　　　　www.paradisespringswinery.com
Closed New Year's, Easter,　　　　E-mail: wine@paradisespringswinery.com
Thanksgiving, Christmas

Paradise Springs was founded in 2007 by Jane Kincheloe and her son Kirk Wiles and opened to the public in 2009. The winery sponsors Friday happy hours, live music on weekends, and a pumpkin carving festival in October. The spacious tasting room offers light fare to have either inside or on the covered deck, which features an outdoor fireplace. The facilities are available for rental for private parties and dinners. Leashed dogs are welcome. Please note that last pours begin thirty minutes before closing.

Sparkling Wines: Après *(Viognier)*, Blanc de Blancs.

White Wines: Chardonnay, Petit Manseng, Sauvignon Blanc, Viognier.

Rosé Wines: Nana's Rosé.

Red Wines: Cabernet Franc, Cabernet Sauvignon, Mélange, Meritage, Pinot Noir, Tannat.

Fortified Wines: Swagger *(port-style)*.

Price Range: $20–$55

Tastings: $15 per person.

Groups: Reservations required for groups of 8 or more; $15 per person.

Wheelchair accessible.

Purchasing: Online or via VinoShipper to AK, AL, CA, DC, FL, ID, IL, LA, MN, MO, NC, ND, NE, NH, NM, NV, OH, OR, VA, WV, and WY..

Directions: From I-66, take Exit 55 onto southbound Fairfax County Parkway (Route 286 South). Drive about 5 miles and take the exit for Route 123 South. Turn right at the second traffic light onto Clifton Road (Route 645). Turn left onto Yates Ford Road before entering the village of Clifton and drive 1.7 miles to the winery on left.

❖ ❖ ❖

Pearmund Cellars
6190 Georgetown Road
Broad Run VA 20137

Hours: Daily 10:00–6:00 (F to 8:30, Apr–Oct)　　　　540-347-3475
Closed New Year's, Easter, Thanksgiving, Christmas　　www.pearmundcellars.com
E-mail: info@pearmundcellars.com

Chris Pearmund founded Pearmund Cellars in 2003 after over a decade of selling grapes to regional wineries from his twenty-five-acre Meriwether Vineyard. The winery sponsors a number of special events, including TGIF nights, Girls Night Out, winemaker dinners, and an SPCA fundraiser. The barrel room is available for rental for parties and dinners. Pearmund welcomes leashed dogs and supervised children, with a "Kid's Corner" inside the tasting room.

White Wines: Chardonnay, Petit Manseng, Riesling, Vidal Blanc, Viognier.

Red Wines: Ameritage, Black Ops, Cabernet Franc, Cabernet Sauvignon, Malbec, Merlot, Petit Verdot.

Sweet/Dessert Wines: Late Harvest Petit Manseng, Late Harvest Traminette.

Price Range: $20–$39

Tastings: $10 per person.

Groups: Reservations required for groups of 6 or more.

Wheelchair accessible.

Directions: From I-66, take Exit 43A (Gainesville/Warrenton) onto U.S. Route 29 South. Drive 7.5 miles and take a right onto Old Alexandria Turnpike, staying straight to go onto Georgetown Road (Route 674) after ¼ mile. The long winery driveway (portions unpaved) will be one mile on the left.

❖ ❖ ❖

Quattro Goomba's Winery
22860 James Monroe Highway
Aldie VA 20105

Hours: W–M 12:00–6:00 (F to 9:00 in summer)   703-327-6052
Closed New Year's, Thanksgiving, Christmas   www.goombawine.com
E-mail: qgw@goombawine.com

Quattro Goomba's is a micro-commercial winery that sources its wines from Virginia and other grape-growing states and countries. After sampling wines, visitors can stay over a glass or bottle and enjoy freshly baked Sicilian-style pizza by the slice. Quattro Goomba's offers live music on weekends and can be rented for weddings and private parties. Children and leashed dogs are welcome. The winery now has a brewery on site.

White Wines: Piney River White *(Virginia)*, Sorelle *(Washington state)*.

Rosé Wines: Piney River Rosé *(Virginia)*.

Red Wines: Curico *(Chile)*, Piney River Red *(Virginia)*, Tradizione *(Virginia)*, Vino di Nonni *(California)*, Vino di San Pietro *(California)*.

Sweet/Dessert Wines: Vino Dolce *(Virginia)*.

Price Range: $20–$29

Tastings: $8 per person.

Groups: Reservations required for groups of 8 or more.

Wheelchair accessible.

Directions: From I-66, take Exit 57B onto U.S. Route 50 West. Follow U.S. Route 50 West for 17 miles through one roundabout. At the second roundabout, take the exit onto James Monroe Highway (U.S. Route 15 North) and drive 1.2 miles to the winery on right.

❖ ❖ ❖

Vint Hill Craft Winery
7150 Lineweaver Road
Warrenton VA 20187

Hours: F–Su 11:00–6:00
Closed New Year's, Thanksgiving, Christmas

540-351-0000
www.vinthillcraftwinery.com
E-mail: info@craftwinery.com

Vint Hill is a custom-crush winery that offers customers a unique opportunity to design and produce a half or full barrel of wine under the guidance of experienced winemakers. Founded in 2009 by Chris Pearmund (Pearmund Cellars) and Ray Summerell, the winery is housed in a restored 1900 dairy barn at Vint Hill Farms, once a secure listening post run by the U.S. military until the 1990s. The winery uses grapes from Virginia, California, and Washington in production; it has no vineyard of its own. Vint Hill's tasting bar overlooks the production floor, offering visitors the chance to see winemaking in action.

Price Range: $22–$29 for a bottle under production

Tastings: $10 per person for a flight of wines under production.

Groups: Reservations requested for groups of 8 or more, $15 per person with souvenir glass.

Purchasing: Contact the winery for details.

Directions: From I-66, take Exit 43A (Gainesville/Warrenton) onto U.S. Route 29 South. Drive 5.2 miles and turn left onto Vint Hill Road (Route 215). After 1.6 miles, turn right onto Kennedy Road (Route 652). Turn left at the stop sign onto Aiken Road; drive ¼ mile. Turn left onto Bludau Drive and then right onto Lineweaver Road to the entrance.

❖ ❖ ❖

Winery at Bull Run
15950 Lee Highway
Centreville VA 20120

Hours: Sa–W 11:00–7:00, Th 11:00–8:00,　　　　　　703-815-2233
F 11:00–9:00 (to 10:00 May–Sep)　　　　　　www.wineryatbullrun.com
Closed New Year's, Easter, Thanksgiving, Christmas

Jon and Kim Hickox opened The Winery at Bull Run on a historic property bordering the Manassas National Battlefield Park; Civil War relics found during construction are on display in the tasting room. Winemaker Ashton Lough uses all Virginia- and estate-grown fruit for the wines. The tasting room features a number of tables and sofas inside, as well as tables and seating outdoors on the veranda and grounds, including covered tables in the Generals' Quarters (reservation only). The winery offers live music on weekends with light fare and food trucks, and may be rented for parties and weddings. Children are welcome but must be supervised at all times. Bull Run offers discounts for military personnel, police, and firefighters.

Sparkling Wines: Stonebridge.

Fruit Wines: Blackberry, Blueberry, Peach, Strawberry.

White Wines: Chardonnay, Delaney, Petit Manseng, Pinot Gris, Riesling, Viognier.

Rosé Wines: Rosé.

Red Wines: Cabernet Franc, Cabernet Sauvignon, Meritage, Merlot, Norton, Petit Verdot.

Price Range: $19–$38

Tastings: $12 per person with souvenir glass.

Groups: Reservations required for groups from 8 to 25; tastings held before 3:00, $15 per person.

Wheelchair accessible.

Purchasing: Online ordering available to most states.

Directions: From I-66, take Exit 52 onto U.S. Route 29 South. Drive 2.8 miles to the winery entrance on the right.

❖ ❖ ❖

Winery at La Grange
4970 Antioch Road
Haymarket VA 20169

Hours: Daily 11:00–6:00 (Sa to 8:00, Su to 7:00 in summer)   703-753-9360
Closed New Year's, Easter, Thanksgiving, Christmas   www.wineryatlagrange.com
E-mail: info@wineryatlagrange.com

The Winery at La Grange was founded in 2006 by Chris Pearmund (Pearmund Cellars, Vint Hill) and is now owned by a group of Chinese investors, with Seth Chambers as winemaker. It is located on the twenty-acre historic La Grange estate, whose manor house dates from the 1790s. The parlor and downstairs lounge offer comfortable seating where guests can relax over a glass of wine or use the winery's Wi-Fi; outdoor seating is also available on the patios. La Grange sponsors a number of special activities and events, including movie nights, Sangria Saturdays, and winemaker dinners. The facilities are available to rent for private parties and weddings.

White Wines: Chardonnay, Cuvée Blanc, Pinot Gris.

Rosé Wines: Rosé.

Red Wines: Benoni's Red, Cabernet Franc, Cabernet Sauvignon, General's Battlefield Red, Meritage, Norton.

Fortified Wines: Snort *(port-style)*.

Price Range: $24–$43

Tastings: $13 per person with souvenir glass.

Groups: Reservations required for groups of 6 or more.

Wheelchair accessible.

Purchasing: Online to VA or via VinoShipper to AK, AL, AZ, CA, CO, DC, FL, GA, HI, IA, ID, IL, IN, KS, LA, MA, MD, ME, MN, MO, NC, ND, NE, NH, NM, NV, NY, OH, OR, PA, SC, TN, TX, WA, WI, WV, and WY.

Directions: From I-66, take Exit 40 (Haymarket) onto U.S. Route 15 South. Turn right at the second light onto Route 55 and drive about one mile. Turn right onto Antioch Road and continue 3 miles to the winery on left.

READING A VIRGINIA WINE LABEL

All wine labels must be approved by the federal Bureau of Alcohol, Tobacco, Firearms, and Explosives (BATFE), which determines the specific guidelines governing each element on those wine labels, down to the font size of the print.

Let's decipher the label of an imaginary Virginia winery.

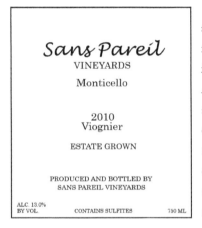

Sans Pareil
VINEYARDS
Monticello

2010
Viognier

ESTATE GROWN

PRODUCED AND BOTTLED BY
SANS PAREIL VINEYARDS

ALC. 13.0%
BY VOL   CONTAINS SULFITES   750 ML

Below the winery name is the name of an American Viticultural Area (AVA). This means that at least 85 percent of the grapes in this particular wine were grown in that AVA. If a county name is included instead, at least 85 percent of the grapes must have come from that county. If the label reads simply "Virginia," then 75 percent or more of the grapes are from Virginia. Look (or ask) for "100% Virginia grown" if you are seeking a pure Virginia wine.

The vintage year and varietal name will also be displayed on the label. If the wine is a blend, the label will show the name of the wine, but the specific grape varieties and their proportions may or may not be listed, depending on the winery's preferences.

"Estate grown" means that all the grapes for this wine were grown on the winery's property.

This particular wine was produced and bottled at the winery itself. A number of small Virginia wineries work with a larger winery or use a "custom crush" facility, such as Michael Shaps Wineworks, to produce their wines. In these instances, the winery will work closely with an expert winemaker to customize the wine and blend it to the winery's specifications.

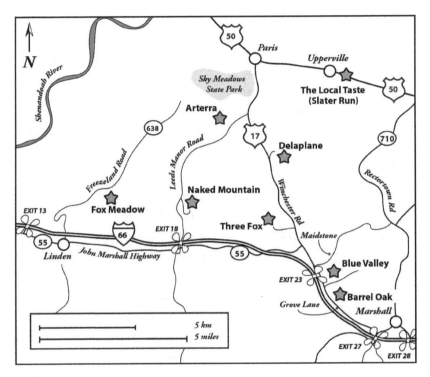

Map 3.7. Delaplane

DELAPLANE

Arterra Vineyard
1808 Leeds Manor Road
Delaplane VA 20144

Hours: F–Su, holiday M 11:00–5:00
Closed New Year's Eve & Day,
Thanksgiving, Christmas

540-422-3443
www.arterrawines.com
E-mail: arterrawines@gmail.com

Arterra was opened in 2015 by Jason Murray and Sandy Gray-Murray who use the winery as both a tasting room and exhibit area for Sandy's Hawkmoth Art. Arterra's tasting bar features river-tumbled rocks under a glass top, and both its indoor and outdoor tables offer a zen view of the surrounding trees, a perfect complement to Jason's organically made wines. Snacks are available for purchase at the winery.

Fruit Wines: Apple, Blueberry-Apple.

White Wines: Chardonnay, Riesling.

Red Wines: Cabernet Franc, Hawkmoth Reserve, Malbec, Petit Verdot, Tannat.

Sweet/Dessert Wines: Late-Harvest Tannat.

Price Range: $29–$49

Tastings: $10 per person for 4 wines, $15 for 6 wines.

Groups: Reservations required for groups over 5; no limos or buses.

Wheelchair accessible.

Purchasing: Online through VinoShipper for residents of AL, AK, AZ, CA, CO, DC, FL, GA, IA, ID, IL, IN, KS, LA, MA, MD, ME, MN, MO,

NE, NV, NH, NM, NC, ND, NY, OH, OR, PA, SC, TN, TX, VA, WA, WI, WV, and WY.

Directions: From I-66, take exit 23 (Delaplane/Paris). Drive north on Winchester Road (U.S. Route 17) for 5.8 miles. Turn left onto Leeds Manor Road (Route 688). Drive 1.4 miles to the winery's gravel drive on the right.

❖ ❖ ❖

Barrel Oak Winery
3623 Grove Lane
Delaplane VA 20144

Hours: Daily 11:00–6:00 (F, Sa to 9:00, May–Nov only), Closed New Year's, Thanksgiving, Christmas

540-364-6402
www.barreloak.com
E-mail: info@barreloak.com

Barrel Oak was founded in 2008 by Brian and Sharon Roeder and has become a popular weekend wine destination. Tastings are held in the winery's modern two-story tasting room, with special reserve tastings also available. In addition to live music and TGI Sunsets, Barrel Oak sponsors a range of special events, including breast cancer fundraisers and special pet adoption weekends. The winery may be rented for private parties. Children and leashed dogs are welcome.

White Wines: BowHaus White, Chardonnay, Petit Manseng, Seyval Blanc, Viognier.

Rosé Wines: Rosé.

Red Wines: BowHaus Red, Cabernet Franc, Cabernet Sauvignon, Meritage, Petit Verdot.

Sweet/Dessert Wines: Chocolate Lab Red.

Fortified Wines: Madeira.

Price Range: $29–$60

Tastings: $7 per person for flight of three wines, $11 for six.

Handicapped accessible.

Purchasing: Online to VA or via VinoShipper for AL, AK, CA, DC, FL, ID, IL, LA, MN, MO, NE, NV, NH, NM, NC, ND, OH, OR, WV, WY.

Directions: From I-66, take Exit 27 (Marshall). Turn north in the direction of Marshall onto Free State Road (Route 55). Make an immediate left onto Grove Lane. The winery entrance will be about 2 miles on the right.

❖ ❖ ❖

Blue Valley Vineyard & Winery
9402 Justice Lane
Delaplane VA 20144

Hours: M–Th 11:00–6:00, F, Su 11:00–7:00 (Apr–Oct) 540-364-2347
Closed New Year's, Thanksgiving, www.bluevalleyvineyardandwinery.com
Christmas Eve & Day E-mail: Events@BlueValleyVA.com

The Zissios family opened their tasting room high on a hill with views of vineyards and hilltops from the spacious stone patios that surround the tasting room. Blue Valley's wines are made with fruit from their 14-acre vineyard as well as from elsewhere in the United States. Breads, cheeses, and dips are available for purchase in the tasting room. The facilities may be rented for special events and weddings.

White Wines: Chardonnay, Heritage, Muscat Ottonel, Pinot Gris, Sauvignon Blanc.

Rosé Wines: Rosé, Virginia Rosé.

Red Wines: Celebration, Merlot, Petit Verdot, Remembrance, Tradition.

Price Range: $20–$39

Tastings: $10 per person.

Groups: Reservations required for groups of 8 or more, $16 per person.

Purchasing: Online via VinoShipper to AK, AL, AZ, CA, CO, DC, FL, GA, HI, IA, ID, IL, IN, KS, LA, MA, MD, ME, MN, MO, NC, ND, NE, NH, NM, NV, NY, OH, OR, SC, TN, TX, WA, WI, WV, and WY.

Directions: From I-66, take Exit 27 (Marshall). Turn north in the direction of Marshall onto Free State Road (Route 55). Make an immediate left onto Grove Lane. Drive 3.1 miles and turn right onto Justice Lane (narrow, portions unpaved). The winery entrance will be about 0.3 miles on the left.

❖ ❖ ❖

Delaplane Cellars
2187 Winchester Road
Delaplane VA 20144

Hours: Th–M 11:00–5:00 (Sa to 6:00) (Mar–Dec);
F–Su 11:00–5:00 (Jan–Feb)
Closed New Year's, Thanksgiving,
Christmas Eve & Day

540-592-7210
www.delaplanecellars.com
E-mail: wine@delaplanecellars.com

Delaplane Cellars was founded by Jim and Betsy Dolphin. The tasting room and terrace both offer a view of the Crooked Run valley. Light food is also available for purchase. In summer, Delaplane sponsors Sunset Saturdays and Easy Like Sunday Afternoons with live music. Vineyard tours ($15 per person) are available in summers (reservations required). Military, veterans, police officers, and firefighters receive a 10 percent discount on wine purchases. The winery is certified Virginia Green.

White Wines: Chardonnay, Mélange Blanc, Sauvignon Blanc, Vidal Blanc, Viognier.

Rosé Wines: Rosé.

Red Wines: Cabernet Franc, Cinq5, Duet, Left Bank, Mélange Rouge, Merlot, Springlot, Syrah, Williams Gap.

Sweet/Dessert Wines: Late Harvest Petit Manseng.

Price Range: $20–$30

Tastings: $8 per person.

Wheelchair accessible.

Restrictions: No buses or limos; no groups over six; no outside food; no visitors under 21.

Purchasing: Online purchasing available for VA residents; please contact the winery for shipping to all other states.

Directions: From I-66, take Exit 23 onto Winchester Road (U.S. Route 17 North) toward Delaplane and Paris. Continue on U.S. Route 17 North for 4 miles and turn right onto the winery's single-lane gravel driveway.

❖ ❖ ❖

Fox Meadow Winery
3310 Freezeland Road
Linden VA 22642

Hours: M–F 11:00–5:00, Sa–Su 11:00–6:00   540-636-6777
Closed New Year's, Easter, Thanksgiving, Christmas   www.foxmeadowwinery.com
E-mail: info@foxmeadowwinery.com

Perched on a hillside over 1,700 feet above sea level, Fox Meadow Winery offers guests a spectacular vista of vineyards and the Blue Ridge from its tasting room and outdoor deck. Originally part of the Freezeland Orchards, Fox Meadow was founded by Dan and Cheryl Mortland and opened to the public in 2006. The tasting room offers visitors two tasting bars from which to sample Fox Meadow's wines, many of which are paired with food samples for extra effect. A side tasting room may be rented for small events. Fox Meadow is available for weddings or private parties.

White Wines: Blue Mountain Mist, Chardonnay, Freezeland White, Le Renard Gris, Pinot Grigio, Pinot Gris, Riesling, Vidal Blanc.

Red Wines: Cabernet Franc, Cabernet Sauvignon, Chambourcin, Freezeland Red, Le Renard Rouge *(Bordeaux-style blend)*, Meritage, Merlot.

Price Range: $19–$29

Tastings: $6 per person.

Groups: Reservations required for groups of 8 or more, $10 per person fee.

Wheelchair accessible.

Purchasing: Online for DC, FL, GA, MD, NC, PA, TX, and VA residents.

Directions: From I-66 West, take Exit 18 (Markham) and turn south onto Leeds Manor Road. Turn west onto John Marshall Highway (Route 55) and drive 4 miles toward Linden. Turn right onto Freezeland Road (Route 638) and continue 3 miles to the winery up the hill and on the right.

❖ ❖ ❖

Naked Mountain Vineyard
2747 Leeds Manor Road
Markham VA 22643

Hours: Daily 11:00–5:00 (F–Su to 6:00, Apr–Oct)   540-364-1609
Closed New Year's Eve & Day, Thanksgiving,   www.nakedmountainwinery.com
Christmas Eve & Day   E-mail: drinknaked@nakedmountainwinery.com

Founded in 1982, Naked Mountain is owned by Randy and Megan Morgan. Located on forty-two acres, it now produces over six thousand cases of wine each year. The tasting room includes a fireplace for chilly days and opens onto a deck offering a splendid view of mountains, valleys, and vines. The winery hosts winemaker dinners and open houses, as well as live music on weekends. Pets are welcome.

White Wines: Aerie White, Birthday Suit, Chardonnay, Chardonnay-Riesling, Riesling, Skinny Dipper.

Rosé Wines: Make Me Blush.

Red Wines: Aerie Red, Cabernet Franc, Cabernet Sauvignon, Catamount Run Red, Raptor Red, Red Light.

Sweet/Dessert Wines: Old Vine Riesling, Soar.

Price Range: $20–$34

Tastings: $10 per person.

Groups: Reservations required for groups of 8 to 15 (maximum size), $15 per person fee; long vehicles and stretch limos will find it difficult to maneuver around the driveway's blind curve.

Wheelchair accessible.

Purchasing: Online via VinoShipper to AK, AL, AZ, CA, CO, DC, FL, GA, IA, ID, IL, IN, KS, LA, MA, MD, ME, MN, MO, NC, ND, NE, NH, NJ, NM, NV, NY, OH, OR, PA, SC, TN, TX, VA, WA, WI, WV, and WY.

Directions: From I-66, take exit 18 (Markham) and drive north on Leeds Manor Road (Route 688) for 1.6 miles. The long winery driveway will be on the right (watch out for the blind curve!).

❖ ❖ ❖

Slater Run Vineyard
(Tasting Room: The Local Taste)
9030 John S. Mosby Highway (U.S. Route 50)
Upperville VA 20185

Hours: Th–Sa 12:00–6:00, Su 12:00–5:00
Closed New Year's Eve & Day, Thanksgiving,
Christmas Eve & Day

540-592-3042
www.slaterrun.com
Tasting room: www.thelocaltaste.net
E-mail: info@thelocaltaste.net

Chris and Kerry Slater Patusky established their winery on 300 acres of land that has been in Kerry's family since the early 1700's. They planted their vineyard in 2010, with a first vintage four years later. Slater Run wines may be sampled at their tasting room in Upperville, The Local Taste, in a historic 19th-century building that features monthly events including an Oyster Fest, guided wine tastings, and book signings for local writers. The vineyard and production facilities are open a few times per year for special occasions; check the winery's Facebook page for announcements. Slater Run produces all estate-grown wines under winemaker Katell Griaud; they also offer a dessert wine produced by Katell's family-run winery in France, Chateau Kalian.

White Wines: Chardonnay, Pinot Gris.

Rosé Wines: Rosé.

Red Wines: Cabernet Franc, First Bridge (*Bordeaux-style blend*).

Sweet/Dessert Wines: Chateau Kalian Monbazillac.

Price Range: $19–$50

Tastings: $10 per person.

Groups: Reservations requested for groups of 8 or more.

Wheelchair accessible.

Purchasing: Online at VinoShipper for AL, AK, AZ, CA, CO, DC, FL, GA, HI, IA, ID, IL, IN, KS, LA, MA, MD, ME, MN, MO, NC, ND, NE, NH, NM, NV, NY, OH, OR, PA, SC, TN, TX, VA, WA, WI, WV, WY.

Directions: From U.S. Route 50, drive west through Middleburg for 8 miles to the Local Taste on the right.

❖ ❖ ❖

Three Fox Vineyards
10100 Three Fox Lane
Delaplane VA 20144

Hours: Th–Sa, M 11:00–5:00, Su 12:00–5:00   540-364-6073
Closed New Year's Eve & Day,   www.threefoxvineyards.com
Thanksgiving, Christmas Eve & Day   E-mail: info@threefoxvineyards.com

Three Fox Vineyards acquired its name when Holli and Jon Todhunter saw three foxes on a hill while first visiting the property. The winery sits on fifty acres of gently rolling hills and includes over ten acres of vines. Three Fox sponsors a range of events, including Vin-Olympics, wine dinners,

SPCA fundraisers, and an annual Blessing of the Harvest. At 1:00 p.m. on summertime Sundays, winemaker Jon leads Winemaker Walkabouts through the vineyard and winery (reservations required). Three Fox may be rented for weddings or private events. Children and dogs are welcome.

Sparkling Wines: T-J Blanc de Chardonnay.

White Wines: Calabrese Pinot Grigio, Gatto Bianco, La Bohème Viognier, La Giocosa Chardonnay, Leggero Chardonnay.

Rosé Wines: Cano Passo Rosé.

Red Wines: Alouette Cabernet Franc, La Trovatella Merlot, Piemontese Nebbiolo, Signor Sangiovese Reserve, Volpe Sangiovese.

Fortified Wines: Rosso Dolce Chambourcin.

Price Range: $21–$29

Tastings: $5 per person.

Groups: Reservations required for groups of 8 to 50; $15 per person.

Restrictions: No buses after 2:00 p.m.

Purchasing: Online at VinoShipper to AL, AK, AZ, CA, CO, DC, FL, GA, HI, IA, ID, IL, IN, KS, LA, MA, MD, ME, MN, MO, NC, ND, NE, NH, NM, NV, NY, OH, OR, PA, SC, TN, TX, VA, WA, WI, WV, and WY.

Directions: From I-66, take Exit 23 (Delaplane/Paris). Turn onto U.S. Route 17 North and continue about one mile. After crossing the railroad tracks, turn left onto Three Fox Lane and the winery entrance on the left.

୬ஓஅ

WHITE, RED, AND PINK WINES

Peel back the skin of a *V. vinifera* grape, and you will find, with few exceptions, that the fruit underneath is light, regardless of the color of the grape skins. It is easy to see that white wines get their color from the grape itself. The color for red and pink wines comes from a different step in the winemaking process.

The juice for red wines becomes red by keeping the grape skins in contact with the juice. This skin contact may range from less than a day to a week or more, depending on the wine being made. In addition to color, the skins also convey flavor and tannins, helping give the finished wine body and structure.

This also means that white wines may be made even from dark-skinned grapes as long as the juice does not come in contact with the skins. The most well-known such wine is Champagne, which is made from Pinot Noir and Pinot Meunier (both dark-skinned grapes) as well as from Chardonnay (a light-skinned grape).

Rosé, or pink, wines are made through one of several methods. In direct press, the grapes are crushed, and the must (juice, pulp, skins, stems) is quickly pressed and the juice put in a fermentation tank. Winemakers may also allow the juice to remain in contact with the skins, a process called maceration. In the saignée method, red grapes are barely crushed and then are left to rest in the tank for a few hours before some juice is drawn, or bled, off for rosé and the rest is then processed as red wine. (Saignée means "bled" in French.) Regardless of method, the color of the final wine will range from pale blush to a deeper pink, depending on how long the juice rested on the skins.

A common practice in the United States and other countries is to blend white and red wines together after fermentation. This approach is illegal in France, though French winemakers sometimes get around the ban by co-fermenting white and red grapes or by blending a light rosé with a darker one.

୬ஓஅ

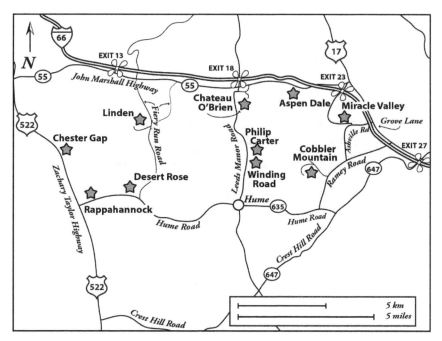

Map 3.8. Northern Blue Ridge

NORTHERN BLUE RIDGE

Aspen Dale Winery at the Barn
11083 John Marshall Highway
Delaplane VA 20144

Hours: M–Th 11:00–5:00, F–Sa 11:00–6:00, Su 12:00–6:00   540-364-1722
Closed New Year's, Thanksgiving,   www.aspendalewinery.com
Christmas   E-mail: reservations@aspendalewinery.com

Aspen Dale Winery is located on a two-hundred-year-old country estate that once belonged to the family of nineteenth-century Supreme Court Chief Justice John Marshall and is now owned by Larry and Kelly Carr. The tasting room is in a restored barn, with tables, sofas, and wing chairs adjoining the tasting bar; live music is featured on weekends. Their Virginia-grown wines are paired with small samplings of food for tastings. Cheeses, sausage, and other foods are also available for purchase. The facilities may be rented for weddings and private events. Children and dogs are welcome.

Ciders: Hard Cider.

White Wines: Hildersham, Islington, Sarah's Chapeau.

Rosé Wines: Mary Madeleine's Rosé.

Red Wines: Bridgetown Red, Parris Country Blend, Rockawalkin' *(Bordeaux-style blend)*.

Price Range: $22–$42

Tastings: $8 per person.

Groups: Reservations required for groups of 8 or more.

Directions: From I-66, take Exit 23 (Paris/Delaplane) onto U.S. Route 17 North for ½ mile. Turn west onto John Marshall Highway (Route 55). Drive 2.4 miles to the winery entrance on the left.

❖ ❖ ❖

Chateau O'Brien at Northpoint
3238 Rail Stop Road
Markham VA 22643

Hours: Th–M 11:00–5:00
Closed New Year's, Easter,
Thanksgiving, Christmas Eve & Day

540-364-6441
www.chateauobrien.com
E-mail: howard@chateauobrien.com

Howard and Debbie O'Brien opened their winery and vineyard to the public in 2006, four years after purchasing the property. Chateau O'Brien's French-style farmhouse home is on a hilltop, and visitors can see it long before they pull into the parking lot. The farmhouse includes three separate tasting rooms and a covered deck with sweeping views of the countryside and vines. Chateau O'Brien regularly hosts murder mystery dinners, an annual crab boil, and various festivals. The winery is also available for private parties or dinners. Active duty military receive a 15 percent discount.

Fruit Wines: Virginia Apple Wine.

White Wines: Chardonnay, Northpoint White, Petit Manseng, Pinot Grigio.

Rosé Wines: April's Apple Rosé, Northpoint Rosé, Tannat Rosé.

Red Wines: Buddy's Bistro Red, Cabernet Franc, Cabernet Sauvignon, Malbec, Northpoint Red, Padlock Red, Petit Verdot, Syrah.

Sweet/Dessert Wines: Ice Apple Wine, Late Harvest Tannat.

Price Range: $25–$79

Tastings: $8 per person for classic; $15 for cellar collection, Sa–Su only.

Groups: Reservations required for groups of 8 or more, $20 per person.

Wheelchair accessible.

Restrictions: No one under 21 permitted in the tasting room or on the winery grounds; buses, vans, and limos by appointment only. No pets.

Purchasing: Online ordering available for most states; see website for details.

Directions: From I-66, take Exit 18 (Markham). Turn south onto Leeds Manor Road and cross John Marshall Highway (Route 55). Turn left onto Old Markham Road and then make a hairpin right onto Rail Stop Road. Drive up the hill to the winery entrance.

❖ ❖ ❖

Chester Gap Cellars
4615 Remount Road
Front Royal VA 22630

Hours: F–Su 11:00–5:00 (F, Sa to 6:00 in summer)   540-636-8086

Memorial Day & Labor Day 11:00–5:00   www.chestergapcellars.com

Closed New Year's, Christmas   E-mail: Bernd@ChesterGapCellars.com

Chester Gap is located near the Shenandoah National Park at over one thousand feet in elevation, offering a lovely view from the tasting room and deck of the gap for which it is named. Owners Bernd and Kristi Jung got their start in the wine business in Florida before moving to Virginia and establishing Chester Gap. The couple planted their first vines on their eight-acre vineyard in 2000 and produced their first wines four years later.

A native of Munich, Germany, Bernd also serves as the winemaker and vineyard manager.

White Wines: Roussanne, Viognier.

Red Wines: Cabernet Franc, Merlot, Petit Verdot, Vintner Red.

Sweet/Dessert Wines: Cuvée Manseng *(Petit Manseng)*.

Price Range: $19–$32

Tastings: $7 per person.

Restrictions: No groups over 6; no buses or limos permitted.

Purchasing: Online shipping for VA residents only.

Directions: From I-66, take Exit 13 (Linden). Turn south onto Apple Mountain Road (Route 79) and then right onto John Marshall Highway (Route 55). Drive 4.7 miles and turn left onto U.S. Route 522 (Remount Road/Zachary Taylor Highway). The winery will be 4.7 miles on the left.

❖ ❖ ❖

Cobbler Mountain Cellars
10363 Moreland Road (GPS address)
5909 Long Fall Lane (street address)
Delaplane VA 20144

Hours: Th–M 11:00–5:00
Closed New Year's,
Thanksgiving, Christmas

540-364-2802
www.cobblermountain.com
E-mail: shop-cobbler@gmail.com

Jeff and Laura McCarthy Louden established Cobbler Mountain Cellars on a ninety-acre farm that Laura's father had originally purchased in 1959. Located high on a hill overlooking Little Cobbler Mountain, the winery offers seating on the patio at the side of the house and on the lawn. Several signs along the long driveway point guests to a creekside picnic area and a hiking trail. Bread and artisanal cheeses are available for purchase. Cobbler Mountain also features live music on many weekends. The facilities may be rented for weddings. Children are welcome.

Ciders: Ginger Peach, Hard Apple Cider, Harvest Pumpkin, Jammin' Cranberry Ginger, Kickin' Cinnamon, Maple Stout, Mountain Top Hop, Original Honey, Smackin' Orange, Traditional Jeffersonian, Wild Blackberry Hop.

White Wines: Chardonnay, Cobblestone White, Vidal Blanc.

Red Wines: Cabernet Franc, Cabernet Sauvignon, Malbec, Meritage, Merlot, Petit Verdot.

Price Range: $10–$40.

Tastings: $10 per person; groups of 8 or more, $12 per person.

Purchasing: Online via VinoShipper to AK, AL, CA, DC, FL, ID, IL, LA, MN, MO, NC, ND, NE, NH, NM, NV, OH, OR, VA, WV, and WY.

Directions: From I-66, take Exit 27 (Marshall) and turn north in the direction of Marshall onto Free State Road (Route 55). Make an immediate left onto Grove Lane. Take the first left onto Ramey Road. Drive 3.2 miles and turn right onto Moreland Road (portions unpaved). Cobbler Mountain's driveway (also unpaved) will be about ⅓ mile on the left; continue up the hill to the tasting room entrance on the left side of the house.

❖ ❖ ❖

Desert Rose Ranch & Winery
13726 Hume Road
Hume VA 22639

Hours: Daily 12:00–6:00 (May–Nov)   540-635-3200
F–Su, M holidays 12:00–6:00 (Dec–Apr)   www.desertrosewinery.com
Closed New Year's, Thanksgiving, Christmas   E-mail: info@desertrosewinery.com

Bob and Linda Claymier established Desert Rose Winery on an eighty-acre farm the couple had purchased with the aim of starting a horse ranch. After deciding to establish a vineyard, they opened their winery to the public in 2011. The tasting room's Western theme reflects Bob's background growing up on a ranch in eastern Oregon. The name of the winery is from the desert rose crystalline formations often found in arid regions. Desert Rose offers live music on weekends. Children have a special place of their own in the tasting room's Kiddie Korner. Pets are welcome.

White Wines: Chardonnay, Ole Moo-Moo.

Rosé Wines: Sparky.

Red Wines: Cabernet Franc, Covert Cab *(Crimson Cabernet)*, Fiery Run Franc, Merlot, Norton, R.E.D.

Sweet/Dessert Wines: Desert Delight *(Vidal Blanc)*, Starboard *(Norton)*.

Price Range: $23–$42

Tastings: $8 per person for 8 wines, $10 for 10 wines.

Groups: Reservations required for groups of 6 or more, $12 per person fee.

Wheelchair accessible.

Restrictions: No buses.

Purchasing: Online to DC and VA residents only.

Directions: From I-66, take Exit 18 (Markham) and turn south onto Leeds Manor Road. Cross John Marshall Highway (Route 55) and continue along Leeds Manor Road for 5 miles. Turn right onto Hume Road and drive 5 miles to the winery entrance on the right, just past Fiery Run Road.

❖ ❖ ❖

Linden Vineyards
3708 Harrels Corner Road
Linden VA 22642

Hours: F–Su 11:00–5:00 (Apr–Nov)
Sa–Su 11:00–5:00 (Dec–Mar)
Closed Easter, mid-Dec–6 Jan

540-364-1997
www.lindenvineyards.com
E-mail: wine@lindenvineyards.com

Owner-winemaker Jim Law founded Linden Vineyards in 1983 and opened his winery to the public five years later. A highly respected vintner, Law is considered a mentor by many fellow Virginia winemakers and offers a two-year wine apprenticeship program. Visitors to Linden may opt for a regular tasting or choose a special reserve cellar tasting on weekends (sign up upon arriving). Bread and cheeses are available for purchase. Please note there are no chairs in the tasting room; deck seating is limited to Case Club members on weekends.

White Wines: Chardonnay, Sauvignon Blanc, Riesling-Vidal, Viognier.

Rosé Wines: Rosé.

Red Wines: Avenius Red, Boisseau Red, Claret, Hardscrabble Red, Petit Verdot, Red.

Sweet/Dessert Wines: Late Harvest Petit Manseng, Late Harvest Vidal.

Price Range: $22–$50

Tastings: $8 per person for basic tasting; $25 per person for cellar tasting.

Restrictions: No limos, buses, or groups over 4. Case Club members only on the deck and grounds on weekends, maximum 3 guests per member.

Purchasing: Online ordering for VA residents only.

Directions: From I-66, take Exit 18 (Markham). Turn south onto John Marshall Highway (Route 55) and drive 4.2 miles to the village of Linden. Turn left onto State Route 638 which will become Harrels Corner Road. The winery's gravel driveway will be 2.2 miles on the right.

❖ ❖ ❖

Miracle Valley Vineyard
3841 Cobbler Mountain Road
Delaplane VA 20144

Hours: Th–M 11:00–5:00   540-364-0228
Closed mid-Dec–Feb   www.miraclevalleyvineyard.com
                                        E-mail: vineyardbusiness@aol.com

Established by Mary Ann and Joe Cunningham, Miracle Valley Vineyard opened in 2007. The winery's tasting room is in a restored 1880's farmhouse featuring a handcrafted wooden tasting bar and an adjoining parlor with a fireplace, tables, and chairs for visitors. The winery's stone patios offer a good view of the vineyards and Cobbler Mountain beyond. Miracle Valley sponsors various events, including Taste of Italy, Sangria Sundays, and live music. The winery may be rented for private parties and events. Children are welcome.

White Wines: Chardonnay, Cobbler Mountain White, Viognier.

Red Wines: Cabernet Franc, Cabernet Sauvignon, Cobbler Mountain Red, Meritage, Merlot.

Sweet/Dessert Wines: Smitten, Sweet Michelle, Symphony.

Price Range: $18–$30

Tastings: $10 per person.

Groups: Reservations required for groups of 9 or more.

Wheelchair accessible.

Restrictions: Groups of 12 or more only at 11:00 am, 12:00 pm, or 1:00 pm. No pets.

Purchasing: Phone ordering for AK, DC, FL, ID, LA, MO, NE, NV, NH, NM, ND, OH, OR, VA, WV, and WY.

Directions: From I-66, take Exit 27 (Marshall). Turn onto Free State Road (Route 55 East) and make an immediate left onto Grove Lane. Drive 2.5 miles and turn left onto Ashville Road, crossing under I-66. Drive about ½ mile and turn right onto Cobbler Mountain Road (Route 731). Continue 0.7 mile to Double J Lane and the winery on the right.

❖ ❖ ❖

Philip Carter Winery
4366 Stillhouse Road
Hume VA 22639

Hours: Daily 11:00–6:00 (Sa to 7:00) (May–Oct)   540-364-1203
Daily 11:00–5:00 (Sa to 6:00) (Nov–Apr)   www.pcwinery.com
Closed New Year's, Thanksgiving, Christmas   E-mail: info@pcwinery.com

Philip Carter Strother purchased the former Stillhouse Winery in 2008, renaming it in honor of the Carter family's long role in Virginia's history. The winery sponsors a range of events, including SPCA fundraisers, Sangria weekends, Movies in the Vineyards, book signings for local authors, and an annual Blessing of the Vines. The winery facilities, which are rated as Virginia Green, are available to rent for private dinners and weddings. Pets and children are welcome.

White Wines: Chardonnay, Governor Fauquier, Viognier.

Rosé Wines: Rosewell.

Red Wines: Cabernet Franc, Cabernet Sauvignon, Corotoman, Falconwood Red.

Sweet/Dessert Wines: Sweet Danielle.

Fortified Wines: 1762 *(port-style)*.

Price Range: $22–$450

Tastings: $8 per person

Groups: Reservations required for groups of 8 or more, $12 per person.

Purchasing: Online via VinoShipper to AK, AL, CA, DC, FL, ID, IL, LA, MN, MO, NC, ND, NE, NH, NM, NV, OH, OR, VA, WV, and WY.

Directions: From I-66, take Exit 18 (Markham) and turn south onto Leeds Manor Road. Drive 4 miles and turn left onto Stillhouse Road (portions unpaved) to the winery on right.

❖ ❖ ❖

Rappahannock Cellars
14437 Hume Road
Huntly VA 22640

Hours: Daily 11:30–5:00 (Sa to 6:00)
Closed New Year's, Easter, Thanksgiving, Christmas

540-635-9398
www.rappahannockcellars.com
E-mail: info@rcellars.com

John and Marialisa Delmare founded Rappahannock Cellars in 1998 after selling their Saratoga Vineyards in California's Santa Cruz Mountains. Light food is available for purchase. Live music and food trucks are often featured on weekends, with seating indoors or outside on the grounds. The winery is available for rental for private parties and weddings. The tasting room includes a children's corner with books and games. Dogs are welcome. Rappahannock Cellars plans to open a distillery in Autumn 2017; see the website for more details.

Sparkling Wines: Fizzy Rosé.

White Wines: Chardonnay, Chard/Vio, Seyval Blanc, Viognier, Vx2 (*Vidal Blanc, Viognier*).

Rosé Wines: Rosé.

Red Wines: Cabernet Franc, Chambourcin, Meritage, Merlot, New World Red, Noblesse Rouge, Norton, Petit Verdot.

Sweet/Dessert Wines: Late Harvest Vidal, Solera *(sherry style)*.

Fortified Wines: Port *(Norton)*.

Price Range: $25–$40

Tastings: $10 per person.

Groups: Reservations required for groups over 7; $12.50 per person.

Wheelchair accessible.

Purchasing: Online to VA or via VinoShipper to AK, AL, CA, FL, ID, IL, LA, MO, ND, NE, NH, NM, NV, OH, OR, WV, and WY.

Directions: From I-66, take Exit 13 (Linden/Front Royal) onto John Marshall Highway (Route 55) toward Front Royal. Drive 4.7 miles and turn left onto U.S. Route 522 South (Remount Road). Drive 6.9 miles and turn left onto Hume Road (Route 635). The winery will be on the left.

❖ ❖ ❖

Winding Road Cellars
4289 Leeds Manor Road
Markham VA 22643

Hours: Th–M 11:00–6:00   540-364-1025
Closed New Year's, Thanksgiving, Christmas   www.windingroadcellars.com
                                                E-mail: info@windingroadcellars.com

Scott and Linda Culver opened Winding Road Cellars in August 2013, fulfilling Scott's long-held dream of having his own winery after retiring from the Fairfax County Police Department. Scott began making wine nearly ten years ago under the mentorship of Louis Papadopoulos (Mediterranean Cellars) and is using grapes from Mediterranean while his own vines mature. The tasting room was built by the same Amish carpenters who restored the barn at Sunset Hills Vineyards in Loudoun County and offers a lovely view of the winery pond from its windows and outdoor deck. Winding Road offers occasional special events, including music and bonfires.

White Wines: Chardonnay, Twilight, Vidal Blanc, Viognier.

Red Wines: Cabernet Franc, Cabernet Sauvignon, Chambourcin, Tribute.

Sweet/Dessert Wines: Semi-sweet Chambourcin.

Price Range: $21–$38

Tastings: $5 per person.

Directions: From I-66, take Exit 18 (Markham) and turn south onto Leeds Manor Road. Follow Leeds Manor Road for 4.1 miles to winery on the left.

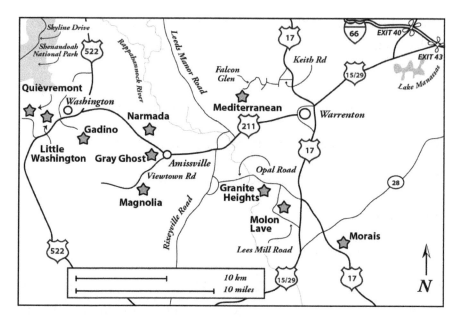

Map 3.9. Warrenton

WARRENTON

Gadino Cellars
92 School House Road
Washington VA 22747

Hours: F, Su–M 11:30–5:00, Sa 11:30–6:00 (Feb–Dec) 540-987-9292
Closed New Year's, Easter, Thanksgiving, Christmas www.gadinocellars.com
E-mail: steph@gadinocellars.com

Longtime wine enthusiasts Bill and Aleta Saccuta Gadino first planted their fifteen-acre vineyard in 1989. Sixteen years later, the couple opened Gadino Cellars to the public outside the historic town of Little Washington, with Bill and daughter Stephanie serving as winemakers. The tasting room offers cheese and sausage for purchase to enjoy either inside or on the trellised deck that overlooks the vines and gardens. Guests can test their skills on the two regulation-size bocce ball courts. Gadino sponsors a number of special events, including fundraisers, live music, and harvest picnics. Gadino is a certified Virginia Green winery. Pets and children are welcome.

White Wines: Chardonnay, Luminoso, Petit Manseng, Pinot Grigio, Sunset, Vidal Blanc, Viognier.

Rosé Wines: Moonrise.

Red Wines: Cabernet Franc, Cabernet Sauvignon, Delfino Rosso, Merlot, Nebbiolo, Petit Verdot.

Sweet/Dessert Wines: Dolce Sofia *(Petit Manseng, Vidal Blanc)*.

Fortified Wines: Finale *(port-style)*.

Price Range: $18–$49

Tastings: $8 per person.

Groups: Reservations required for groups of 7 or more, Tu–Th only.

Wheelchair accessible.

Purchasing: Online via VinoShipper to AK, AL, AZ, CA, CO, DC, FL, GA, HI, IA, ID, IL, IN, KS, LA, MA, MD, ME, MN, MO, MT, NC, ND, NE, NH, NM, NV, NY, OH, OR, PA, SC, TN, TX, VA, WA, WI, WV, and WY.

Directions: From Warrenton, take U.S. Route 29 South. Turn onto U.S. Route 211 West toward the Shenandoah National Park. Drive 23.3 miles and turn left onto School House Road (Route 636). The winery driveway (portions unpaved) will be about ½ mile on the left.

❖ ❖ ❖

Granite Heights Vineyards
8141 Opal Road
Warrenton VA 20186

Hours: F 1:00–6:00, Sa–Su Noon–5:00 (Apr–Nov) 540-349-5185
Closed Dec–Mar www.graniteheightsorchard.com
E-mail: TR@gh.wine

Granite Heights was established by Luke and Toni Kilyk on a working farm and orchard that has now expanded to 53 acres. Granite Heights produced its first vintage in 2010 and opened to the public two years later. Luke serves as the winemaker for the winery's all-Virginia grown wines, with a focus on Bordeaux-style blends. The tasting room is in a restored farmhouse with several tasting areas for visitors. Sandwiches and other light fare are available for purchase, as are several jams from Granite Heights Orchard fruit and honey from beehives on the property. Well-behaved children are welcome.

White Wines: Chardonnay, Petit Manseng, Shadow White.

Rosé Wines: Rosé.

Red Wines: Barbelo, Cabernet Franc, Cabernet Sauvignon, Evening Serenade, Humility, Lomax Reserve, Merlot.

Sweet/Dessert Wines: Intemporel *(Petit Manseng)*.

Fortified Wines: Ashby *(port-style)*.

Price Range: $17–$29

Tastings: $8 per person.

Groups: Reservations required for groups over 8 or any group arriving by limo or van; $11 per person.

Purchasing: Online via VinoShipper to AK, AL, AZ, CA, CO, DC, FL, GA, HI, IA, ID, IL, IN, KS, LA, MA, MD, ME, MN, MO, NC, ND, NE, NH, NM, NV, NY, OH, OR, PA, SC, TN, TX, VA, WA, WI, WV, and WY.

Directions: From Warrenton, drive south onto U.S. Route 15/17/29 about 7 miles to the village of Opal. Turn right onto Opal Road and continue 2.7 miles to the winery driveway on the left.

❖ ❖ ❖

Gray Ghost Vineyards & Winery
14706 Lee Highway
Amissville VA 20106

Hours: F–Su, M holidays 11:00–5:00 (Mar–Dec),
Sa–Su, M holidays 11:00-5:00 (Jan-Feb)
Closed New Year's, Easter, Thanksgiving, Christmas

540-937-4869
www.grayghostvineyards.com

Gray Ghost was founded by Al and Cheryl Kellert, who named their winery after Confederate Colonel John S. Mosby, known during the Civil War as the Gray Ghost. (Al's family is related to the Mosbys.) The winery, which now produces about a dozen estate-grown wines, celebrated the twentieth anniversary of its opening in 2014. Seating is available upstairs on the second floor of the tasting room or outdoors on the deck or gazebos. Visitors may enjoy cheese and crackers purchased at the winery or may bring their own picnic fare. Gray Ghost offers a range of activities at the winery, including a Valentine's Day tasting, a volunteer harvest program, an annual food drive, and a Civil War authors day. In December, the winery also puts on a Holiday Open House that features statues and scenes made from over sixty thousand wine corks. Children are welcome.

White Wines: Chardonnay, Gewurztraminer, Riesling, Seyval Blanc, Victorian White, Vidal Blanc.

Red Wines: Cabernet Franc, Cabernet Sauvignon, Petit Verdot, Ranger Reserve *(Bordeaux-style blend)*, Victorian Red.

Sweet/Dessert Wines: Adieu *(late-harvest Vidal Blanc)*.

Price Range: $17–$50

Tastings: $5 per person.

Groups: Reservations required for groups of 8 or more.

Directions: From Warrenton, take U.S. Route 29 South and turn onto U.S. Route 211 West toward the Shenandoah National Park. Drive 11.5 miles to Woods Edge Lane at the Amissville Volunteer Fire & Rescue. Make a U-turn on the highway to the winery entrance on the right.

❖ ❖ ❖

Little Washington Winery & Vineyards

72 Christmas Tree Lane

Washington VA 22747

Hours: F-Su, holiday M 11:00–5:00 (to 6:00 in summer)   540-987-8330

Closed New Year's, Christmas   www.littlewashingtonwinery.com

E-mail: info@littlewashingtonwinery.com

Little Washington Winery is located just outside the historic town of "little" Washington. Opened in 2011 by Carl and Donna Henrickson, the winery is on a twenty-five-acre farm with scenic views from its decks. Tastings include Little Washington's own wines as well as wines from other small-lot producers in the United States and elsewhere. Visitors are welcome to bring their own picnic lunches to enjoy on the grounds. Art and jewelry by local artists are often available in the tasting room. Light fare is available in the certified Virginia Green winery. Children and pets are welcome.

White Wines: Chardonnay, Viognier.

Rosé Wines: Funky Flamingo, Pink, Pink Cadillac.

Red Wines: Cabernet Franc, George *(Bordeaux-style blend)*, Que Syrah.

Price Range: $18–$34

Tastings: $7 per person.

Groups: Please call ahead for groups for 8 or more.

Wheelchair accessible.

Purchasing: Online via VinoShipper to AK, AL, AZ, CA, CO, DC, FL, GA, HI, IA, ID, IL, IN, KS, LA, MA, MD, ME, MN, MO, NC, ND, NE, NH, NM, NV, NY, OH, OR, PA, SC, TN, TX, VA, WA, WI, WV, and WY.

Directions: From Warrenton, take U.S. Route 29 South. Turn onto U.S. Route 211 West toward the Shenandoah National Park. Drive 24 miles and turn right onto Christmas Tree Lane. The winery driveway will be about ½ mile on the right.

❖ ❖ ❖

Magnolia Vineyards
200 Viewtown Road
Amissville VA 20106

Hours: F 12:00–6:00, Sa–Su 11:30–5:30
Closed New Year's, Easter, Christmas

703-785-8180
www.magnoliavineyards.com
E-mail: info@magnoliavineyards.com

Magnolia Vineyards is owned by Glenn and Tina Marchione who bought the 50-acre property with a winery in mind. They planted their first vineyard in 2008 and now have seven acres under vine, with plans to expand. At the moment, the tasting room is located in the walk-out basement of their home, with a kid's corner as well as seating indoors and outside on the patio and grounds. The Marchiones' two rescue dogs, Olie and Maggie, are likely to be on hand to welcome visitors; one dollar from each bottle sold of the Hawkins Run Red is donated to the Rappahannock animal shelter in their honor.

White Wines: Black Walnut White, Viognier.

Red Wines: Cabernet Franc, Hawkins Run Red *(Bordeaux-style blend)*.

Sweet/Dessert Wines: Pazzo.

Price Range: $18–$24

Tastings: $10 per person.

Groups: Reservations required for groups of 6 to 15, $12 per person.

Restrictions: No buses, no groups over 15.

Purchasing: Online via VinoShipper to AK, AL, AZ, CA, CO, DC, FL, GA, HI, IA, ID, IL, IN, KS, LA, MA, MD, ME, MN, MO, NC, ND, NE, NH, NM, NV, NY, OH, OR, PA, SC, TN, TX, VA, WA, WI, WV, and WY.

Directions: From Warrenton, take U.S. Route 29 South and turn onto U.S. Route 211 West toward the Shenandoah National Park. Drive 11 miles to Viewtown Road and turn left. (If you reach the Amissville Volunteer Fire & Rescue, you have gone too far). Continue 3.2 miles on Viewtown Road to the winery driveway on the left.

❖ ❖ ❖

Mediterranean Cellars
8295 Falcon Glen Road
Warrenton VA 20186

Hours: Daily 11:00–6:00 (F-Sa to 8:00, Su to 7:00, summer only) 540-428-1984
Closed New Year's, Thanksgiving, Christmas www.mediterraneancellars.com
E-mail: info@mediterraneancellars.com

Mediterranean Cellars was opened in 2003 by Louis Papadopoulos, who first began making wine in his native Greece before moving to Virginia in 1984. The winery is located on a hillside that offers visitors a charming view of the valley and vineyards below from its stone patio. Inside the tasting room are a small tasting bar and larger tasting room with several tables and chairs for seating. In addition to its wide selection of mostly estate-grown varietals, Mediterranean offers a retsina-style white wine in a tribute to the Papadopoulos family's ancestral origins. Light fare is available for purchase. Children and pets are welcome.

White Wines: Belleview Blanc, Chardonnay, Moscato, Pinot Crigio, Rechina *(retsina-style)*, Riesling, Vidal Blanc, Viognier.

Rosé Wines: Calypso, Matina's Rosé.

Red Wines: Cabernet Franc, Cabernet Sauvignon, Chambourcin, Merlot, Romance.

Sweet/Dessert Wines: Sweet Lucia, Sweet Romance Reserve.

Price Range: $16–$45

Tastings: $5 per person.

Groups: Please call ahead for groups for 8 or more.

Wheelchair accessible.

Directions: From Warrenton, take U.S. Route 17 North for about 3 miles. Turn left onto Keith Road (Route 628) and drive 1.1 miles. At the end of the road, turn left onto Cannonball Gate Road and drive about 1 mile. Turn right onto Falcon Glen Road (portions unpaved) to the winery driveway ½ mile on the left.

❖ ❖ ❖

Molon Lave Vineyards
10075 Lees Mill Road
Warrenton VA 20186

Hours: Daily 11:00–6:00
Closed New Year's, Easter, Thanksgiving, Christmas

540-439-5460
www.molonlavevineyards.com
E-mail: info@molonlavevineyards.com

Molon Lave was founded by Louis Papadopoulos, son of the owner of nearby Mediterranean Cellars. The winery's name is rooted in ancient Greek history in honor of the family's heritage: At the battle of Thermopylae, Persian King Xerxes called on Spartan King Leonidas to surrender his greatly outnumbered force. Leonidas replied, "Come and take them [molon lave]." The winery's tasting room includes two spacious areas with several tasting bars as well as a wraparound patio and outdoor pavilion. As at Mediterranean Cellars, Molon Lave offers a retsina-style wine in honor of the family's Greek heritage. Tastings also include small food pairings. Snacks are available for purchase at the winery, which may be rented for weddings and private events. Kosher wine tastings are available by reservation.

White Wines: Autumn Nectar, Chardonnay, Petit Manseng, Riesling, Vidal Blanc.

Rosé Wines: Kokineli *(retsina-style)*.

Red Wines: Cabernet Franc, Cabernet Sauvignon, Chambourcin, Kate's Charm, Merlot.

Price Range: $22–$38

Tastings: $8 per person.

Groups: Reservations required for groups over 7 and all buses, limos, and vans; $12 per person.

Wheelchair accessible.

Purchasing: Online via VinoShipper to AL, CA, ID, IL, LA, MO, NC, ND, NE, NH, NM, NV, OH, OR, WV, and WY.

Directions: From Warrenton, drive south onto U.S. Route 15/17/29 about 7 miles to the village of Opal. Turn right onto Opal Road and continue one mile. Turn left onto Lees Mill Road. Winery entrance will be on the left in 0.7 miles.

❖ ❖ ❖

Morais Vineyards
11409 Marsh Road
Bealeton VA 22712

Hours: F 1:00–7:00, Sa–Su 12:00–6:00   540-326-6336
Closed New Year's, Easter, Thanksgiving, Christmas   www.moraisvineyards.com
E-mail: moraisvineyards@aol.com

José and Josephine Morais [*more-ice*] established Morais Vineyards in 2004, when they planted the first vines on the property. The winery opened to the public eight years later, offering all estate-grown wines from grapes grown on the 100-acre property. Several of the wines honor the family's Portuguese heritage, including Jeropiga, a Portuguese-style dessert wine. The winemaker also crushes the grapes by foot in the traditional Portuguese manner. Visitors can relax in the tasting area around a fireplace or outside on the patios, which feature a view of the vines. The facilities include a ballroom for weddings and other events.

Morais also offers a satellite tasting room, Aroma, in Manassas (9249 Center Street, W–Th 4:00–7:00, F 4:00–9:00, Sa 1:00–8:00, Su 1:00–6:00).

Fruit Wines: Cherry.

White Wines: Battlefield White, Sauvignon Blanc, White Select *(Rkatsiteli)*.

Rosé Wines: Rosé.

Red Wines: Cabernet Franc, Red Select *(Merlot, Cabernet Franc)*, Merlot, Touriga Nacional.

Sweet/Dessert Wines: Jeropiga *(Merlot)*, Moscatel *(Muscat)*.

Fortified Wines: Tawny Port.

Price Range: $10–$24

Tastings: $8 per person.

Groups: Reservations appreciated for groups of 6 or more.

Wheelchair accessible.

Restrictions: Reservations required for buses, limos, and vans.

Directions: From Warrenton, drive south onto U.S. Route 15/17/29 about 7 miles to the village of Opal. Turn left to continue following U.S. Route 17. Drive 4.9 miles and make a U-turn at the Sunoco station; the winery driveway will be 0.1 mile on the right.

❖ ❖ ❖

Narmada Winery
43 Narmada Lane
Amissville VA 20106

Hours: Th–F, M 12:00–5:00, Sa 11:00–7:00, Su 11:00–6:00
Closed New Year's, Thanksgiving, Christmas

540-937-8215
www.narmadawinery.com
E-mail: info@narmadawinery.com

Narmada brings a taste of India to Virginia's wine country. The winery was established by Sudha and Pandit Patil, who planted their first vines in 2005. Sudha serves as the winemaker, and Pandit handles the business end. The Patils named their winery in honor of Pandit's mother, Narmada. In addition to cheeses, cold cuts, and breads, Narmada also offers small plates featuring Indian specialties on weekends. The winery is available for rental for private parties of up to one hundred people and offers occasional yoga events. Children and pets are welcome.

White Wines: Chardonel, Chardonnay, Dream *(Traminette)*, MOM *(Chardonel, Vidal Blanc)*, Viognier.

Rosé Wines: Gulabi *(Chambourcin, Chardonel)*

Red Wines: Cabernet Franc, Cabernet Sauvignon, Jubilee, Malbec, Mélange *(Bordeaux-style blend)*, Merlot, Midnight *(Chambourcin)*, Reflection *(Chambourcin)*, Tannat, Yash-Vir *(Bordeaux-style blend)*.

Sweet/Dessert Wines: Lotus *(Vidal Blanc)*, Primita *(Chambourcin, raspberry)*.

Fortified Wines: Allure *(port-style)*.

Price Range: $20–$36

Tastings: $8 for 5 wines, $10 for reserve wines, $30 for all on the list.

Groups: Reservations required for groups of 8 or more, $15 per person.

Wheelchair accessible.

Purchasing: Online to AZ, AK, CA, DC, FL, MD, NY, MN, VA, and WA or via VinoShipper to AL, CA, ID, IL, LA, MO, NC, ND, NE, NM, NV, OH, OR, WV, and WY.

Directions: From Warrenton, take U.S. Route 211 West for 13 miles to the winery entrance on the right.

❖ ❖ ❖

Quièvremont Winery
162 Gidbrown Hollow Road
Washington VA 22747

Hours: Th–Su 12:00–6:00 (F, Sa to 7:00, Apr–Oct)   540-987-3192
Closed New Year's, Thanksgiving, Christmas   www.quievremont.com
                                        E-mail: info@quievremont.com

John and Teri Guevremont established their winery next to the 250-year-old Reality Farm property that they purchased after John retired from a long career as a Marine Corps aviator. They opened Quièvremont [*KEE-ver-mont*] several years later and named it in honor of the family name's ancient origins in Normandy, France. The spacious tasting room includes multiple tables for seating indoors as well as a wide back deck overlooking the winery pond and hills beyond. A range of crackers and various cheeses are available for purchase. The winery frequently offers live music on weekends and may be rented for private events.

White Wines: Chardonnay.

Rosé Wines: Rosé.

Red Wines: Cabernet Franc, Cabernet Sauvignon, Meritage, Vin de Maison.

Price Range: $24–$32

Tastings: $16 per person.

Purchasing: Online ordering to DC, MD, and VA, and via VinoShipper to AK, AL, CA, DC, FL, ID, IL, LA, MD, MN, MO, NC, ND, NE, NH, NM, NV, OH, OR, VA, WV, and WY.

Directions: From Warrenton, take U.S. Route 29 South. Turn onto U.S. Route 211 West toward the Shenandoah National Park. Drive 24.8 miles and turn right onto Gidbrown Hollow Road. The winery entrance will be about ½ mile on the right.

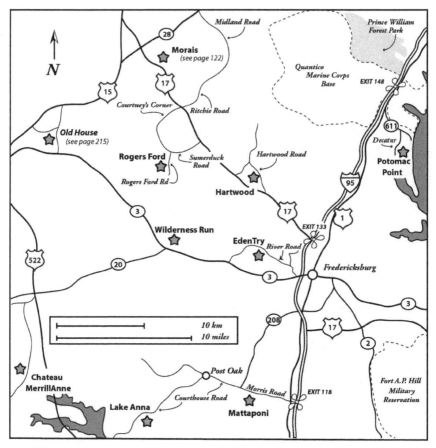

Map 3.10. Fredericksburg

FREDERICKSBURG

Chateau MerrillAnne
16234 Marquis Road
Orange VA 22960

Hours: F–Sa, M holidays 11:00–5:00, Su 12:00–5:00 (Mar–Nov)   540-656-6177
(Open also Th 11:00–5:00, Jun–Aug only)   www.chateaumerrillanne.com
Closed Dec–Feb, Easter, Thanksgiving   E-mail: ChateauMerrillAnne@gmail.com

Kenny and Emily White transformed a 117-acre farm previously owned by Kenny's father into a vineyard in 2008 when they planted their first vines, with their first harvest four years later. The winery is named to honor Kenny's parents, Merrill and Anne, and the black cat on the wine labels was inspired by a cat on the property. The tasting room is in a renovated barn, with ample seating inside and out. Children and leashed pets are welcome.

White Wines: Chardonnay, Palace White, Viognier.

Rosé Wines: Grimalkin, Vin Gris.

Red Wines: Cabernet Franc, Cabernet Sauvignon, Governor Spotswood Red, Palace Red, Petit Verdot.

Price Range: $18–$24

Tastings: $6 per person.

Groups: Reservations required for groups of 8 or more, $10 per person.

Restrictions: No buses; limos only before 1:00.

Directions: From I-95, take Exit 130B toward Culpeper and drive 13 miles. Turn left onto Constitution Highway (VA 20) and drive 13.4 miles. Turn left onto U.S. Route 522 South and make an immediate right onto Village

Road (VA 671). After 0.8 miles, turn left onto Marquis Road (VA 669). The winery will be 5.6 miles on the right.

❖ ❖ ❖

Eden Try Estate & Winery
6818 River Road
Fredericksburg VA 22407

Hours: Su 12:00–5:00 (Apr–mid-Nov)　　　　　　　　540-786-0057
Closed Easter　　　　　　　　　　　　　　　　www.edentrywinery.com
　　　　　　　　　　　　E-mail:　events@edentryevents.com

Eden Try Estate is owned and operated by Linda Morrison and Gary Gratopp, and was named by the original owner who wanted to "try at the Garden of Eden." The property is primarily a wedding venue and includes a small tasting room where visitors can sample the estate's wines on Sunday afternoons. There is a small gazebo and other shaded outdoor seating that offers a view of the estate.

White Wines: Serpentine White.

Rosé Wines: Eve's Delight Rosé.

Red Wines: Fig Leaf Red, Forbidden, Paradise, Temptation.

Price Range: $18–$22

Tastings: $5 per person.

Directions: From I-95, take Exit 130B (Culpeper) onto VA Route 3 West (Plank Road). After ½ mile, turn right onto Bragg Road. Drive about one mile and turn left onto River Road. Continue 3.6 miles to the winery's gravel drive on the left.

❖ ❖ ❖

Hartwood Winery

345 Hartwood Road

Fredericksburg VA 22406

Hours: W–F, M holidays 11:00–5:00, Sa–Su 11:00–6:00   540-752-4893

Closed New Year's, Easter, Thanksgiving, Christmas   www.hartwoodwinery.com

E-mail: J-B@hartwoodwinery.com

Hartwood is a small family-owned and operated winery just outside Fredericksburg. The winery has seven acres under vine on site, with twenty-five additional acres of vineyards across the state; all its wines are Virginia-grown. Opened in 1989, the winery takes its name from the surrounding Hartwood community, known for its large deer population. In addition to regular tastings, owner-winemakers Jim and Beverly Livingston offer private tastings and tours. Hartwood also sponsors special winery events, include festivals, barrel tastings, open houses, and wine appreciation seminars. The tasting room includes a small gift shop. Children and pets are welcome.

White Wines: Chardonnay, Deweese White, Hartwood Station White, Rappahannock White, Seyval Blanc, Viognier.

Rosé Wines: Blushing Hart, Rappahannock Rose.

Red Wines: Cabernet Franc, Cabernet Sauvignon, Claret, Merlot, Petit Verdot, Rappahannock Red, Tannat.

Sweet/Dessert Wines: Blushing Heart.

Price Range: $15–$23

Tastings: $5 per person.

Groups: Private tastings for up to 40; contact winery for details.

Purchasing: Online via VinoShipper to AK, AL, DC, FL, ID, IL, LA, MN, MO, NC, ND, NE, NH, NM, NV, OH, OR, WV, and WY.

Directions: From I-95, take Exit 133 (Warrenton) onto U.S. Route 17 North. Drive 6 miles and turn right onto Hartwood Road (Route 612). Winery will be on left in 1.5 miles.

❖ ❖ ❖

Lake Anna Winery
5621 Courthouse Road
Spotsylvania VA 22551

Hours: W–Sa 11:00–5:00, Su 1:00–5:00
Closed New Year's, Thanksgiving, Christmas

540-895-5085
www.lawinery.com
E-mail: info@lawinery.com

Lake Anna Winery had its origins as a vineyard established by Bill and Ann Heidig in 1983 to sell grapes to local wineries. Seven years later, the Heidigs decided to produce their own wines and opened Lake Anna. Now under the ownership and management of sons Jeff and Eric, Lake Anna produces about seven thousand cases of wine annually. The tasting room includes a tasting bar, tables for extra seating, and a gift shop. The winery also offers free Wi-Fi for visitors. Special events include live music, a "Wine and Whiskers" SPCA fundraiser, and annual Octoberfest. The facility may be rented for private events and weddings. Children and pets are welcome.

White Wines: Chardonnay, Lake Side White, Seyval Blanc, Totally White.

Rosé Wines: Lake Side Sunset.

Red Wines: Cabernet Franc, Lake Side Red, Merlot, Petit Verdot, Spotsylvania Claret.

Sweet/Dessert Wines: Concerto (*Chambourcin, cherry*), Essensual (*Vidal Blanc*).

Price Range: $14–$38

Tastings: $5 per person.

Wheelchair accessible.

Directions: From I-95, take Exit 118 (Thornburg) and turn west onto Morris Road (Route 606) which will become Courthouse Road (Route 208). At the Post Oak community, turn left to continue following Courthouse Road and drive 7.5 miles to winery entrance on left.

❖ ❖ ❖

Mattaponi Winery
7530 Morris Road
Spotsylvania VA 22551

Hours: W–Su 10:00–6:00 (summer/fall),
W–Su 11:00–6:00 (winter)
Closed New Year's, Thanksgiving, Christmas

540-582-2897
www.mattaponiwinery.com
E-mail: mattaponiwinery@aol.com

Mattaponi *(matta-poe-NIGH)* is one of only two Native American-owned wineries in the United States (North Carolina's Native Vines is the other). Owners Mike and Janette Evans began as home winemakers over twenty years ago before eventually opening their winery on the grounds of their Christmas tree farm near Fredericksburg. The Evanses chose Algonquin names for several wines to honor the Native Americans who originally settled Virginia. Proceeds from their Tibik-Kizismin wine support the Avon Cancer Foundation.

Fruit Wines: Kizismin *(peach)*, Makadewamin *(blackberry)*, Odeimin *(strawberry)*, Pow Wow *(chocolate, strawberry)*, Tibik-Kizismin *(blueberry)*, Wematin *(strawberry, grapefruit)*, Wojape *(strawberry)*.

White Wines: Chardonnay, Wabamin *(Niagara)*, Riesling.

Red Wines: Cabernet Franc, Cabernet Sauvignon, Chambourcin, Freedom *(Cabernet Franc, White Moore's Diamond, Concord)*, Merlot, Miskwamin *(Concord)*.

Price Range: $13–$18

Tastings: $2 per person.

Groups: Reservations required for groups of 10 or more.

Directions: From I-95, take Exit 118 (Thornburg) and turn west onto Morris Road (Route 606). Drive 4 miles to winery entrance on left and follow the gravel driveway to the tasting room entrance at the rear of the house.

❖ ❖ ❖

Potomac Point Vineyard & Winery
275 Decatur Road
Stafford VA 22554

Hours: W–M 11:00–6:00 (F–Sa to 9:30, summer only)   540-446-2266
Closed New Year's, Thanksgiving, Christmas   www.potomacpointwinery.com
E-mail: info@potomacpointwinery.com

Since opening in 2007 under the ownership of Skip and Cindi Causey, Potomac Point has become a popular venue for weekend wine tourism. The winery's tasting room opens onto an outdoor courtyard; outdoor seating is also available upstairs on a rooftop patio. The winery sponsors special events, including Ladies' Nights and live music on Fireside Fridays and on Sundays (with cover charge). Children are welcome to play in the "Little Buds" room. Potomac Point offers several rooms, including a ballroom, for private parties and weddings. Pets are welcome.

White Wines: Chardonnay, La Belle Vie White, Viognier.

Rosé Wines: La Belle Vie Rosé.

Red Wines: Abbinato, Cabernet Franc, Coyote Cave Red, Richland Reserve *(Bordeaux-style blend)*, Merlot, Norton, Petit Verdot.

Sweet/Dessert Wines: Dolce Rubus, Moscato Dolce, Vin de Paille *(Petit Manseng)*.

Fortified Wines: Rabelos Port *(port-style)*.

Price Range: $15–$33

Tastings: $7 for classic, $12 for premium (with souvenir glass).

Groups: Reservations required for groups of 10 or more; $12 for classic and $17 for premium.

Wheelchair accessible.

Purchasing: Online orders to many states; see website for details.

Directions: From I-95, take Exit 148 toward Quantico. Turn east onto Russell Road and merge onto U.S. Route 1 South. Drive 1.4 miles. Turn left onto Telegraph Road (Route 736). After ½ mile, turn left onto Widewater Road (Route 611). Drive 2.8 miles and turn right onto Decatur Road. The winery driveway (portions unpaved) will be 1 mile on the left.

❖ ❖ ❖

Rogers Ford Farm Winery
14674 Rogers Ford Road
Sumerduck VA 22742

Hours: F–Su 11:00–5:00 (Mar–Dec) 540-439-3707
Closed Jan–Feb, Christmas www.rogersfordwine.com
E-mail: john@rogersfordwine.com

Rogers Ford Farm Winery is located on a 55-acre property that has been a working farm since 1825. Owner-winemaker John Puckett is happy to share his knowledge of the farm's Civil War history with visitors and welcomes those who arrive on horseback (a hitching post is outside). The intimate tasting room has two small tasting bars and offers snacks for purchase. The property extends to the Rappahannock River, with outdoor seating for visitors. Rogers Ford collaborates with a nearby equestrian center to offer wine trail rides and with the Inn at Kelly's Ford to sponsor murder mystery dinners and wine tastings.

Sparkling Wines: Cuvée Julia.

White Wines: Jacob Christopher Chardonnay, Goldvein, Vidal Blanc.

Rosé Wines: Sumerduck Rosé.

Red Wines: Cabernet Franc, Cabernet Sauvignon, Petit Verdot.

Sweet/Dessert Wines: Brandy Station Dulce, First Frost Vidal.

Fortified Wines: Snake Castle *(port-style)*.

Price Range: $16–$29

Tastings: $8 per person.

Groups: Reservations required for groups of 8 or more; $10 per person.

Purchasing: Online via VinoShipper to AK, AL, AZ, CA, CO, DC, FL, GA, HI, IA, ID, IL, IN, KS, LA, MA, MD, ME, MN, MO, NC, ND, NE, NH, NM, NV, NY, OH, OR, PA, SC, TN, TX, VA, WA, WI, WV, and WY.

Directions: From I-95, take Exit 133 (Warrenton) onto U.S. Route 17 North. Drive 12.5 miles and turn left onto Sumerduck Road (Route 651). After 3.7 miles, turn left onto Rogers Ford Road. The winery is 2 miles on the right.

❖ ❖ ❖

Wilderness Run Vineyards
11109 Plank Road
Spotsylvania VA 22553

Hours: Th–Sa 11:00–9:00, Su 11:00–5:00   540-842-0199
Closed New Year's, Thanksgiving, Christmas   www.wildernessrunvineyards.com
E-mail: harry@wildernessrunvineyards.com

Harry Pagan and his father, Robert, were inspired by a trip to Tuscany to start a vineyard on their 150-acre working farm on the fringes of the historic Wilderness Battlefield where General Ulysses Grant began the long final campaign against Confederate General Robert E. Lee that ended the Civil War. Wilderness Run's tasting list includes wines made from its own vineyards as well as from other Virginia wineries. The owners have also launched the 1781 Brewery on the site. Seating is available both inside the tasting room and outside, with food available for purchase. The winery sponsors live music on weekends. Leashed pets are welcome.

White Wines: Chardonnay.

Rosé Wines: Pink Chair Rosé.

Red Wines: Monroe Merlot, Red Table Wine, Tool Shed Red.

Price Range: $17–$32

Tastings: $8 per person.

Groups: Please call ahead for groups of 6 to 25 (maximum size).

Directions: From I-95, take Exit 133 (Warrenton) onto U.S. Route 17 North. Drive 12.6 miles to the winery entrance on the right.

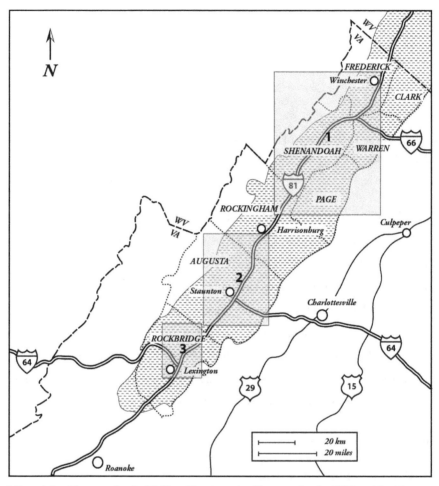

Map 4.1. Shenandoah Valley Region & Shenandoah AVA: (1) Upper Shenandoah Valley; (2) Lower Shenandoah Valley (Staunton); (3) Lower Shenandoah Valley (Rockbridge).

4. SHENANDOAH VALLEY REGION & AVA

The Shenandoah Valley offers visitors both rich history and stunning scenic beauty. Stretching from the Virginia-Maryland line to just past the town of Lexington, it is bordered on the east by the Blue Ridge Mountains and on the west by the Alleghany and Appalachian Plateaus. Much of the region is underlain by limestone, and the entire valley is pockmarked by numerous caverns. Sitting in the rain shadow of the Appalachians, summers here are drier than elsewhere in Virginia, although winters can be snowy and quite cold at times.

The Shenandoah region has two dozen wineries scattered the length of the valley. Large or small, all combine a serene wine tasting opportunity with picturesque natural settings. The valley is bisected by I-81, a busy north-south highway that provides easy access to wineries and other sites. Visitors with more time may prefer instead to take U.S. Route 11 which parallels the interstate but is a more tranquil way to experience the small towns and scenic countryside of the Shenandoah.

❖ ❖ ❖

<u>Things to see and do</u>: There is something for nature lovers of all ages here: caverns for exploring, trails for hiking and camping, mountains for skiing, and lakes and rivers for fishing. Underground caverns are particularly numerous. Visitors can explore Luray Caverns, Shenandoah Caverns,

or the granddaddy of them all, Grand Caverns, which has been open to the public since 1806. All three are open year-round and are great places for adults and children alike.

The 50-mile-long Massanutten Mountain splits the valley from Strasburg to Harrisonburg and offers hiking and skiing, depending on the season. Hiking trails include the Stony Man Mountain Hike near Luray and the Massanutten Storybook Trail, the latter accessible even for children. Further south, visitors can explore the Natural Bridge, an ancient twenty-story-high natural arch that was a sacred site for the Native American Monacan tribe. Some historians believe the young George Washington visited the site around 1750 on a surveying trip for Lord Fairfax.

As the breadbasket of Virginia, the Shenandoah is also rich in Civil War history. The area saw frequent clashes as General Thomas "Stonewall" Jackson led his troops in an extended campaign up and down the Valley. Among the battlefields are New Market, where cadets from the Virginia Military Institute (VMI) participated; Cedar Creek, near Middletown; and Kernstown, near Winchester. Self-guided driving tours can be downloaded at www.civilwartraveler.com/EAST/VA [case sensitive].

The town of Lexington is home to both VMI and to Washington and Lee University, the ninth oldest university in the country. Originally founded in 1749 as the Augusta Academy, the institution's leaders changed its name to Washington Academy in appreciation for George Washington's gift of stock in the James River Canal. In 1865, Robert E. Lee became president of then-Washington College, serving for five years before his death in 1870. The college then changed its name to honor Lee, who is entombed on the campus; his favorite horse, Traveller, is buried just outside the Lee Chapel.

Visitors may also experience the region's cultural history in Staunton [STAN-ton] at the open-air Frontier Culture Museum, a living history site that includes farmsteads from England, Germany, Ireland, and West

Africa, as well as a traditional Shenandoah Valley farm. Check the website (www.frontiermuseum.org) for details on events and openings. For theater lovers, the American Shakespeare Center offers year-round performances at its Blackfriars Playhouse, a reproduction of the first indoor theater in the English-speaking world. The ASC website provides more information on performances (www.americanshakespearecenter.com).

❖ ❖ ❖

<u>Wine Trails</u>: Several wine trails center around the Shenandoah Valley, including the Shenandoah County Wine Trail, and the Shenandoah Valley Wine Trail. See Appendix 1 for more details.

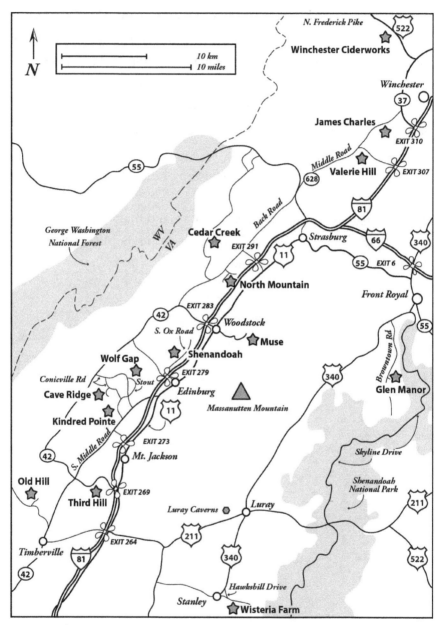

Map 4.2. Upper Shenandoah Valley

UPPER SHENANDOAH VALLEY

Cave Ridge Vineyard
1476 Conicville Road
Mt. Jackson VA 22842

Hours: M, W–Su 12:00–6:00 (F, Sa to 7:00 in summer)   540-477-2585
Closed New Year's, Thanksgiving, Christmas   www.caveridge.com
                            E-mail: caveridgewines@caveridge.com

Owner and winemaker Randy Phillips established Cave Ridge in 2000, opening the winery to the public six years later. The winery name comes from a cave on the property, and the fossil on the wine labels is a photo of a large fossil uncovered when the vines were being planted. Visitors can relax over one of the estate-grown wines on the deck or the cobblestoned courtyard outside the tasting room and may either bring their own food or purchase snacks on site. The winery may be rented for dinners, weddings, and special events. Cave Ridge sponsors occasional live music, chili Saturdays, and holiday open houses. Children and leashed dogs are welcome.

White Wines: Chardonnay, Traminette, Riesling, Viognier.

Rosé Wines: Rambling Rose.

Red Wines: Cabernet Sauvignon, Chambourcin, Fossil Hill Reserve, Mount Jackson Rouge, Syrah.

Sweet/Dessert Wines: La Petite Traminette.

Fortified Wines: Fandango *(port-style)*.

Price Range: $16–$35

Tastings: $6 for regular, $18 for reserve.

Wheelchair accessible.

Reservations required for groups of 7 or more.

Purchasing: Online to DC, FL, NC, PA, and VA only.

Directions: From I-81, take Exit 283 (Woodstock) and turn west onto Reservoir Road (Route 42). Continue for 10.4 miles and turn left onto Conicville Road. The winery's single-lane gravel drive is on the right after 1.6 miles (be careful at the semi-blind curve at the end!).

❖ ❖ ❖

Cedar Creek Vineyard
7384 Zepp Road
Star Tannery VA 22654

Hours: F–Su 11:00–5:00 (Apr–Nov)   540-436-8394
Closed Dec–Mar   www.cedarcreekvineyard.com
E-mail: wine@cedarcreekvineyard.com

Longtime weekend visitors to the Shenandoah, Ron and Chris Schmidt purchased their 77-acre property on the slopes above Cedar Creek after Ron retired as a U.S. Park Police officer. Visitors have the opportunity for vertical tastings of Cedar Creek's wines, especially Ron's highly-rated Cabernet Francs. While no food is available for purchase, guests are welcome to bring their own and sit on the deck or lawn to enjoy the view of the vineyards and mountain peaks, including Three High Heads and Half Moon. Ron is retiring and recommends that visitors call first to confirm he is open.

White Wines: Chardonnay.

Red Wines: Cabernet Franc.

Price Range: $19–$21

Tastings: $5 per person.

Groups: Reservations requested for groups over six.

Directions: From I-81, take Exit 296 (Stanley) and turn onto VA Route 55 West. Drive 8.4 miles. Turn left onto Star Tannery Road (VA 604). Follow Star Tannery Road through its many twists and turns for 7.3 miles. Turn left into the winery's narrow gravel drive and cross over Cedar Creek up to the tasting room.

❖ ❖ ❖

Glen Manor Vineyard
2244 Browntown Road
Front Royal VA 22630

Hours: W–Sa 11:00–5:00, Su 12:00–5:00 (Apr–Nov); 540-635-6324
F, Sa 11:00–5:00, Su 12:00–5:00 (Dec–Mar) www.glenmanorvineyards.com
Closed Easter, Thanksgiving, E-mail: gmvwine@glenmanorvineyards.com
Christmas through New Year's

Glen Manor Vineyards, on the western flank of the Blue Ridge Mountains, is a 212-acre working farm that has been in the same family for over one hundred years. Jeff White established Glen Manor's first vineyards in 1995, opening his winery in 2008 after working with neighboring Linden Vineyards for twelve years. Jeff's wife, Kelly, is often on hand to welcome visitors in the winery's tasting room and to talk about Glen Manor's award-winning estate-grown wines. While no food is available for sale, visitors are welcome to bring their own. Leashed dogs are welcome.

White Wines: Petit Manseng, Sauvignon Blanc.

Rosé Wines: Morales Rosé.

Red Wines: Cabernet Franc, Hodder Hill, Petit Verdot, St. Ruth, Vin Rouge.

Sweet/Dessert Wines: Raepheus.

Price Range: $21–$35

Tastings: $4 or $8 per person, depending on number of wines tasted.

Restrictions: No limos, buses, or groups over six.

Wheelchair accessible.

Directions: From I-66, take Exit 6 (Front Royal) and follow U.S. Route 340 South for 4.5 miles. Just after passing the entrance to Skyline Drive and the Shenandoah National Park, turn left onto Browntown Road and continue 5.2 miles to the winery's gravel driveway on the left.

❖ ❖ ❖

James Charles Winery & Vineyard
4063 Middle Road
Winchester VA 22602

Hours: M–Th 12:00–5:00, F 12:00–9:00
Sa 12:00–8:00, Su 12:00–5:00
Closed New Year's, Thanksgiving, Christmas

540-931-4386
www.jamescharleswine.com
E-mail: info@jamescharleswine.com

James Charles is the newest endeavor by the Bogaty family, which also owns Veramar and Bogati Wineries. Named after the family patriarch, James Charles offers wines made by son Justin Bogaty using Virginia-grown grapes from the family's vineyards as well as others in the area. The winery offers seating indoors as well as on a patio with sweeping views of vines and hills. Breads, cheeses, and spreads are available for purchase. The facilities may be rented for weddings or private parties. Leashed pets are welcome.

White Wines: Chardonnay, Cuvée de la Reine, Pinot Gris, Riesling, Sauvignon Blanc, Viognier.

Red Wines: Arrivato Ameritage, Petit Verdot, Syrah.

Price Range: $24–$35

Tastings: $10 per person.

Groups: Reservations required for groups of 8 or more, $18 per person.

Directions: From Winchester, drive south on Middle Road (Route 628) south for 5 miles to the winery entrance on the left.

❖ ❖ ❖

Muse Vineyards
16 Serendipity Lane
Woodstock VA 22664

Hours: F 12:00–8:00, Sa–Su 12:00–6:00
Closed Christmas, New Year's

540-459-7033
www.musevineyards.com
E-mail: info@musevineyards.com

Robert Muse and Sally Cowel first purchased the property that was to become Muse Vineyards in 2003, prompted by a desire to own a vineyard, ultimately opening their tasting room in late 2016. Over the years, they expanded their holdings and now have twenty-two acres of vines. Working with winemaker Tim Rausse, Robert produces Rhone-style blends from varieties including Grenache, Mourvedre, and Gamay. Muse offers a range of cheese, meats, and spreads for purchase in the tasting room.

White Wines: Chardonnay, Thalia.

Red Wines: Clio, Calliope.

Price Range: $19–$40

Groups: Reservations requested for groups of 8 or more.

Purchasing: Online to DC, GA, IL, IN, VA, and NY.

Directions: From I-81, take Exit 283 (Woodstock) and turn east onto Reservoir Road (VA 610). After 1.5 miles, turn right onto Hollingsworth (Route 609) just after passing the Shenandoah Animal Hospital. Follow Route 609 through a hairpin curve to a single-lane concrete bridge across Shenandoah River. Turn right into the winery drive on the right.

❖ ❖ ❖

North Mountain Vineyard & Winery
4374 Swartz Road
Maurertown VA 22644

Hours: W–Su 11:00–5:00
Closed New Year's, Thanksgiving, Christmas

540-436-9463
www.northmountainvineyard.com
E-mail: wine@northmountainvineyard.com

North Mountain has been owned and operated since 1998 by Brad Foster and Krista Jackson-Foster, whose son, John Jackson, serves as winemaker. The tasting room includes picture windows that open onto decks, where visitors can sit and enjoy the view over a glass of wine and a snack. The winery offers barrel room tours and tastings with advance reservations. North Mountain sponsors several events, including live music on weekends, chili cook-offs, winemaker's dinners, Mother's and Father's Day events, and an annual Oktober Wein Festival. The facilities are available for weddings and private parties. Children and pets are welcome.

Fruit Wines: Apple.

White Wines: Chardonnay, Grüner Veltliner, Oktoberfest, Riesling, Vidal Blanc.

Blush Wines: Sweet Caroline's Blush.

Red Wines: Cabernet Franc, Cabernet Sauvignon, Chambourcin, Claret, Tom's Brook Red *(Cabernet Franc)*, Zweigelt.

Sweet/Dessert Wines: Mountain Midnight *(Chambourcin)*, Mountain Sunset.

Price Range: $14–$45

Tastings: $5 per person.

Groups: Reservations required for groups of 8 or more, $15 per person.

Directions: From I-81, take Exit 291 (Tom's Brook) and turn west onto Mount Olive Road. Drive 1.4 miles and turn left onto Back Road (Route 623). Continue 2 miles and turn left onto Harrisville Road (Route 655). After 0.4 miles, turn right onto Swartz Road and the winery entrance.

❖ ❖ ❖

Old Hill Hard Cider
17768 Honeyville Road
Timberville VA 22853

Hours: M–Sa 11:00–5:00 (opens at 9:00 in summer)   540-896-7582
Closed New Year's, Thanksgiving, Christmas   www.oldhillcider.com
E-mail: info@oldhillcider.com

Sharon and Shannon Showalter were inspired to open their cidery after purchasing the Showalter Orchard from Shannon's father, who had started the orchard fifty years earlier. They host tastings of their cider offerings, as well as an annual apple harvest festival and an apple school. They make their ciders using a century-old apple press to extract the juices and ferment their ciders in old bourbon barrels. Children and leashed dogs are welcome.

Ciders: Betwixt, Cidermaker's Barrel, Heritage, Yesteryear.

Sweet/Dessert Ciders: Season's Finish.

Price Range: $18–$20

Tastings: $5 per person.

Groups: Reservations requested for groups of 8 or more.

Directions: From I-81, take Exit 264 (New Market) and turn west onto Old Cross Road (VA Route 211). Drive 5.6 miles into the town of Timberville and turn right onto South Main Street. Continue 0.7 miles and make a left onto Orchard Drive. Drive another 2.6 miles and turn right onto Honeyville Road and the orchard entrance.

❖ ❖ ❖

Shenandoah Vineyards
3659 South Ox Road
Edinburg VA 22824

Hours: Daily, 10:00–5:00 (to 6:00 in summer)
Closed New Year's, Thanksgiving, Christmas

540-984-8699
www.shenandoahvineyardsva.com
E-mail: shenvine@shentel.net

Founded in 1976, Shenandoah Vineyards is one of Virginia's oldest wineries. All their wines are estate-grown and are produced by Michael Shaps Wineworks. The tasting room is in a Civil War-era barn that offers visitors two balcony decks from which to appreciate the views of the vineyards and nearby Massanutten Mountain. The winery holds special Valentine's Day tastings, wine and cheese weekends, country cookouts, an annual Harvest Festival, and a holiday open house. Children are welcome.

White Wines: Chardonnay, Johannisberg Riesling.

Red Wines: Cabernet Sauvignon, Chambourcin, Rebel Red.

Price Range: $18–$35

Tastings: $8 per person, including tour (hourly).

Wheelchair accessible.

Purchasing: Online via VinoShipper for AK, AL, CA, DC, FL, ID, IL, LA, MN, MO, NC, ND, NE, NH, NM, NV, OH, OR, WV, and WY.

Directions: From I-81, take Exit 279 and turn west onto Stoney Creek Road. Make an immediate right onto South Ox Road. The winery will be 1.6 miles on the left.

❖ ❖ ❖

Third Hill at DeMello Vineyards
2110 Quicksburg Road
Quicksburg VA 22847

Hours: M, Th 11:00–5:00 (Jun–Oct only), F 12:00–8:00,
Sa 12:00–8:30, Su 11:00–5:00
Closed New Year's, Thanksgiving, Christmas

540-740-8464
www.demellovineyardsthirdhillwinery.com

Edward and Wendy DeMello opened their winery in late 2016, naming it for Third Hill, a peak just visible from the winery's deck and that served as a signal station during the Civil War. They are using grapes from other Virginia vineayrds while their own vines mature. The tasting room offers cheese plates that visitors can take on the winery deck to enjoy the view of the mountains in the distance.

White Wines: Riesling, Traminette, Viognier.

Rosé Wines: Rosé.

Red Wines: Cabernet Franc, Cabernet Sauvignon, Petit Verdot.

Price Range: $19–$28.

Tastings: $5 to $10 per person.

Directions: From I-81, take Exit 269 (Shenandoah Caverns) and turn west onto Caverns Road which bends sharply to the right. After 1.2 miles, turn left onto Turkey Knob Road (Route 698) and continue 1.3 miles. After crossing Holmans Creek, turn right onto Quicksburg Road (Route 767) and drive 0.7 miles to the entrance on the left.

❖ ❖ ❖

Valerie Hill Winery
1687 Marlboro Road
Stephens City VA 22655

Hours: M–Th 11:00–6:00, F 11:00–8:00,   540-869-9567
Sa 11:00–7:00, Su 11:00–5:00   www.valeriehillwinery.com
Closed New Year's Eve & Day,   E-mail: info@valeriehillwinery.com
Thanksgiving, Christmas Eve & Day

Valerie Hill opened to the public in 2012 on an 18-acre property just south of Winchester. The tasting room is housed in an early nineteenth-century manor house that features a stone patio and fire pit for chilly afternoons. Winemaker Justin Bogaty (Bogati Bodega, Veramar) is producing Valerie Hill's wines from all Virginia-grown grapes while the winery's own vineyard matures. A selection of cheeses, cold cuts and spreads is available for purchase. Live music is featured on select Friday evenings. Children and pets are welcome.

White Wines: Antebellum, Chardonnay, Manor House White, Seyval Blanc, Vidal Blanc.

Red Wines: Chambourcin, Merlot, Petit Verdot.

Price Range: $27–$29

Tastings: $9 per person.

Groups: Reservations required for groups of 10 or more, $12 per person.

Directions: From I-81, take Exit 307 (VA Route 277) toward Stephens City/ Route 340. Turn right after 0.3 miles onto Fairfax Pike which will become Marlboro Road. Drive 3.7 miles in all to the winery entrance on the left.

❖ ❖ ❖

Vineyard at Kindred Pointe
3575 Conicville Road
Mt. Jackson VA 22842

Hours: W–F, Su 12:00–6:00, Sa 12:00–7:00 (summer) 540-447-3570
W–Su 12:00–5:00 (winter) www.kindredpointe.com
Closed New Year's, Thanksgiving, Christmas E-mail: info@kindredpointe.com

Kindred Pointe, owned and operated by Amy and Bruce Helsley, started out as Kindred Pointe stables but morphed into a winery after the Helsleys planted a five-acre vineyard in 2008. They converted the horse barn into a tasting room, which now offers two fireplaces to keep visitors warm on chilly days and outdoor seating for warmer weather. The winery sponsors live music on weekends. The facilities may be rented for private parties and weddings. Children and dogs are welcome.

Ciders: Hard Core, Hard Luck, Hard Times.

White Wines: Chardonnay, Oscar *(Vidal Blanc)*.

Red Wines: Malbec, Merlot, Picasso.

Price Range: $23–$30

Tastings: $6 per person.

Purchasing: Online via VinoShipper to AK, AL, CA, DC, FL, ID, IL, LA, MN, MO, NC, ND, NE, NH, NM, NV, OH, OR, VA, WV, and WY.

Directions: From I-81, take Exit 273 (Mt. Jackson). Turn west onto Mt. Jackson Road (VA Route 703) for 1.3 miles. Turn right onto South Middle Road (VA Route 614) and drive 0.9 mile. Turn left onto Conicville Road, continuing for 1.5 miles to the winery entrance on the left.

❖ ❖ ❖

Winchester Ciderworks
2502 North Frederick Pike
Winchester VA 22603

Hours: Sa, Su 12:00–5:00 (spring–fall) 540-550-3800
Closed New Year's, Christmas www.winchesterciderworks.com
E-mail: stephen@winchesterciderworks.com

Stephen Schuurman began making ciders after arriving in Virginia in 2004 from his native England, eventually joining forces with local apple grower Diane Kearns of Fruit Hill Orchard to expand his production. Ciders are made from Virginia fruit and include several that are aged in different types of barrels to give added flavor and complexity.

Ciders: Malice, Wicked Wiles *(aged in either bourbon, brandy, rum, or rye barrels)*.

Price Range: Varies depending on size of container

Tastings: $5 per person.

Directions: From I-81, take Exit 310 (Kernstown) and turn onto VA 37 North after 0.2 miles. Continue 6.7 miles and take the exit for U.S. 522 (Berkeley Springs), which becomes North Frederick Pike. Drive 2.5 miles and turn into the entrance on the right.

❖ ❖ ❖

Wisteria Farm & Vineyard
1126 Marksville Road
Stanley VA 22851

Hours: Th–M 12:00–6:00 (Mar–Dec)
Closed Thanksgiving, Christmas, Jan–Feb

540-742-1489
www.wisteriavineyard.com
E-mail: info@wisteriavineyard.com

Wisteria Vineyard is part of a working farm owned by Sue and Moussa Ishak, a native of Lebanon. The tasting room is next to the farm's Victoria-era farmhouse, with an outdoor deck and firepits. Guests may either bring their own picnic or purchase cheese and snacks. The winery hosts a number of special events, such as SPCA fundraisers, live music, an annual Blessing of the Vines, and Wine & Ewe Shearing Days. Wisteria Farm is a certified Virginia Green winery. Children and dogs are welcome.

White Wines: Chardonnay, Pinot Gris, Seyval Blanc, Traminette, Viognier.

Red Wines: Adonis, Carmine, Merlot, Norton, Velvet.

Sweet/Dessert Wines: Sweet Daisy.

Price Range: $16–$18

Tastings: $5 per person.

Wheelchair accessible.

Directions: From Luray, take U.S. Route 340 South for 6 miles and bear left onto Hawksbill Road. After ½ mile, turn left onto Marksville Road. The winery will be on the right after about ¼ mile.

❖ ❖ ❖

Wolf Gap Vineyard & Winery
123 Stout Road
Edinburg VA 22824

Hours: F–M 12:00–7:00 (Apr–Nov);
Sa, Su 1:00–5:00 (Dec–Mar)
Closed New Year's, Christmas

540-984-3306
www.wolfgapvineyard.com
E-mail: admin@wolfgapvineyard.com

Wolf Gap Winery was founded in 2007 by Will and Diane Elledge, who named it after Wolf Gap, which can be seen to the west along the Virginia-West Virginia state line. The two-story winery has a tasting deck and events patio for warm weather seating and scenic views of the Allegheny Mountains. Private winery and vineyard tours are available with advance reservations. The facilities may be rented for special events and weddings. Wolf Gap offers discounts for active-duty military personnel.

Fruit Wines: Blueberry Wine.

White Wines: Chardonnay, Traminette.

Rosé Wines: Lobo Loco.

Red Wines: Cabernet Franc, Cabernet Sauvignon, Chambourcin, Mariage.

Price Range: $16–$34

Tastings: $5 per person.

Groups: Reservations required for groups of 8 or more.

Purchasing: Online purchasing available for residents of AK, AZ, CA, DC, FL, GA, KS, MN, MO, NC, NM, RI, and TX.

Directions: From I-81, take Exit 279 east onto Stoney Creek Road (Route 185). Drive 1 mile. Turn right onto South Main Street (U.S. Route 11 South). Drive 1.7 miles and turn right onto South Middle Road. After 2.8 miles, turn right onto Headquarters Road. Drive 2.4 miles; turn right onto Stout Road; the winery will be on the left.

BORDEAUX-STYLE BLENDS

Bordeaux, Bordeaux-style, Meritage—do these terms all mean the same thing? Well, yes and no.

True Bordeaux wines are only from the area around Bordeaux, France. Specifically, the Bordeaux region encompasses vineyards along both banks of France's Gironde River, which flows through the city of Bordeaux, and its tributaries, the Garonne and Dordogne. Wine grapes have been cultivated here since at least the 1st century AD, when the Roman aristocrat and naturalist Pliny the Elder wrote about the grape-growing and wines he encountered in the area.

Also called Claret, red Bordeaux is generally a blend of Cabernet Sauvignon, Merlot, Cabernet Franc, Petit Verdot, and, to a much lesser extent, Malbec. (A sixth grape, Carmenère, is used only rarely.) The individual grape varieties are first fermented, then aged separately in oak barrels for over a year before being blended and bottled. High-quality Bordeaux wines are rich, powerful wines that age beautifully, becoming more complex and refined over time.

Wines said to be "Bordeaux-style" also are blends of two or more of the five classic Bordeaux red wine varieties. Because Bordeaux reds are considered by many to rank among the world's greatest wines, a winery's Bordeaux-style wine will often be held up as that winery's finest production. The specific grapes and proportions in the blend vary somewhat from year to year, depending on the vintage quality, and the winery may or may not reveal its specific blend.

Meritage (rhymes with "heritage") is a trademarked name for Bordeaux-style American wines. Coined in 1981, the name is a combination of "merit" to signify grape quality and "heritage" to denote the historical tradition of wine blending. To use the term Meritage on the label, the wine must be a blend of two or more of the five classic Bordeaux varieties; St. Macaire, Gros Verdot, and Carmenère grapes may also be used. No single grape variety may account for more than 90% of the blend. The winery must also join the Meritage Alliance and pay an annual licensing fee to the group.

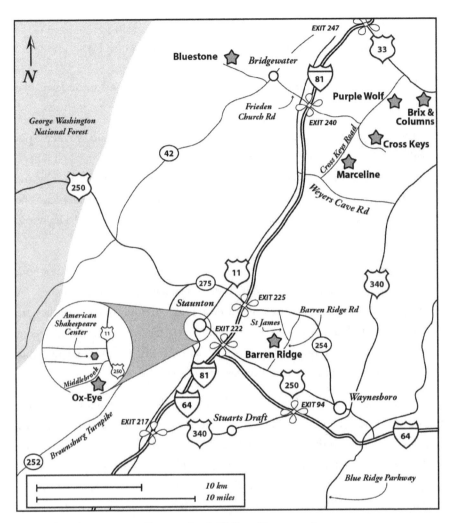

Map 4.3. Lower Shenandoah Valley (Staunton)

LOWER SHENANDOAH VALLEY

Barren Ridge Vineyards
984 Barren Ridge Road
Fishersville VA 22939

Hours: M–W 11:00–6:00, Su 1:00–6:00,
Th–Sa 11:00–9:00 (Apr–Aug), to 8:00 (Sep–Mar)
Closed New Year's, Easter,
Thanksgiving, Christmas

540-248-3300
www.barrenridgevineyardsva.com
E-mail: info@barrenridgevineyards.com

Barren Ridge is owned by John and Shelby Higgs, who established their winery on an apple orchard in John's family since 1934, converting the property's old apple barn into the tasting room. Guests may purchase cheese and sausage plates to have inside or on the patio while enjoying the view of the vines and neighboring hills. Barren Ridge sources its wines from its own vines and from other Shenandoah vineyards. In addition to live music on weekends, the winery holds an annual Swedish Fire Festival in winter and a Pork & Cork Festival on the 4th of July. The facilities may be rented for private parties or weddings. Children and dogs are welcome.

White Wines: Chardonnay, Harmony, Tinkling Spring, Traminette, Vidal Blanc, Viognier.

Red Wines: Cabernet Franc, Merlot, Petit Verdot, Red Barren, Touriga Nacional.

Sweet/Dessert Wines: Christof *(Viognier, Vidal Blanc)*.

Price Range: $17–$32

Tastings: $5 per person for basic red or white tasting, $8 for reserve tasting.

Groups: Reservations required for groups of 8 or more, $10 per person.

Purchasing: Online via VinoShipper to AK, AL, AZ, CA, CO, DC, FL,

GA, HI, IA, ID, IL, IN, KS, LA, MA, MD, ME, MN, MO, NC, ND, NE, NH, NM, NV, NY, OH, OR, PA, SC, TN, TX, VA, WA, WI, WV, and WY.

Directions: From I-81, take Exit 225 onto Woodrow Wilson Parkway (Route 275) east toward Fishersville. After 1 mile, the road becomes Hermitage Road (Route 254). Continue 1.2 miles and turn right onto St. James Road. Drive 2.3 miles and turn right onto Barren Ridge Road and then to the winery entrance on the right.

❖ ❖ ❖

Bluestone Vineyard
4828 Spring Creek Road
Bridgewater VA 22812

Hours: M–Sa 11:00–6:00, Su 1:00–6:00   540-828-0099
Closed New Year's, Thanksgiving, Christmas   www.bluestonevineyard.com
E-mail: info@bluestonevineyard.com

Bluestone Vineyard was opened to the public in 2011 by Curt and Jackie Hartman. After Curt retired several years earlier, he began developing Bluestone's vineyard in 2002, inspired in part by his friendship with the owners of MistyRay Winery *(by appointment only)*. Bluestone produces all Virginia-grown wines from their own vines or other vineyards. The tasting room is located in the two-story winery production building and overlooks the barrel room. Bluestone sponsors occasional live music and charity benefits.

White Wines: Chardonnay, Petit Manseng, Vidal Blanc, Viognier.

Rosé Wines: Rosé.

Red Wines: Cabernet Franc, Cabernet Sauvignon, Merlot, Steep Face.

Sweet/Dessert Wines: Beau, Blue Ice *(Traminette)*, Crooked and Weedy, Moscato.

Fortified Wines: Dry Dock *(port-style)*.

Price Range: $15–$26

Tastings: $5 per person for white or red flight, $10 for full.

Reservations required for groups of 8 or more.

Wheelchair accessible.

Purchasing: Online purchases are available for residents of AK, CA, DC, FL, MN, MO, NV, NC, PA, and VA.

Directions: From I-81, take Exit 240 and turn west onto Friedens Church Road (Route 257). Drive 3.3 miles into the town of Bridgewater and turn left onto North Main Street (Route 42). After ½ mile, turn right onto Spring Creek Road. Continue 1.7 miles to the winery on the right.

❖ ❖ ❖

Brix and Columns
1501 Dave Berry Road
McGaheysville VA 22840

Hours: W, Th 11:00–6:00, F 11:00–9:00,   540-828-0099
Sa 11:00–5:00, Su 12:00–6:00   www.bluestonevineyard.com
Closed New Year's, Thanksgiving, Christmas   E-mail: info@bluestonevineyard.com

Shenandoah natives Stephanie and Steve Pence opened Brix and Columns in early 2017 on the grounds of their 160-acre Six Penny Farm near Massanutten Mountain. They planted their first vines in 2016 and currently work with Michael Shaps (*Michael Shaps Wineworks*) to produce their wines. Brix and Columns sponsors live music on weekends, as well as outdoor yoga and zumba sessions, weather permitting. The facilities are available for rental for weddings and private events. Leashed dogs are welcome.

White Wines: Chardonnay, Viognier, White Brix.

Rosé Wines: Rosé.

Red Wines: Cabernet Franc, McGahey Reserve Red, Petit Verdot.

Price Range: $18–$33

Tastings: $8 per person.

Reservations required for groups of 7 or more.

Purchasing: Online purchases are available for several states; contact winery for details.

Directions: From I-81, take Exit 247A (Elkton) east onto E. Market Street (U.S. Route 33 East). Drive 9.6 miles and turn right onto New Hope Road. Make an immediate left onto McGaheysville Road, then take the first right onto Dave Berry Road. The winery will be 1.2 miles on the left.

❖ ❖ ❖

Cross Keys Vineyards
6011 East Timber Ridge Road
Mt. Crawford VA 22841

Hours: Daily 11:00–7:00 (Apr–Oct), 540-234-0505
11:00–5:00 (Nov–Mar) www.crosskeysvineyards.com
Closed New Year's, Thanksgiving, Christmas E-mail: info@crosskeysvineyards.com

Cross Keys was founded by Bob and Nikoo Bakhtiar, who came to the US from their native Iran as university students. They planted their first vines in 2002 and opened the winery to the public six years later. The winery's twenty-five-acre vineyard is under the supervision of winemaker Stephan Heyns from South Africa. Cross Keys offers "Grape to Glass" tours each day at 12:00, 2:00, and 4:00. The winery's various events rooms can be rented for private parties or weddings. Cross Keys also hosts a variety of special programs, including live music, special festivals, a holiday illumination in December, and a New Year's Eve party. Dogs are welcome.

White Wines: Chardonnay, Joy White *(Vidal Blanc)*.

Rosé Wines: Fiore.

Red Wines: Cabernet Franc, Joy Red *(Chambourcin)*, Meritage, Merlot, Petit Verdot, Pinot Noir, Touriga.

Sweet/Dessert Wines: Ali d'Oro *(Chardonel)*.

Fortified Wines: Tavern *(Touriga Nacional)*.

Price Range: $20–$38

Tastings: $12 to $15 per person, depending on flight selected.

Groups: Reservations required for groups of 10 or more, $15 per person.

Wheelchair accessible.

Directions: From I-81, take Exit 240 and turn east onto Friedens Church Road (Route 682). Drive 4 miles and turn right onto Cross Keys Road (Route 276). Continue ½ mile to East Timber Ridge Road and turn left. The winery will be 1.2 miles on the left.

❖ ❖ ❖

Marceline Vineyards
5887 Cross Keys Road
Mt. Crawford VA 22841

Hours: Th–Sa 11:00–6:00, Su 1:00–6:00 (Apr–Oct),   540-212-9798
Th–Sa 11:00–5:00, Su 1:00–5:00 (Nov–Mar)   www.marcelinevineyards.com
Closed New Year's, Thanksgiving, Christmas   E-mail: info@marcelinevineyards.com

Susan Rudolph Pleasant and her family opened Marceline [*mar-seh-leen*] Vineyards in December 2016, ten years after planting their first vines. Named for Susan's mother, Marceline is housed in a restored horse barn at the top of a hill overlooking the vineyards. Tim and Peter Rausse serve as consultants, with Tim as the winemaker for Marceline's all-Virginia wines. The winery offers crackers and cheeses for purchase; guests may enjoy these either inside the tasting room or out on the deck with its views of Massanutten Mountain. The facilities may be rented for private events or weddings.

White Wines: Chardonnay.

Rosé Wines: Rosé.

Red Wines: Cabernet Franc, Cabernet Sauvignon.

Sweet/Dessert Wines: Cabernet Franc Dessert.

Price Range: $20–$38

Tastings: $5 per person.

Restrictions: No dogs or pets allowed.

Directions: From I-81, take Exit 247A (Elkton) and turn east onto East Market Street (U.S. Route 33 East). Drive 4 miles, then turn right onto Cross Keys Road (VA 276). The winery will be 5.7 miles on the left.

❖ ❖ ❖

Ox-Eye Vineyards
44 Middlebrook Avenue
Staunton VA   24401

Hours: M–Th 12:00–6:00, F 12:00–7:00,
Sa 10:00–7:00, Su 12:00–5:00
Closed New Year's, Easter,
Thanksgiving, Christmas

540-849-7926
www.oxeyevineyards.com
E-mail: info@OxEyeVineyards.com

Ox-Eye Vineyards was founded by John and Susan Kiers, who opened to the public in 2011 after selling grapes for many years to other wineries. They named their winery after the ox-eye daisies that proliferate in the valleys around the town of Swoope where their vineyards are located. The tasting room is in Staunton in a restored railroad weigh station in the town's core restaurant and tourism district. After tasting Ox-Eye's estate-grown wines, visitors can relax over a glass or bottle at one of the tables upstairs or outside on the patio. The tasting room features exhibits by local artists on the walls. Light fare is offered for purchase. Free Wi-Fi is available.

Sparkling Wines: Ox-Eye Sparkling (*Chardonnay*).

White Wines: Chardonnay, Riesling, Scale House Reserve Riesling, Traminette, White Ox.

Blush Wines: Shy Ox.

Red Wines: Cabernet Franc, Lemberger, Pinot Noir.

Price Range: $17–$35

Tastings: $7 per person.

Purchasing: Online via VinoShipper to AK, AL, AZ, CA, CO, DC, FL, GA, HI, IA, ID, IL, IN, KS, LA, MA, MD, ME, MN, MO, NC, ND, NE, NH, NM, NV, NY, OH, OR, PA, SC, TN, TX, VA, WA, WI, WV, and WY.

Directions: From I-81, take Exit 222 onto U.S. Route 250 West. Drive two miles into Staunton. Bear right onto Greenville Avenue, where U.S. Route 250 and U.S. Route 11 merge. Take the first left onto Commerce Road to continue following U.S. Route 250. Take the third left onto Middlebrook Avenue. The winery will be on the left in 0.1 mile; parking is available on the street or in the town parking lot across the street from the tasting room.

❖ ❖ ❖

Purple Wolf Vineyards
2644 Cross Keys Road
Harrisonburg VA   22801

Hours: M–Sa 12:00–6:00, Su 1:00–6:00 (Mar–Dec),
M–Sa 12:00–5:00, Su 1:00–5:00 (Jan–Feb)
Closed New Year's, Easter,
Thanksgiving, Christmas

540-421-6345
www.purplewolfvineyard.com
E-mail: whiteoaklavender@gmail.com

Purple Wolf, located next to the White Oak Lavender Farm, offers several Virginia-grown wines infused with lavender. Opened in 2015 by Julie Houshalter, Purple Wolf's wines are made by Randy Phillips of nearby Cave Ridge Vineyard. After tasting, visitors can either linger over a glass or bottle of wine or check out the many lavender-based products in the farm store.

White Wines: Imperial Gem, Riesling, Thumbelina, Viognier.

Rosé Wines: Butterfly Kisses.

Red Wines: Cabernet Franc, Chambourcin, Pardon My Purple.

Fortified Wines: Royale Velvet.

Price Range: $18–$24

Tastings: $5 per person for white or red flight, $9 for full.

Directions: From I-81, take Exit 247A (Elkton) and turn east onto East Market Street (U.S. Route 33 East). Drive 4 miles, then turn right onto Cross Keys Road (VA 276). The winery will be 2.4 miles on the right.

❖ ❖ ❖

Rockbridge Vineyard

35 Hill View Lane

Raphine VA 24472

Hours: Tu–Sa 10:00–6:00, Su–M 12:00–5:00

Closed New Year's Eve & Day, Thanksgiving,

Christmas Eve & Day

540-377-6204

www.rockbridgevineyard.com

E-mail: rockbridgewine@gmail.com

Rockbridge Vineyard was established in 1992 by Shepherd Rouse and Jane Millott-Rouse. Shep, who serves as the winemaker, worked at several California wineries, including Chateau St. Jean, Schramsburg, and Carneros Creek, before returning to his native Virginia. Rockbridge's name comes from the county in which it is located as well as from the county's most

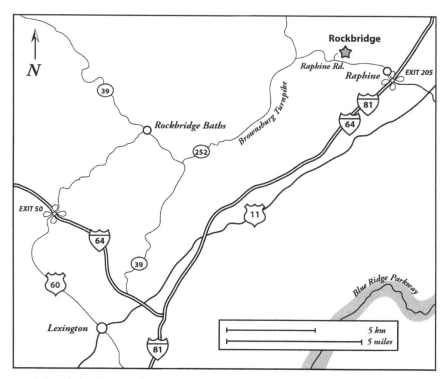

Map 4.4. Lower Shenandoah Valley (Rockbridge)

famous natural feature, the Natural Bridge, whose depiction adorns many of the winery's labels. The DeChiel label of some of Rockbridge's wines is in honor of Shep's French Huguenot lineage. The winery and tasting room are in a large, red barn, with a small deck just outside the tasting room entrance. Light fair is available for purchase. The facility is available for rental for private parties and weddings. Rockbridge frequently sponsors live music, winemaker dinners, and harvest festivals. Children and dogs are welcome.

Fruit Wines: Vin de Pomme *(apple)*.

White Wines: Chardonnay, St. Mary's Blanc, Traminette, Tuscarora White, Vignoles, Viognier, White Riesling.

Rosé Wines: Rose Hill Rosé, Jeremiah's Blush *(Concord, Vidal Blanc)*, Pinot Noir Blanc.

Red Wines: Cabernet Franc, Chambourcin, Meritage, Merlot, Pinot Noir, Syrah, Virginia Claret *(Norton)*, Lexington & Concord, Tuscarora Red.

Sweet/Dessert Wines: V d'Or.

Price Range: $12–$25

Tastings: $5 per person.

Groups: Please call ahead for reservations and per person fee.

Purchasing: Online purchasing is available for AZ, CA, CO, DC, FL, GA, HI, IA, ID, IL, IN, KS, LA, MO, NC, NM, OH, OR, TX, VA, WA, WI, WV, and WY.

Directions: From I-81, take Exit 205 (Raphine) onto Route 606 West. The winery will be one mile on the right, past the village of Raphine.

SPARKLING WINES

Few things add a more festive and elegant touch to any celebration than sparkling wine. Sparkling wine as we know it originated and was perfected in France's Champagne region by, as tradition has it, the Benedictine monk Dom Perignon.

Only sparkling wines made in Champagne may be called by that name; all others are more correctly termed "sparkling" wines although they may indicate on their labels if they were made using the *méthode champenoise*, or champagne method. (The official term in Europe is now traditional or classic method, the European Union bureaucracy having banned the phrase "champagne method.")

In this champagne method, sparkling wine gets its bubbles through a second fermentation in the bottle. After the grapes have been pressed and the base wine fermented and blended, a sugar-yeast mixture is added to the wine, which is then put into the familiar thick, dark bottles we see on wine store shelves. After this second fermentation has been completed, the yeast sediments are frozen and removed through a process called disgorgement, and the bottles are then corked and sealed.

While sparkling wine may be made from a range of different grapes, the classic varieties used in the Champagne region are Chardonnay, Pinot Noir, and Meunier (also called Pinot Meunier). Classic champagne is often a blend of wines from two or more of these grapes. However, if the label includes the phrase "blanc de blancs" (French for "white from white"), the wine was made solely from Chardonnay grapes. If the label indicates "blanc de noirs" ("white from black") then only Pinot Noir was used.

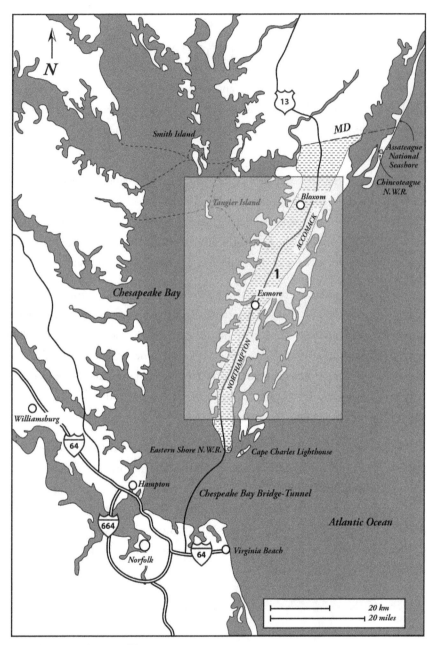

Map 5.1. Eastern Virginia

5. EASTERN SHORE REGION & AVA

The Eastern Shore of Virginia is a narrow finger of land accessible from Virginia only by way of the 17.6-mile Chesapeake Bay Bridge-Tunnel (CBBT) or by passenger ferry across the Chesapeake Bay. (For drivers with a fear of bridges, a CBBT employee can drive your car across the bridge with advance reservations.) With the Atlantic Ocean on one side and the Chesapeake Bay on the other, the region is marked by sandy, well-drained soils and a temperate climate. At its broadest point, the peninsula is only twenty-two miles wide and stretches seventy miles from the Maryland border down to its southern tip.

The Eastern Shore's sole remaining winery produces AVA-designated wines, allowing wine aficionados to conduct their own horizontal tastings at home to compare the range of character and personality in wines from across Virginia.

❖ ❖ ❖

<u>Things to see and do</u>: The Eastern Shore is blessed with exceptional natural beauty and offers many options for bird-watching, kayaking, boating, and fishing. Two of its national wildlife refuges (NWR)—the Eastern Shore of Virginia NWR and the Chincoteague NWR—along with the Assateague Island National Seashore and Virginia Coast Reserve translate to perhaps the longest stretch of protected coastline on the Atlantic.

The Eastern Shore NWR at the southern tip of the peninsula is well known as a waystation for migratory birds, particularly in the autumn, as well as for raptors and butterflies. Bird lovers and photographers can use the observation decks and photography blinds in the refuge to observe and photograph birds in their habitat. The refuge's visitor center at Cape Charles has various displays and exhibits to introduce visitors to the region's wildlife. A "Please Touch" table is particularly popular with children, and the summertime Butterfly Garden is a photographer's delight.

The region also offers numerous biking trails, such as a self-guided walking and biking tour on Chincoteague, several trails at Kiptopeke State Park, and the newly opened Southern Tip Bike and Hike Trail. Special bike tours include the annual Between the Waters Bike Tour, a fundraiser hosted by Citizens for a Better Eastern Shore.

In addition, Assateague is famous for its wild ponies which can be seen wandering and grazing on the island. In the Chincoteague Pony Swim in late July, about 150 ponies swim across Assateague Channel in an annual event memorialized by Marguerite Henry in her 1947 children's book, *Misty of Chincoteague*. After some of the foals are sold, the ponies then swim back to Assateague, where visitors can see them in the wild on pony-watching cruises or kayak tours.

❖ ❖ ❖

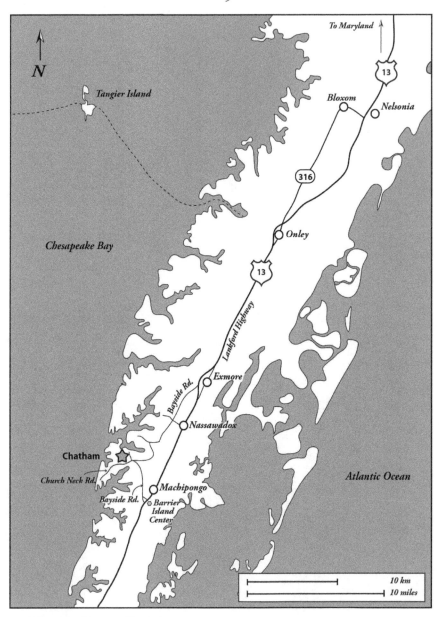

Map 5.2. Eastern Virginia

EASTERN VIRGINIA

Chatham Vineyards & Winery
9232 Chatham Road
Machipongo VA 23405

Hours: Daily 10:00–5:00 (Apr–Dec) 757-678-5588
Th–Sa, M 10:00–5:00, Su 12: 00–5:00 http://chathamvineyards.net
Closed New Year's, Easter, Thanksgiving, Christmas E-mail: info@chathamvineyards.net

Chatham Vineyards is owned by second-generation vintner Jon Wehner who worked in his parents' Great Falls Vineyard while growing up in northern Virginia's Fairfax County. The wines are all bottled under the Church Creek label, named for the stream that flows next to the farm. Chatham Vineyards hosts several special winery events, including kayak tours and "Girls Days Out." The winery may be rented for events and weddings. Children and pets are welcome.

White Wines: Chardonnay.

Rosé Wines: Rosé.

Red Wines: Cabernet Franc, Merlot, Vintner's Blend *(Bordeaux-style blend).*

Sweet/Dessert Wines: Late Harvest Dessert Wine.

Price Range: $14–$25

Tastings: $5

Wheelchair accessible.

Purchasing: Online sales for AK, DC, FL, MD, MI, NY, and VA.

Directions: From U.S. Route 13, turn west at the Barrier Islands Center onto Young Street then right on Bayside Road. Drive 3 miles. Turn left onto Church Neck Road and right onto Chatham Road. The winery is on the left.

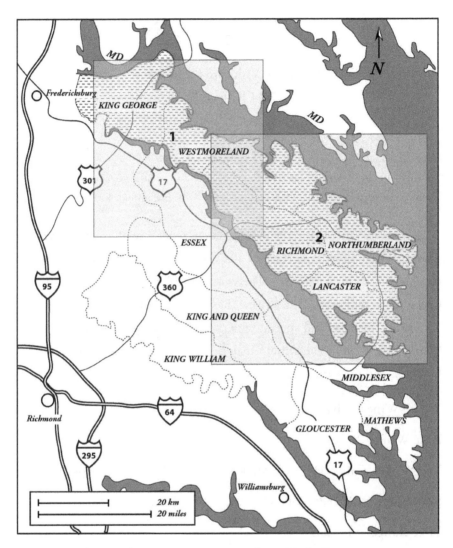

Map 6.1. Chesapeake Bay Region & Northern Neck-George
Washington Birthplace AVA: (1) Northern Neck (northern section);
(2) Northern Neck (southern section).

6. CHESAPEAKE BAY REGION & NORTHERN NECK-GEORGE WASHINGTON BIRTHPLACE AVA

Virginia's three long peninsulas jutting into the Chesapeake Bay were the first to be colonized by the English in the seventeenth century. The northernmost of these, the Northern Neck, is bounded on the north by the Potomac River and on the south by the Rappahannock. The Middle Peninsula is next, bounded by the Rappahannock to the north and the York River to the south.

The name of the AVA is generally given simply as Northern Neck, the original longer title having been a compromise between the two names originally proposed. The AVA is characterized by relatively flat terrain and light, sandy, well-drained soils. It has a comparatively mild climate, especially during winter: the moderating influence of the Chesapeake Bay keeps frost days at a minimum, and river breezes help temper summertime heat and humidity.

The region's wineries produce the full range of wine types, from sparkling to dessert and even fortified. For their largely estate-grown production, Northern Neck wineries use varietals that are also grown elsewhere in Virginia, but the nature and essence of their wines will be distinctly different precisely because of the AVA's unique climate and soil combinations. Reds, for instance, can be lighter than those from central Virginia where the climate and soils are different.

❖ ❖ ❖

<u>Things to See and Do</u>: The Chesapeake Bay region was first explored by a European in 1608 when Captain John Smith led two expeditions from Jamestown northward to map the Chesapeake and its native American settlements. The region's agricultural and fishing resources attracted a growing number of planters and colonists from England who settled in the area.

A number of these families rose to prominence during the American War of Independence. Presidents George Washington, James Madison, and James Monroe were born on the Northern Neck, as were Francis Lightfoot Lee and Richard Henry Lee, signers of the Declaration of Independence. The Lee brothers' cousin, Henry Lee, was the grandfather of General Robert E. Lee, commander of the South's Army of Northern Virginia, who was born at Stratford Hall, the family plantation on the banks of the Potomac.

The Northern Neck boasts a rich variety of outdoor activities for nature lovers to enjoy, including boating, camping, and hiking trails. Northern Neck wetlands welcome over 200 species of migratory birds each year and are home to one of the largest populations of bald eagles on the eastern U.S. coast, making the region a bird-watcher's paradise.

❖ ❖ ❖

<u>Wine Trails</u>: The Chesapeake Bay Wine Trail includes all the wineries in the Northern Neck and Middle Peninsula. Please see Appendix 1 for more details.

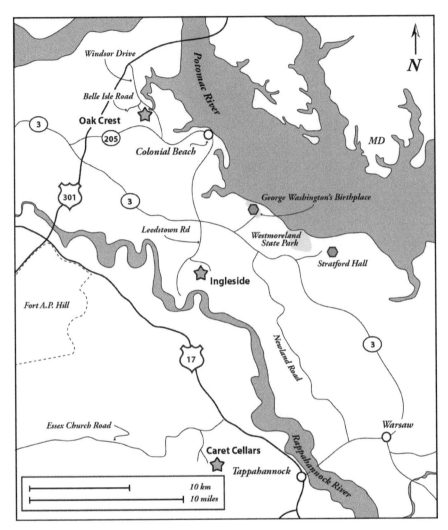

Map 6.2. Northern Neck (northern section)

NORTHERN NECK

Caret Cellars
495 Meadow Landing Lane
Caret VA 22436

Hours: Th–M 12:00–6:00
Closed New Year's, Thanksgiving, Christmas Eve & Day

540-413-6454
www.caretcellars.com
E-mail: caretcellars@hughes.net

Rich and Junghee Thompson opened Caret Cellars (*kah-rett*] in early September 2015 after first planting their vineyards eight years earlier. They work with winemaker Floyd Oslin to produce a range of wines using estate- or Virginia-grown grapes. The tasting room offers seating indoors as well as tables outdoors overlooking the vineyard where visitors can enjoy live music and food truck barbecue on weekends. The facilities are available for private events. Children and leashed dogs are welcome.

White Wines: Chardonnay, Viognier, White Merlot.

Rosé Wines: Rosato di Sangiovese.

Red Wines: Chambourcin, Merlot, Rivah Red, Sangiovese, Super Tuscan, .

Price Range: $15–$24

Tastings: $5 per person.

Purchasing: Online via VinoShipper to AK, AL, CA, DC, FL, ID, IL, LA, MN, MO, NC, ND, NE, NH, NM, NV, OH, OR, VA, WV, and WY.

Directions: From U.S. Route 17, turn onto Essex Church Road (VA 624). Drive 0.5 mile and turn left onto Belmont Road (unpaved). After another half-mile, Belmont curves left and turns into Meadow Landing (unpaved). Continue on to the winery entrance on the left.

❖ ❖ ❖

The Dog and Oyster Vineyards
170 White Fences Drive
Irvington VA 22480

Hours: Daily 11:00–5:00 (Apr–Sep)

F-Su 11:00–5:00 (mid-Sep–Feb)

Th-M 11:00–5:00 (Mar only)

Closed New Year's, Thanksgiving, Christmas

804-438-9463

www.dogandoyster.com

E-mail: dudley@hopeandglory.com

The Dog and Oyster is owned by Doug and Peggy Patterson who named the winery after their dogs who shoo deer away from the vines and after the oysters of the Chesapeake Bay. The winery is easily recognizable from the road by the pair of giant corkscrews on either side of the drive leading to the six-acre vineyard. The small tasting room includes both a covered patio with several chairs and tables, as well as an interior room with a tasting bar and small shop.. Dogs are welcome.

Guests may stay at the Pattersons' Hope and Glory Inn in Irvington, including the Tents at Vineyard Grove, adjacent to the Dog and Oyster.

White Wines: Oyster White *(Chardonel)*, Pearl *(Vidal Blanc)*.

Rosé Wines: Rosie.

Red Wines: Merlot, Shelter Dog Red.

Price Range: $25–$33

Tastings: $7 per person, on the hour and half-hour.

Groups: Call ahead for groups over six.

Wheelchair accessible.

Directions: From U.S. Route 17, take U.S. Route 360 East into the town of Tappahannock. Cross the Rappahannock River and turn right onto Route 3 at the town of Warsaw. Drive 29.6 miles and turn right onto Route 200 (Irvington Road). Drive 4 miles and turn left into White Fences Lane.

❖ ❖ ❖

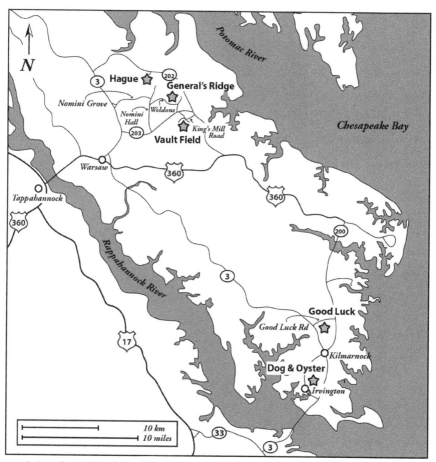

Map 6.3. Northern Neck (southern section)

General's Ridge Vineyard & Winery
1618 Weldons Drive
Hague VA 22469

Hours: Th, Su , holiday M 12:00–5:00, F, Sa 12:00–6:00   804-472-3172

Closed New Year's, Thanksgiving, Christmas   http://generalsridgevineyard.com

E-mail: tastingroom@generalsridgevineyard.com

Founded by retired General Rick Phillips and his wife, Linda, General's Ridge began operations ten years ago as a vineyard selling its production to nearby wineries. The Phillipses decided to start their own winery and to the public in 2011. They currently have about thirty acres under vine and work with Michael Shaps Wineworks which handles their production. Snacks and light food may be purchased in the tasting room. General's Ridge offers various events, including wine pairings and dinners.

General's Ridge also offers two guest houses for overnight stays, private parties, and weddings. The Manor House is a restored, two-story, nineteenth-century house; the smaller Carriage House can hold small conferences or wedding receptions.

White Wines: Chardonnay, GRV White, Pinot Grigio, Viognier.

Rosé Wines: Rosé.

Red Wines: Cabernet Franc, GRV Red, Merlot, Petit Verdot.

Sweet/Dessert Wines: General's Nightcap.

Fortified Wines: General's Last Call *(port-style)*.

Price Range: $11–$20

Tastings: $6 per person for white, $8 for reds, $9 for full tasting list.

Wheelchair accessible.

Directions: From U.S. Route 17, turn onto U.S. Route 360 East at the town of Tappahannock. Drive 6.6 miles and turn left onto Route 3 at the town of Warsaw. Continue following Route 3 for 6 miles. Turn right onto Nomini Grove Road (Route 621, which will become Route 600). Drive 3.7 miles until Nomini Grove Road until it ends at Nomini Hall Road and turn right. Take the second left onto Weldons Drive. The winery entrance will be about a mile on the left.

❖ ❖ ❖

Good Luck Cellars
1025 Good Luck Road
Kilmarnock VA 22482

Hours: M, Th 11:00–5:00, F 11:00–8:00,
Sa 11:00–6:00, Su 12:00–5:00
Closed January, Thanksgiving, Christmas

804-435-1416
www.goodluckcellars.com
E-mail: info@goodluckcellars.com

Good Luck Cellars was established by Paul and Katie Krop, longtime wine enthusiasts from Virginia Beach. The Krops planted their 12-acre vineyard on the site of a reclaimed sand and gravel pit. The winery opened to the public in 2011 and includes a tasting room with both indoor and outdoor seating, including a wrap-around veranda where visitors can linger. The facilities may be rented for special events.

White Wines: Chardonel, Chardonnay, Four Blonds, Vidal Blanc, Vignoles.

Rosé Wines: Rip Rap Rosé.

Red Wines: Cabernet Sauvignon, Chambourcin, Radiant Red *(Chambourcin)*.

Sweet/Dessert Wines: Sweet Shamrock Red.

Price Range: $16–$28

Tastings: $5 per person.

Wheelchair accessible.

Directions: From U.S. Route 17, turn east onto Route 33 and drive 7 miles. Turn left onto Greys Point Road (Route 3) and cross the Rappahannock River. Follow Route 3 for 14 miles and turn right onto Good Luck Road. The winery will be about one mile on the right.

❖ ❖ ❖

The Hague Winery
8268 Cople Highway
Hague VA 22469

Hours: Daily 11:00–5:00 (Apr–Nov)   804-472-5283
Closed Dec–Mar   www.thehaguewinery.com
                              E-mail: cmadey@thehaguewinery.com

Stephen and Cynthia Madey purchased the historic Buena Vista plantation, which dates to 1835, just outside the hamlet of Hague, Virginia, and established their five-acre vineyard soon afterward. The first vines were planted in 2005, and the first estate-grown wines released in 2009 under the guidance of Lucie Morton, one of Virginia's pioneering viticulturists. The Hague's tasting room is in a renovated barn with several tables and chairs indoors as well as a covered patio outside where guests may enjoy light snacks over a glass or bottle of wine. Visitors may also rent The Cottage, a two-bedroom restored guest house on the property, for overnight stays.

White Wines: Chardonel.

Rosé Wines: Rosé.

Red Wines: Cabernet Franc, Meritage, Merlot, Petit Verdot.

Dessert Wines: Cynthia *(Muscat Ottonel).*

Price Range: $17–$29

Tastings: $6 per person.

Groups: Reservations encouraged for groups of 8 or more.

Purchasing: Online for AK, AZ, CA, CO, CT, DC, FL, GA, HI, IA, ID, IL, IN, KS, LA, ME, MI, MN, MO, NC, ND, NE, NH, NV, NY, OH, OR, SC, TN, TX, VA, VT, WA, WI, WV, and WY.

Directions: From U.S. Route 17, turn onto U.S. Route 340 East at the town of Tappahannock. Drive 6.6 miles and turn left onto Route 3 at the town of Warsaw. Continue following Route 3 for 3.3 miles and turn right onto Oldhams Road (Route 203). Drive 7.5 miles and turn left onto Cople Highway (Route 202). Drive 4.6 miles to the winery entrance on left.

❖ ❖ ❖

Ingleside Vineyards
5872 Leedstown Road
Oak Grove VA 22443

Hours: M–Sa 10:00–5:00, Su 12:00–5:00   804-224-8687
(Memorial Day to Labor Day, open until 6:00)   www.inglesidevineyards.com
Closed New Year's, Easter,   E-mail: info@inglesidevineyards.com
Thanksgiving, Christmas

One of Virginia's earliest wineries, Ingleside Vineyards is also one of the largest in terms of acreage, with about 60 acres under vine. The winery sponsors a range of special events, including live music, barrel tastings, and harvest festivals, and can host private parties or weddings for up to

150 guests on the grounds. The tasting room is in an old dairy barn and includes a patio with tables and chairs where visitors may enjoy a picnic lunch. Children will find a small natural history museum at one end of the patio. Pets are welcome.

Sparkling Wines: Virginia Brut.

White Wines: Albariño, Blue Crab Blanc, Chardonnay, Colonial White, Pinot Grigio, Viognier.

Rosé Wines: Blue Crab Blush, Sweet Virginia Rosé.

Red Wines: Blue Crab Red, Cabernet Franc, Cabernet Merlot, Left Bank *(Cabernet Sauvignon)*, Petit Verdot, Right Bank *(Merlot)*, Sangiovese.

Dessert Wines: October Harvest *(Petit Manseng, Riesling)*, Virginia Gold.

Price Range: $15–$40

Tastings: $5 per person for basic; $7 per person for premium.

Groups: Reservations required for groups of 8 or more.

Wheelchair accessible.

Purchasing: Online to VA and via VinoShipper to AK, AL, AZ, CA, CO, DC, FL, GA, HI, IA, ID, IL, IN, KS, LA, MA, MD, ME, MN, MO, NC, ND, NE, NH, NM, NV, NY, OH, OR, PA, SC, TN, TX, WA, WI, WV, and WY.

Directions: From U.S. Route 301, turn south onto Route 3. Drive 10 miles and turn right onto Leedstown Road (Route 638). Drive 2.2 miles to the winery's gravel driveway on the left.

❖ ❖ ❖

Oak Crest Vineyard & Winery
8215 Oak Crest Drive
King George VA 22485

Hours: W–Su 10:00–5:00 (Mar–Dec), Sa–Su 11:00–4:00 (Jan, Feb)   540-663-2813
Closed Easter, Thanksgiving, Christmas   www.oakcrestwinery.com
E-mail: winery@oakcrestwinery.com

Oak Crest Vineyard & Winery was opened in 2002 by Conrad and Dorothy Brandt. The Brandts use the Symphony grape for most of their white wines, which vary in taste depending on the specific yeasts used in production. The tasting room and winery are built into the side of a hill, with the barrel room literally carved into the ground. Guests may purchase snacks in the tasting room or bring their own picnics to enjoy on the decks and patio that adjoin the tasting room. The winery may be rented for private parties and weddings. Children and pets are welcome.

White Wines: Moonlight Sonata *(Symphony)*, Symphony, Viognier.

Rosé Wines: Summer Rose *(Cabernet Franc)*.

Red Wines: Cabernet Franc, Cabernet Sauvignon, Cannon Ridge Red, Rhapsody.

Sweet/Dessert Wines: Finale *(Symphony)*, Summer Medley *(Symphony, straw-berries)*, Symphony (sweet).

Fortified Wines: Ruby *(port-style)*.

Other: Hot Jazz *(Symphony, jalapeño peppers)*.

Price Range: $16–$23

Tastings: $5 per person.

Groups: Reservations requested for groups of 8 or more.

Restrictions: Reservations required for buses and limos (parking lot is very small).

Purchasing: E-mail purchases for residents of Virginia only.

Directions: From U.S. Route 301 North, turn south onto Windsor Drive (Route 218). Drive 2.5 miles and turn right onto Belle Isle Road. Make an immediate left onto Oak Crest Drive and the winery's gravel driveway.

❖ ❖ ❖

Vault Field Vineyards
2953 Kings Mill Road
Kinsale VA 22488

Hours: Th–Su 11:00–5:00 (to 6:00 in summer) (Apr–Dec)   804-472-4430
Closed Easter, Thanksgiving, Christmas,   www.vaultfield.com
Also closed Jan–Mar (call to see if open on Sa)   E-mail: info@vaultfield.com

After a career in the insurance industry, Keith and Joanne Meenan decided to purchase the historic Vault Field Farm and start a vineyard and winery. The Meenans and their son Dan manage all operations on the vineyard, with Keith also serving as winemaker. The tasting room is inside the winery building. The winery sponsors fall barrel tastings and a spring open house featuring music and light food; proceeds from the events are donated to the local volunteer fire department. Vault Field offers private tastings by appointment.

White Wines: Chardonnay, Conundrum *(Chardonnay, Vidal Blanc, Chardonel)*, Vidal Blanc.

Rosé Wines: Rosé.

Red Wines: Merlot, Red *(Merlot, Cabernet Sauvignon, Chambourcin)*, Reserve Red.

Price Range: $17–$22

Tastings: $5 per person.

Wheelchair accessible.

Purchasing: Online for all states *except* AL, AK, AR, DE, HI, MA, MT, NJ, NM, OK, PA, SD, and UT.

Directions: From U.S. Route 17, turn onto U.S. Route 340 East at the town of Tappahannock. Drive 6.6 miles and turn left onto Route 3 at the town of Warsaw. Continue following Route 3 for 3.3 miles and turn right onto Oldhams Road (Route 203). Drive 7.5 miles and turn right onto Cople Highway (Route 202). Take the first right onto Kings Mill Road. The winery driveway will be about 1 mile on the right.

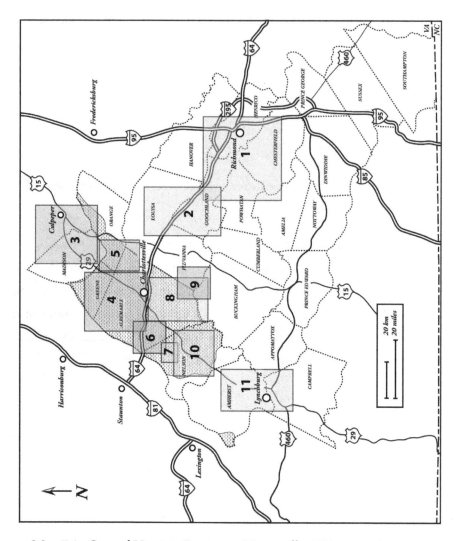

Map 7.1. Central Virginia Region & Monticello AVA: (1) Richmond; (2) Louisa; (3) Madison; (4) Upper Monticello (Free Union-White Hall); (5) Upper Monticello (Stony Point); (6) Afton-Crozet; (7) Rockfish Gap; (8) Lower Monticello (North Garden); (9) Lower Monticello (Scottsville); (10) Lower Monticello (Lovingston); (11) Lynchburg.

7. CENTRAL VIRGINIA REGION & MONTICELLO AVA

Bounded by the Blue Ridge on the west and Tidewater on the east, the Central Virginia Region is rich in history and natural attractions. The topography of this region varies considerably, rising from the flat terrain of the fall line at Richmond to the Blue Ridge Mountains. The Monticello AVA is centered around Charlottesville in the western part of the larger region. While summers throughout Central Virginia are warm, the Blue Ridge helps moderate winter temperatures in the AVA, protecting it from the lower temperatures that can sometimes occur in the Shenandoah Valley immediately to the west.

The Central Virginia region is second only to Northern Virginia in the number of wineries, with over five dozen that are regularly open to the public. Roughly two-thirds of these are in the Monticello AVA, whose vineyards produce twenty-four separate varieties of grapes, including less commonly known ones such as Rkatsiteli, Touriga Nacional, and Pinotage. As of 2016, 145 wines were labeled with the Monticello AVA designation, which means that 85 percent of the grapes used to produce them originated in the AVA. Soils here are generally clay underlain by granite and can produce quite full-bodied wines.

❖ ❖ ❖

<u>Things to see and do</u>: There are numerous historical attractions spread throughout the region, ranging from homes of the founding fathers

(Thomas Jefferson's Monticello and James Monroe's Ash Lawn) to the central campus of the University of Virginia in Charlottesville, designed by Thomas Jefferson and the sole American university to be named a World Heritage Site.

Virginia's capital of Richmond offers a number of interesting sites for visitors. The Church Hill district, located immediately to the east of the downtown area, is a colonial-era neighborhood that includes the historic St. John's Church, where Patrick Henry gave his famous "Give me liberty or give me death!" speech in 1775. The Virginia state capitol building was designed by Thomas Jefferson, who used the Roman-era Maison Carrée in Nîmes, France, as his architectural inspiration. Near the Capitol is the Virginia Civil Rights Memorial that commemorates the student strike led by Barbara Rose Johns of Farmville, Virginia; the students' actions at their high school ultimately led to the Brown v. Board of Education lawsuit that mandated equal educational opportunities for all.

The entire region is particularly rich in Civil War history. The Richmond area includes, among other sites, the Museum of the Civil War Soldier, located near Petersburg on the battlefield where General Ulysses S. Grant's forces shattered General Robert E. Lee's lines in April, 1865. The Sailor's Creek battlefield, just east of Farmville, was the last major battle of the Civil War in the Virginia theater. Three days after losing 7,700 men in combat there against Union forces, General Lee surrendered to General Grant at Appomattox Court House 46 miles to the west. The Lee's Retreat Trail is a self-guided driving tour that traces Lee's last moves in retreating from Petersburg to Appomattox (www.varetreat.com/lee.asp).

Richmond's Jackson Ward neighborhood offers a walking tour where visitors may explore the area called the Harlem of the South that was home for many African-American entrepreneurs after the Civil War. Jackson Ward also was the residence of Maggie Walker, the first woman to found and preside over a bank; her home is now a national historic site run by the

National Park Service. Further south in Lynchburg is the home of Anne Spencer, the noted Harlem Renaissance poet who was the second African-American to be included in the Norton Anthology of Literature.

The region also includes part of Virginia's Civil Rights in Education Heritage Trail (www.varetreat.com/CivilRights.asp), a self-guided driving tour of key sites in the struggle of African-Americans, Native Americans, and women to attain greater access and rights to educational resources.

❖ ❖ ❖

<u>Wine Trails</u>: There are several wine trails for Central Virginia wineries, among them the Heart of Virginia Wine Trail, the Monticello Wine Trail, the Foothills Scenic Wine Way, and Nelson 151. More details are available in Appendix 1.

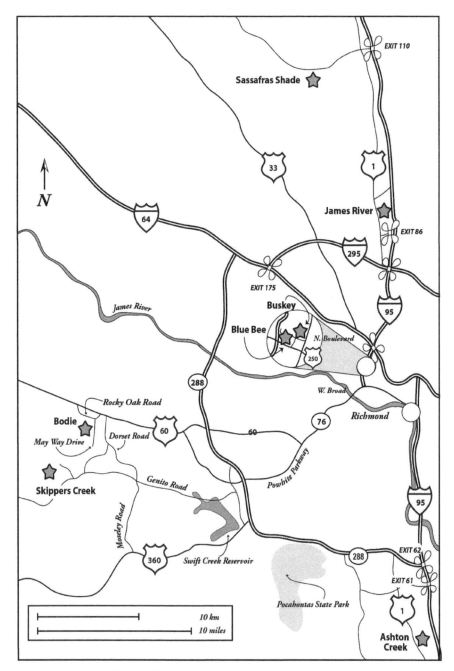

Map 7.2. Richmond

RICHMOND

Ashton Creek Vineyard
14501 Jefferson Davis Highway
Chester VA 23831

Hours: W–F,12:00–8:00, Sa-Su 11:00–6:00 (summer–fall)   804-896-1586
Closed New Year's, Thanksgiving, Christmas   www.ashtoncreekvineyard.com
E-mail: info@ashtoncreekvineyard.com

Ashton Creek Vineyard opened in early 2017 as the Richmond area's newest winery. Kirk and Lori Thibault are using grapes from other Virginia wineries while their own vines mature; LeeHartman (Bluestone Vineyards) and Sudha Patil (Narmada Vineyards) are assisting as winemakers. Ashton Creek offers a range of food, from flatbreads to cheese platters and soups, as well as live music on weekends. Ashton Creek also offers several Potter's Craft ciders in addition to their wines on the tasting menu. The winery has quickly become a popular wedding venue as well. Well-behaved children are welcome.

Ciders: Farmhouse Dry, Farmhouse Saison, Grapefruit-Hibiscus, Mosaic, Oak Barrel Reserve, Sorachi Ace.

White Wines: Willie's White, Seyval Blanc, Traminette.

Red Wines: Cabernet Sauvignon, Cannonball Red.

Sweet/Dessert Wines: Sweet Summertime (*Tannat, Cabernet Sauvignon, blackberry*).

Price Range: $12–$26

Tastings: $10

Directions: From Richmond, take I-95 Southbound for 13 miles to Exit 61B (Chester). Drive west on West Hundred Road (VA 10 West) for ½ mile. Turn left onto Jefferson Davis Highway (U.S. Route 1 South). The winery entrance will be 2.3 miles on the left.

❖ ❖ ❖

Blue Bee Cider
1320 Summit Avenue
Richmond VA 23230

Hours: M–F 1:00–9:00, Sa 12:00–10:00,
Su 12:00–8:00
Closed New Year's, Thanksgiving, Christmas

804-231-0280
www.bluebeecider.com
E-mail: admin@bluebeecider.com

Blue Bee Cider, Virginia's first urban cidery, was founded in 2013 by Courtney Mailey whose interest in cidermaking was initially sparked by an high school aptitude test that pointed to a farming career. After working for various economic development agencies in Washington, D.C., Courtney switched careers, graduating from Cornell University's cider school and apprenticing at Albemarle Ciderworks before opening her cidery. Named after Virginia's native blue orchard bees, Blue Bee is located in the historic Scott's Addition neighborhood in Richmond just a short walk from Buskey Cider. They offer various breads and spreads for visitors to enjoy over a cider after their tastings. The specific ciders on the tasting line-up will vary, depending on availability.

Ciders: Aragon 1904, Charred Ordinary, Gold Dominion, Harrison, Hierophant, Hopsap Shandy, Rocky Ridge Reserve.

Dessert Ciders: Firecracker, Harvest Ration.

Price Range: $10–$33

Tastings: $10 to $15 per person.

Purchasing: Online for DC, MD, NC, and VA only.

Directions: From Interstate 95, take Exit 78 onto South Boulevard. Drive about one mile to Clay Street and turn right. At the third intersection, turn left onto Summit Avenue. The cidery will be on the right.

❖ ❖ ❖

Bodie Vineyards
1809 May Way Drive
Powhatan VA 23139

Hours: M-Sa 1:00–5:00 (until 6:00 in summer)   804-598-2240
Closed New Year's, Thanksgiving, Christmas   www.bodievineyards.com
E-mail: bodievineyards@rocketmail.com

Clyde and Mary Bodie are longtime home winemakers who established their small farm winery in 2008, opening it to the public two years later. The facilities include an outdoor pavilion and picnic tables, where guests are welcome to enjoy a picnic from home. The winery sponsors annual harvest festivals that welcome volunteers to help bring in the grapes. The facilities are available for private parties and events. Children and dogs are welcome.

White Wines: Michaux Blanc *(Cayuga)*.

Red Wines: Rochette Rouge *(Buffalo)*.

Price Range: $15–$20

Directions: From Route 288, turn west onto U.S. Route 60. Drive 8 miles and turn south onto Rocky Oak Road. After about half a mile, turn left onto May Way Drive. The winery driveway will be ⅓ mile on the right.

❖ ❖ ❖

Buskey Cider
2910 West Leigh Street
Richmond VA 23230

Hours: Tu–Th 5:00–9:00, F 3:00–10:00,   804-355-0100
Sa 12:00–10:00, Su 12:00–9:00   www.buskeycider.com
Closed New Year's, Thanksgiving, Christmas   E-mail: buskey@buskeycider.com

Will Correll, along with partner Matthew Meyer, head winemaker at Williamsburg Winery, opened Richmond's second cidery in 2016 in the historic Scott's Addition neighborhood that is becoming a hub for craft brewing and ciders. Cidermaker Alec Steinmetz uses organically-grown apples from an orchard near Harrisonburg in the Shenandoah Valley to make a range of ciders, including some infused with such ingredients as cherry, lemongrass, or jalapeño. The facilities may be rented for special events. The tasting room tables have slate tops and chalk for guests to use for doodling. The cidery name comes from an old Colonial American slang term for someone who is tipsy.

Ciders: 45 and Trying, Belgian Candi, Citra Hop, Dry Hop, Randall'd Ciders, RVA, Tart Cherry.

Price Range: Varies depending on size.

Directions: From Interstate 95, take Exit 78 onto South Boulevard. Drive about one mile to Leigh Street and turn right. The cidery will be on the right.

❖ ❖ ❖

James River Cellars
11008 Washington Highway
Glen Allen VA 23059

Hours: M–Sa 11:00–7:00, Su 11:00–5:00;   804-550-7516
(F to 8:00 in summer)   www.jamesrivercellars.com
Closed New Year's, Thanksgiving, Christmas   E-mail: winery@jamesrivercellars.com

James River was founded by Ray Lazarchic in 2001 and is now owned by James and Mitzi Batterson, Ray's daughter and son-in-law; James also serves as winemaker. James River offers a picnic area and patio just outside the tasting room, where it hosts Fridays on the Patio on the fourth Friday of every month, as well as a harvest wine festival. The facility can be rented for weddings and private events. The winery hosts special events to support various charities, including the American Cancer Society and the Richmond SPCA. Children and leashed dogs are welcome.

White Wines: Chardonel, Chardonnay, Gewurztraminer, Petit Manseng, Vidal Blanc.

Red Wines: Cabernet Franc, Cabernet Sauvignon, Chambourcin, Colonial Red, Hanover, Meritage, Merlot, Monitor vs. CSS Virginia, Petit Verdot, Pinot Noir, Rad Red, Touriga Nacional.

Sweet/Dessert Wines: Hanover White, Montpelier Blush.

Price Range: $16–$45

Tastings: $8 per person.

Groups: Reservations required for groups of 10 or more, $15 per person.

Wheelchair accessible.

Purchasing: Online ordering available to CA, DC, FL, MO, NC, and VA.

Directions: From I-95, take Exit 86B (Elmont) and drive west on Sliding Hill Road. Turn right at the second traffic light onto Washington Highway (U.S. Route 1 North). The winery will be on the right in about 1 mile.

❖ ❖ ❖

Sassafras Shade Vineyard
4492 Ladysmith Road
Ruther Glen VA 22546

Hours: W-Su 11:00–5:00 (F to 7:00 in summer)
Closed New Year's, Easter,
Thanksgiving, Christmas

804-598-7291
www.sassafrasshade.com
E-mail: info@sassafrasshade.com

After growing grapes on their vineyards north of Richmond for 15 years, Gary and Ann Dudley decided to open a tasting room in 2014. The winery is named after the stand of sassafras trees that they found when they first cleared some of the brush from the property. All their wines are from Virginia-grown grapes, most from their own vineyards. Guests are welcome to bring snacks to enjoy on the porch after their tastings.

Fruit Wines: Granny Smith Apple.

White Wines: Caroline White, Cayuga White, Chardonnay, Vidal Blanc, White Chambourcin.

Red Wines: Cabernet Franc, Caroline Red, Chambourcin.

Price Range: $12–$14

Tastings: $5 per person.

Directions: From Interstate 95, take Exit 110 (Ladysmith) and drive west onto Ladysmith Road. Continue 3.9 miles and turn left onto the winery's gravel driveway.

❖ ❖ ❖

Skippers Creek Vineyard
965 Rocky Ford Road
Powhatan VA 23139

Hours: Sa–Su 1:00–5:00 (Apr–Oct)
Closed Nov–Mar

804-598-7291
www.skipperscreekvineyard.com
E-mail: contact@skipperscreekvineyard.com

Chuck and Debbie Zacharias opened their winery west of Richmond after planting a five-acre vineyard on farmland that has been in Debbie's family for over 75 years. The couple plans to expand their plantings in the future, particularly after they retire from their careers in the medical field. Skippers Creek offers tours of the facilities as well as outdoor seating where guests may stay over a glass or bottle of wine.

White Wines: Blonde, Chardonnay, Viognier.

Rosé Wines: Lily (*Chardonnay, Viognier, Cabernet Franc*).

Red Wines: Malbec, Meriwether, Merlot.

Price Range: $16–$22

Purchasing: Email ordering available for residents of AK, CA, DC, FL, NC, MD, MN, MO, NM, and VA.

Directions: From U.S. Route 60, drive west 7 miles and turn left onto New Dorset Road. Drive 0.8 miles. Turn left onto Dorset Road. After 1 mile, turn right onto Schroeder Road and drive 3.3 miles. Turn right again onto Dorset Road (VA 604) and drive another 0.8 miles. Turn right onto Rocky Ford Road (VA 603) and continue 0.7 miles to the winery drive on the left.

ॐ

FORTIFIED WINES

Fortified wines, quite simply, are wines whose alcohol strength has been raised by adding some form of grape spirit, such as brandy. During fermentation, the grape juice's natural sugar is converted into alcohol through the action of yeasts. If left uninterrupted, this process will continue until all the sugar has been consumed. In fortified wine production, extra alcohol is added before, during, or after fermentation.

The most well-known fortified wines are from the Iberian peninsula and the Portuguese island of Madeira.

Sherry originated in southwest Spain in the area around the city of Jerez, from which it draws its name. Made from the Palomino, Pedro Ximénez, and Muscat of Alexandria grapes, sherry is fortified after fermentation has occurred. Classic Spanish sherries are dry and range from the light and elegant Fino to the more concentrated Oloroso.

Port wines take their name from the Portuguese city of Oporto in the Douro region. Grape varieties traditionally used for port include Touriga Nacional, Touriga Francesa, Tinta Cão, Tinta Barroca, and Tinta Roriz. Because port wine is fortified during the fermentation process, the result is a sweet and strong wine.

Madeira is from the island of the same name. It originated by chance in the seventeenth century when merchants discovered that wine transported by ship across the tropics was transformed into a rich, sweet wine with an exceptional shelf life. Madeiras now are fortified during fermentation and then heated to caramelize the sugars. Madeira was very popular among American colonists in the seventeenth and eighteenth centuries. Indeed, patriots at the Second Continental Congress toasted the signing of the Declaration of Independence in 1776 with glasses of madeira.

ॐ

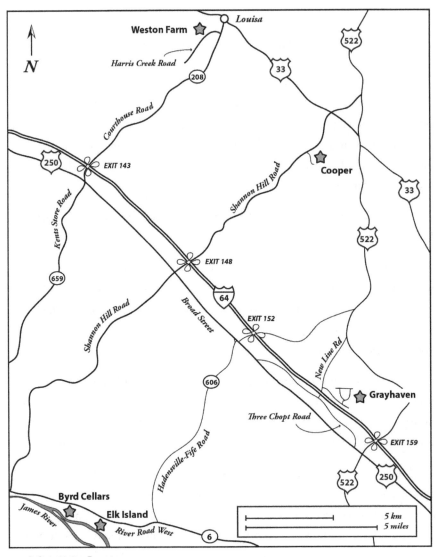

Map 7.3. Louisa

LOUISA

Byrd Cellars
5847 River Road West
Goochland VA 23063

Hours: Sa–Su 12:00–5:00
Closed New Year's, Christmas

804-652-5663
www.byrdcellars.com
E-mail: info@ByrdCellars.com

Byrd Cellars was established in 2008 by Bruce Murray initially as a collaborative venture with two other Goochland County vineyard owners (Murray now operates it alone). The tasting room offer visitors a light-filled space with scenic views of the James River. Byrd Cellars wines are all organically grown Virginia grapes, including from their own fifteen acres of vines. Guests are welcome to sit indoors or outside with a glass or bottle of wine. The facilities are available for small private events and parties. Children and pets are welcome.

Fruit Wines: Apple Concord, Dry Apple, Meadowsweet, Sweet Apple.

White Wines: Chardonnay, Muscat, White Cat.

Rosé Wines: Vin Rosé.

Red Wines: Cabernet Sauvignon, Dahlgren's Raid Red, Merlot, Norton, Pete's Red, Raven Red, Syrah, Velvet *(Norton).*

Price Range: $12–$19

Tastings: $5 per person.

Purchasing: Online to Virginia residents only.

Directions: From I-64, take Exit 152 (Hadensville). Turn left onto Old Fredericksburg Road and drive 0.8 miles. Make a right onto Broad Street (U.S. Route 250 West) and an immediate left to stay on Old Fredericksburg Road which becomes Three Chopt and then Hadensville-Fife Road. After 8 miles in all, turn right onto River Road West (VA 6) and drive 2.7 miles to the winery entrance on the left.

❖ ❖ ❖

Cooper Vineyards
13372 Shannon Hill Road
Louisa VA 23093

Hours: Daily 11:00–5:00
Closed New Year's, Thanksgiving, Christmas

540-894-5474
www.coopervineyards.com
E-mail: info@coopervineyards.com

Geoffrey Cooper and Jacque Hogge established their family-owned and operated winery in scenic Louisa County. Working with winemaker Graham Bell, the winery produces a range of wines including their Noche dessert wine, a blend of Norton and chocolate, and two ice wines. Cooper sponsors an annual mini-Cooper rally, fundraisers for the local SPCA, "Jazz and Chocolate" festivals, and a holiday open house, among other activities. Visitors are welcome to bring their own picnic food to enjoy on the grounds. Cooper's two-story, LEED-certified tasting facilities opened in 2011 and include an outdoor tasting area, weather permitting. Guests are welcome to sit on the veranda overlooking the vines. The facilities are available for private events and parties. Children and pets are welcome.

White Wines: Chardonel, Chardonnay, Coopertage Blanc, Pinot Grigio, Traminette, Vidal Blanc, Viognier.

Rosé Wines: St. Stephen's Rosé.

Red Wines: Cabernet Franc, Cabernet Sauvignon, Chambourcin, Coopertage, Norton, Petit Verdot.

Sweet/Dessert Wines: Noche *(Norton, chocolate)*, Rhapsody *(Vidal Blanc, Chardonel, Viognier)*, Sweet Louisa *(Norton, Concord, Merlot)*, Vida *(Vidal Blanc)*.

Price Range: $16–$28

Tastings: $5 per person.

Purchasing: Online purchasing is available for DC, FL, GA, MD, MN, MT, NC, NJ, PA, and VA.

Directions: From I-64, take Exit 148 (Shannon Hill Road). Drive north on Shannon Hill Road (Route 605) about 8 miles to the winery's gravel driveway on right.

❖ ❖ ❖

Elk Island Winery
5759 River Road West
Goochland VA 23063

Hours: Sa–Su 12:00–6:00 (summer–fall)
Closed New Year's

540-627-3929
www.elkislandwinery.com
E-mail: info@elkislandwinery.com

Named for a nearby 1,300-acre island in the James River, Elk Island Winery takes its name from the original name of the property that once belonged to Thomas Jefferson. The winery is owned and operated by Paul and Sue Anne Klinefelter whose winemaking venture began through their affiliation with Byrd Cellars. The Klinefelters ultimately opted to found their own winery and tasting room, where visitors are welcome to stay on the deck or enclosed porch. The facilities are available for private events and parties. The winery produces several wines under the Terroirier label, which was designed to honor their three rescue terriers; proceeds from their sale benefit terrier rescue organizations. Children and pets are welcome.

Fruit Wines: Cranberry, Eleanor's Red Currant, Island Sunset *(pineapple, pear)*.

White Wines: Chardonnay, Merge White, Sauvignon Blanc, Terroirier White, Vidal Blanc.

Rosé Wines: Chambourcin Rosé.

Red Wines: Cabernet Sauvignon, Chamborton *(Chambourcin, Norton)*, Chambourcin, Confluence Red, Merlot, Norton, Petit Verdot, Ramey's Dream Dornfelder, Terroirier Red.

Price Range: $14–$18

Groups: Reservations requested for groups of 8 or more.

Purchasing: Online purchasing is available for VA residents; please contact the winery for shipping to other states.

Directions: From I-64, take Exit 152 (Hadensville). Turn left onto Old Fredericksburg Road and drive 0.8 miles. Make a right onto Broad Street (U.S. Route 250 West) and an immediate left to stay on Old Fredericksburg Road which becomes Three Chopt and then Hadensville-Fife Road. After 8 miles in all, turn right onto River Road West (VA 6) and drive 2.2 miles to the winery entrance on the left.

❖ ❖ ❖

Grayhaven Winery
4675 E. Grey Fox Circle
Gum Spring VA 23065

Hours: Th–M 11:00–5:00 (Sa to 6:00 in summer)   804-556-3917
Closed New Year's, Thanksgiving, Christmas   www.grayhavenwinery.com
E-mail: max@grayhavenwinery.com

Established by Chuck and Lyn Peple and their daughters, Max and Mallory, Grayhaven was named after the Elvish port of Gray Havens in J.R.R. Tolkien's *Lord of the Rings* trilogy. The winery opened to the public in 1995 and offers a range of estate-grown wines. As a small-lot producer, the variety of Grayhaven wines available for tasting may vary significantly from month to month, depending on which wines have been released or are still available. Visitors are welcome to linger over a glass or bottle after their tastings to enjoy the grounds, including the patio or small deck overlooking a koi pond. The winery hosts occasional special tastings, including a South Africa tasting weekend, and live music. The facilities may be rented for weddings and other special events for up to two hundred people. Children and dogs are welcome.

White Wines: Chardonnay Fumé Blanc, Moonlight White, Riesling, Sauvignon Blanc, Seyval Blanc, Voyager.

Blush Wines: Eventide.

Red Wines: Cabernet Franc, Cabernet Sauvignon, Pinotage, Rendezvous, Touriga, Trekker, Sojourn.

Price Range: $15–$35

Tastings: $4 per person.

Groups: Reservations required for groups of 8 or more, and all bus tours.

Wheelchair accessible.

Purchasing: Online ordering for Virginia residents only.

Directions: From I-64, take Exit 159 (Gum Spring) and turn south onto Cross County Road (Route 522). Turn right onto Broad Street (U.S. Route 250 West) and make the first right onto Three Chopt Road (Route 700). Drive 2.3 miles and turn right onto New Line Road (Route 619). Make a right onto Sheppard Spring Road and then left onto Fox Chase Run. Turn right onto East Grey Fox Circle. The winery entrance will be on the right.

❖ ❖ ❖

Weston Farm Vineyard & Winery
206 Harris Creek Road
Louisa VA 23093

Hours: W–Sa 11:00–5:00
Closed New Year's, Thanksgiving,
Christmas

540-967-4647
www.westonfarmvineyardandwinery.com
E-mail: pennymlouisa@aol.com

Bobby and Penny Martin opened Weston Farm Vineyard to the public in 2010. Working with Virginia vintner Gabriele Rausse, the Martins began making wine in 2009 after planting their vineyard four years earlier. Visitors are welcome to bring a picnic lunch to enjoy on the grounds after their tastings. Weston Farm has a number of animals on the property, with winery dogs Charlie and Suzie often on hand to greet visitors to the tasting room, and rescue horses, miniature donkeys, and cows on the farm. The winery sponsors live music and fundraisers on selected weekends. Children and pets are welcome.

Fruit Wines: Peach, Raspberry, Strawberry, Watermelon.

White Wines: Petit Manseng, Pinot Grigio.

Rosé Wines: Rosé.

Red Wines: Cabernet Franc, Cabernet Sauvignon, Meritage, Norton, Petit Verdot.

Sweet/Dessert Wines: Cherry.

Price Range: $19–$25

Tastings: $10 per person.

Directions: From I-64, take Exit 143 onto Courthouse Road (Route 208) north toward Louisa. Drive 8 miles and turn left onto Harris Creek Road (Route 630). The winery entrance will be on the right.

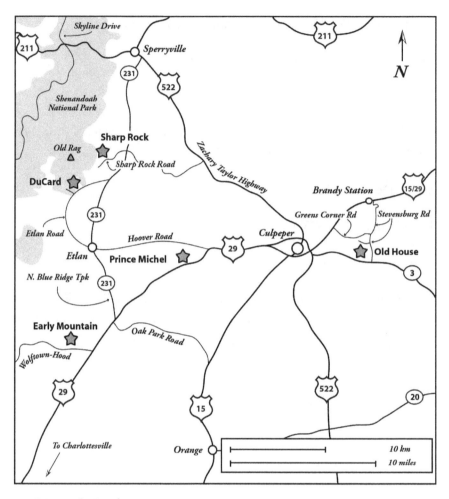

Map 7.4. Madison

MADISON

DuCard Vineyard
40 Gibson Hollow Lane
Etlan VA 22719

Hours: Daily 11:00–6:00 (Sep–Nov)　　　　　　　540-923-4206
F–Su, M holidays 11:00–6:00 (Dec–Aug)　　　www.ducardvineyards.com
Closed Thanksgiving, 20 Dec–6 Jan　　　E-mail: scott@ducardvineyards.com

Scott and Karen Elliff started their vineyard on the site of an old apple orchard in Madison County, opening their winery to the public in 2010 after ten years of producing wines for private sale. The Elliffs named their winery by flipping the name of Scott's favorite single malt scotches, Cardhu. (Ironically, Scott later learned he is distantly related to Cardhu's founders.) The winery offers a scenic view of the Shenandoah National Park from the tasting room and the outdoor patios; the Elliffs donate a portion of the sale proceeds from their Shenandoah White to the park's trust. Winery and vineyard tours are also available for groups up to ten. DuCard offers light snacks and sponsors occasional live music festivals; check the website for details. Pets and children are welcome.

White Wines: Chardonnay, Cuvée 719, Gibson Hollow White, Shenandoah White, Viognier.

Rosé Wines: Rosé.

Red Wines: Cabernet Franc, Merlot, Norton, Petit Verdot, Popham Run *(Bordeaux-style blend)*, Triskele *(Bordeaux-style blend)*.

Fortified Wines: C'Est Trop *(Norton)*, Mon Chéri *(sherry style)*.

Price Range: $24–$42

Tastings: $10 per person.

Groups: Reservations required for groups of 9 or more, $15 per person.

Wheelchair accessible.

Purchasing: Online via VinoShipper to AK, AL, AZ, CA, CO, DC, FL, GA, IA, ID, IL, IN, KS, LA, MA, MD, ME, MN, MO, MT, NC, ND, NE, NH, NM, NV, NY, OH, OR, PA, TN, TX, VA, WA, WI, WV, and WY.

Directions: From U.S. Route 29, turn north onto North Blue Ridge Turnpike (Route 231) and continue for about 6 miles to the village of Etlan. Turn left onto Etlan Road (Route 643). Drive 2.7 miles and turn right onto Gibson Hollow Lane. The winery entrance will be immediately on the right.

❖ ❖ ❖

Early Mountain Winery
6109 Wolftown Hood Road
Madison VA 22727

Hours: W–M 11:00–6:00 (F until 8:00, Sa until 5:00)   540-948-9005
Closed New Year's Eve & Day, Easter,   http://earlymountain.com
Thanksgiving, Christmas Eve & Day   E-mail: cheers@earlymountain.com

Early Mountain is owned by Steve and Jean Case who purchased the former Sweeley Estate Vineyards in late 2011, renaming it in honor of Revolutionary War patriot Joseph Early who was the original owner of the land on which the winery now stands. The facilities include a tasting room with numerous sofas and chairs, a small gift shop, and an events room for weddings and private parties. Wine tastings include both Early Mountain's own production and select wines from other Virginia wineries. Early Mountain sponsors various activities, including live music on Friday evenings. Food is available for purchase at the winery; menus are listed on the website. Children and leashed pets are welcome.

Early Mountain's Guest Cottage is now available for overnight stays; see the website for details.

Sparkling Wines: Pétillant *(Syrah)*.

White Wines: Chardonnay, Five Forks, Pinot Gris, Vidal Blanc, Viognier.

Rosé Wines: Rosé.

Red Wines: Eluvium *(Bordeaux-style blend)*, Foothills, Novum.

Price Range: $22–$38

Tastings: $12 to $22 per person for a red, white, or mixed flight.

Groups: Reservations required for groups of 10 or more.

Wheelchair accessible

Purchasing: Online to VA and many other states; see the website for details.

Directions: From Culpeper, take U.S. 29 South for about 17 miles. Turn right onto Wolftown Hood Road (Route 230). The winery will be 1.2 miles on the right.

❖ ❖ ❖

Old House Vineyards
18351 Corkys Lane
Culpeper VA 22701

Hours: M, W–Th 12:00–5:00, F 12:00–6:00, Sa 11:00–6:00, Su 12:00–6:00 (Memorial Day–Labor Day)
M, W–F, Su 12:00–5:00,
Sa 11:00–6:00 (Labor Day–Memorial Day)
Closed New Year's, Thanksgiving, Christmas

540-423-1032
www.oldhousevineyards.com
E-mail: info@oldhousevineyards.com

Old House was founded in 1998 by Patrick and Allyson Kearney on a farm within the boundaries of the Brandy Station Civil War battlefield. They opened their tasting room in a restored 1800s-era farmhouse which offers a distant view of the house where George Armstrong Custer honeymooned with his bride in 1864. Old House offers several tables on the grounds, which are open for family picnics. The winery sponsors a range of special events, including live music, an annual chili cook-off, and Harvest Days festivals. Old House is also available for rental for private parties, weddings, and corporate events. Children are welcome.

Sparkling Wines: Pétillante.

White Wines: Chardonnay, Clover Hill, Vidal Blanc.

Rosé Wines: Rosie's Rosé *(Cabernet Franc)*.

Red Wines: Bacchanalia *(Cabernet Franc, Chambourcin, Tannat)*, Cabernet Franc, Wicked Bottom *(Chambourcin)*.

Sweet/Dessert Wines: Arctica *(Vidal Blanc)*.

Fortified Wines: Chambourcin Dessert.

Price Range: $18–$35

Tastings: $5 per person.

Groups: Reservations required for groups of 8 or more, $10 per person.

Wheelchair accessible.

Purchasing: Online to AK, CA, FL, MN, and VA.

Directions: From U.S. Route 15/29 at Brandy Station, turn south onto Alanthus Road. Make an immediate left onto Brandy Road and take the first right onto Mount Dumpling Road, which will bend to the left and become Stevensburg Road. Drive 3.2 miles and turn right onto Corkys Road (narrow, gravel drive), which is the driveway to the winery. Continue about ½ mile to the winery parking lot.

❖ ❖ ❖

Prince Michel Vineyard & Winery
154 Winery Lane
Leon VA 22725

Hours: Daily 10:00–6:00 (F–Sa to 7:00) (Apr–Dec);   1-800-800-WINE (9463)
M–Th 10:00–5:00, F–Su 10:00–6:00 (Jan–Mar)   www.princemichel.com
Closed New Year's, Thanksgiving, Christmas   E-mail: info@princemichel.com

Established in 1982, Prince Michel is one of the largest commercial wineries in Virginia, producing well over forty thousand cases annually from both Virginia and other American grapes. Now owned by Kristin Holzman, Prince Michel offers private labels for resorts, companies, and special events, such as weddings. Winemaker Brad Hansen has overseen Prince Michel's production since 1999. The tasting room includes a tasting bar in the middle of an extensive gift shop and free Wi-Fi. The winery offers a free self-guided tour, as well as private group tours by reservation only. Prince Michel has several suites for overnight stays. The facilities may be rented for private meetings, parties, and weddings.

Prince Michel wines are also available for tasting at the Carter Mountain Wine Shop at 1435 Carter's Mountain Trail in Charlottesville. The shop is open from June through November (M-Sa 11:00-6:00, Su to 5:00) and weekends from mid-April through May (F–M 11:00–5:00).

Fruit Wines: Rapidan River Apple-Blackberry, Rapidan River Peach, Rapidan River Raspberry.

Sparkling Wines: Prince Michel Pet Nat.

White Wines: Chardonnay, Mount Juliet Chardonnay, Mount Juliet Petit Manseng, Pinot Grigio, Rapidan River Chardonnay, Rapidan River Dry Riesling, Rapidan River Semi-Dry Riesling, Viognier.

Rosé Wines: Dry Rosé, Rapidan River Rosé.

Red Wines: Cabernet Franc, Cabernet Sauvignon, Merlot, Mountain View Cabernet Franc, Mount Juliet Petit Verdot, Quaker Run Farm Syrah, Symbius *(Bordeaux-style blend)*, Rapidan River Merlot.

Sweet/Dessert Wines: Trés Bien *(Petit Manseng)*, Prince Michel Dessert, Rapidan River Sweet White Reserve, Rapidan River Sweet Red Reserve, Rapidan River Chocolate.

Price Range: $14–$56

Tastings: $5 per person.

Groups: Reservations required for groups of 8 or more; $20 per person for groups of up to 10, $10 per person for groups of 10 to 50.

Wheelchair accessible.

Purchasing: Online for CA, CO, DC, FL, GA, IA, LA, MD, MI, MN, MO, NC, ND, NH, NJ, NY, OH, PA, SC, TX, VA, WI, WA, and WY.

Directions: From Culpeper, take U.S. Route 29 South for 8 miles to the winery on right.

❖ ❖ ❖

Sharp Rock Vineyards
5 Sharp Rock Road
Sperryville VA 22740

Hours: F–Su, M holidays 11:00–5:00 (mid-Feb–Dec)   540-987-8020
Th–M 11:00–5:00 (Oct)   www.sharprockvineyards.com
Closed Jan–mid-Feb, Christmas   E-mail: jeast@sharprockvineyards.com

Sharp Rock Vineyards is located at the base of Old Rag Mountain, one of the most popular hiking destinations in Virginia, and has been a working farm since the late 1700s. Owners Jimm and Kathy East first planted their vineyards in 1992 and now make twelve estate-grown wines. Tastings are held in the upper level of their restored barn. Breads and cheeses are available for purchase. There will generally be several winery dogs on hand to greet visitors. The winery is available for rental for private parties and weddings. Children and pets are welcome.

Sharp Rock also has two riverside cottages for overnight stays. Charges include a complimentary wine tasting and bottle of wine, breakfast, and snacks. The cottages are the closest accommodations available to Old Rag.

White Wines: Chardonnay, Chamois Blanc *(Chardonnay, Vidal Blanc)*, Pinnacle Blanc, Sauvignon Blanc.

Rosé Wines: Rosé, Rosé Noir.

Red Wines: Cabernet Franc, Cabernet Sauvignon, Chamois Rouge, Malbec, Old Rag Red, Petit Verdot, Pinnacle *(Bordeaux-style blend)*.

Price Range: $16–$28

Tastings: $3 per person.

Purchasing: Online purchasing available to AL, AK, CA, CO, CT, DC, HI, ID, IL, IA, MN, MO, NE, NV, NM, ND, OH, OR, RI, VT, VA, WA, WV, and WI.

Directions: From Sperryville, drive south on Route 231 for 8 miles. Turn right onto Sharp Rock Road (Route 601) and drive 1 mile. At the intersection with Nethers Road (Route 707), the winery will be the farm on the right.

❧⊱◈⊰❧

NORTON

One of Virginia's most noteworthy contributions to American wine was the Norton grape. Propagated by amateur horticulturist Dr. Daniel N. Norton on his farm near Richmond, the grape was first listed as Norton's Virginia Seedling in 1822 in the annual catalog of the Linnean Botanic Garden and Nurseries of Long Island, New York, perhaps the country's foremost horticultural institution at that time. The Princes' 1830 Treatise on the Vine described the grape as *Vitis nortoni* and credited the doctor with its cultivation.

It was through the efforts of German viticulturists—George Husmann, in particular—that the Norton grape rose to prominence as a wine grape in the United States. In 1846, German settlers in the central Missouri town of Hermann planted Norton cuttings, producing the first bottle of Norton wine two years later. As the Missouri wine industry grew, becoming at one point the largest producer in the United States, so also grew the cultivation and renown of the Norton grape.

Interest in the Norton peaked in 1870, when Hermann vintner Michael Röschel and business partner John Scherer entered their Norton wine in the 1873 Universal Exhibition in Vienna, Austria. The influential English wine critic Henry Vizately awarded a medal of merit to the Norton, one of only three American wines to be so decorated. It was also during this time that German vineyardists in Virginia established the Monticello Wine Company whose production was based heavily on Norton grapes.

The two Virginia winemakers who have been most influential in bringing Norton back to its native state are Dennis Horton of Horton Vineyards and Jennifer McCloud of Chrysalis. A Missouri native, Horton grew up in Hermann and was introduced to Norton in his college days. He first planted Norton cuttings in his Orange County vineyard in 1988. McCloud became fascinated by the Norton grape and its history after hearing Horton speak at a conference. After establishing Chrysalis, she began planting Norton in her vineyards and now has the single largest planting of this native Virginia grape in the country.

❧⊱◈⊰❧

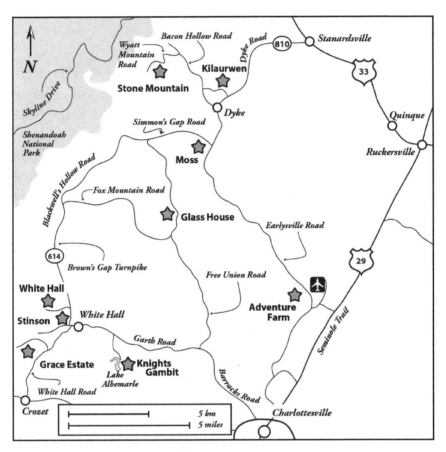

Map 7.5. Upper Monticello (Free Union-White Hall)

UPPER MONTICELLO

Adventure Farms Vineyards
1135 Clan Chisholm Lane
Earlysville VA 22936

Hours: Th–Su 12:00–6:00 (F to 9:00 in summer)
Closed New Year's, Easter, Christmas

434-971-8796
www.adventurefarm.net
E-mail: info@adventurefarm.net

Adventure Farm was founded by the Chisholm family on a farm that has been in their family for over 60 years; in addition to vines, they also raise grass-fed beef cattle and other livestock. The winery made its first wines in 2013, with Michael Shaps as winemaker. (Some of his Michael Shaps Wineworks wines are also available in the tasting room.) The winery sponsors local bands for live music on weekends, with visitors welcome to sit over a glass of wine out on the covered patio. Children are welcome.

Sparkling Wines: Sparkling Brut, Sparkling Rosé.

White Wines: Chardonnay, Viognier.

Rosé Wines: Rosé.

Red Wines: Cabernet Franc, Cabernet Sauvignon, Chambourcin, Gigi's Red Blend, Petit Verdot.

Price Range: $19–$34

Tastings: $8 per person.

Directions: From U.S. Route 29, turn west onto Town Center Road by the Charlottesville Airport. Drive 0.7 miles and turn left onto Dickerson Road. After ½ mile, enter the roundabout and take the first exit onto Earlysville Road. Drive 2.6 miles and turn left into the winery entrance on the left.

❖ ❖ ❖

Barboursville Vineyards
17655 Winery Road
Barboursville VA 22923

Hours: M–Sa 10:00–5:00, Su 11:00–5:00   540-832-3824
Closed New Year's, Thanksgiving, Christmas   www.bbvwine.com

E-mail: bvvy@barboursvillewine.com

Barboursville Vineyards is one of the largest and oldest farm wineries in Virginia. Owned by Gianni and Silvana Zonin, who purchased the historic Barboursville estate in 1976, Barboursville produces thirty-seven thousand bottles of wine annually from its 185-acre vineyard under the guidance of winemaker Luca Paschina, a native of Italy. The tasting room looks onto the octagonal ruins of the Barbour family mansion that was designed by Thomas Jefferson and destroyed by fire on Christmas Day 1884. The ruins feature on the label of the winery's flagship Octagon wine. Winery tours are offered on Saturday and Sunday from noon to 4:00 p.m. The facilities may be rented for private events and weddings. Children are welcome.

The winery's Palladio Restaurant is open for lunch Wednesday to Sunday (reservations recommended) and dinner Friday and Saturday (reservations required). The winery grounds also include two restored buildings—the 1804 Inn and Vineyard Cottage—that are available for overnight stays.

Sparkling Wines: Brut Cuvée, Brut Rosé Cuvée.

White Wines: Chardonnay, Fiano, Pinot Grigio, Sauvignon Blanc, Vermentino, Viognier.

Rosé Wines: Vintage Rosé.

Red Wines: Barbera, Cabernet Franc, Cabernet Sauvignon, Merlot, Nebbiolo, Octagon *(Bordeaux-style blend)*, Petit Verdot, Sangiovese.

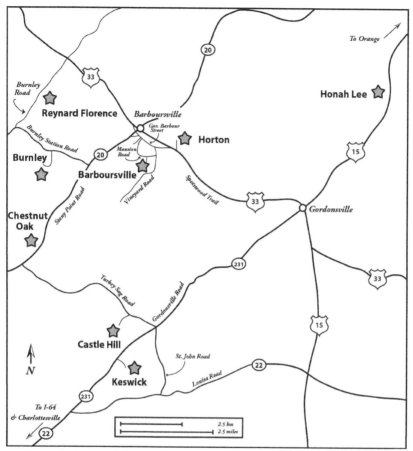

Map 7.6. Upper Monticello (Stony Point)

Sweet/Dessert Wines: Malvaxio Paxxito, Philéo.

Price Range: $15–$55 Tastings: $7 per person.

Groups: Reservations required for group tour buses and limos.

Wheelchair accessible.

Purchasing: Online purchasing available for CA, DC, FL, IL, MA, MD, MI, MN, NH, NM, NC, NY, SC, VA, and WA.

Directions: From U.S. Route 33, turn south onto Route 20 (Constitution Highway). Make an immediate left onto Governor Barbour Street. Take the third right onto Mansion Road. After 3/4 mile, turn right onto Winery Road and the winery parking lot.

❖ ❖ ❖

Burnley Vineyards
4500 Winery Lane
Barboursville VA 22923

Hours: Th–M 11:00–5:00 (Apr–Dec);
F–M 11:00–5:00 (Jan–Mar)
Closed: New Year's, Thanksgiving,
Christmas Eve & Day

434-960-4411
www.burnleywines.com
E-mail: bvwinery@gmx.com

Burnley Vineyard was opened to the public in 1984 by the Reeder family, who first planted their vineyard in 1977. Visitors may purchase snacks, bread, and cheese to enjoy with a glass or bottle of one of Burnley's estate-grown wines. Burnley hosts a number of special winery events, including wine and cheese weekends, an annual Thanksgiving Open House (Friday–Sunday), a holiday open house in December, and special vertical tastings. The facility may be rented for private parties. Children are welcome.

Burnley also offers overnight stays at its Fernando's Hideaway, a furnished guest house with room for four.

Fruit Wines: Peach Fuzz.

White Wines: Chardonnay, Rivanna White, Riesling.

Blush Wines: Rivanna Sunset *(Chambourcin)*.

Red Wines: Barbera, Cabernet Sauvignon, Chambourcin, Dog Gone Red, Norton, Rivanna Red.

Sweet/Dessert Wines: Aurora *(red wine with chocolate, raspberries)*, Somerset.

Fortified Wines: Rubix *(Norton port-style)*.

Price Range: $15–$18

Tastings: $5 per person.

Wheelchair accessible.

Purchasing: Online ordering for many states; see website for details.

Directions: From U.S. Route 33, turn south onto Route 20 (Constitution Highway) and drive 2 miles. Turn right onto Burnley Station Road (Route 641). The winery entrance will be ⅓ mile on the left.

※ ※ ※

Castle Hill Cider
6065 Turkey Sag Road
Keswick VA 22947

Hours: Daily 11:00–5:00 (Apr–Nov);
W–Su 11:00–5:00 (Dec–Mar)
Closed New Year's, Thanksgiving, Christmas

434-296-0047
www.castlehillcider.com
E-mail: info@castlehillcider.com

Castle Hill Cider opened to the public in 2011 on the grounds of the historic Castle Hill estate. The estate's manor house was built in 1764 as the home of Colonel Thomas Walker, who was appointed as Thomas Jefferson's guardian after his father's death. The cidery barn includes the tasting and tank rooms, and an events facility. Cidermaker Stuart Madany is using kvevri terracotta vessels to make Castle Hill's Levity cider; kvevri originated over eight thousand years ago in the Republic of Georgia, where they are still used in traditional wine production. Castle Hill's facilities may be rented for weddings and private events.

Sparkling Ciders: Celestial, Celestial Merret, Levity, Serendipity, Terrestrial.

Still Ciders: Black Twig, Gravity.

Fortified Ciders: 1764 *(cider port).*

Price Range: $17–$25

Tastings: $8 per person.

Groups: Reservations requested for groups of 8 or more.

Wheelchair accessible.

Purchasing: Online for AK, CA, DC, FL, MI, MN, NC, OR, and VA, or via VinoShipper to AL, AZ, CO, GA, HI, IA, ID, IL, IN, KS, LA, MA, MD, ME, MO, ND, NE, NH, NM, NV, NY, OH, PA, SC, TN, TX, WA, WI, WV, and WY.

Directions: From I-64, take Exit 124 onto U.S. Route 250 East (Shadwell). Drive 1.9 miles and turn onto Route 22 East. After 5.4 miles, stay straight to go onto Gordonsville Road (Route 231). Continue 3.3 miles and turn left onto Turkey Sag Road (Route 640). Drive 3/4 mile and turn left into the cidery driveway between the white stone posts.

❖ ❖ ❖

Chestnut Oak Vineyards
5050 Stony Point Road
Barboursville VA 22923

Hours: F–Su 12:00–6:00   434-964-9104
Closed New Year's, Easter, Christmas   www.chestnutoakvineyard.com
                                E-mail: info@chestnutoakvineyard.com

Chestnut Oak was opened by Janet Bolla on her property just north of Charlottesville. The winery focuses on two varietals, Petit Manseng and Cabernet Sauvignon, and its estate-grown production is grown under the guidance of Michael Shaps. The tasting room offers tables and seating for relaxing over a glass of wine, with lovely murals reminiscent of Latin American art.

White Wines: Alba-Vidal, Chardonnay, Petit Manseng.

Rosé Wines: Rosé *(Petit Manseng, Cabernet Sauvignon)*.

Red Wines: Cabernet Franc, Cabernet Sauvignon, Red Table Wine.

Sweet/Dessert Wines: Cabernet Franc, Cabernet Sauvignon, Red Table Wine.

Price Range: $18–$25

Tastings: $5 per person with souvenir glass.

Purchasing: Online via VinoShipper to AK, AL, AZ, CA, CO, DC, FL, GA, HI, IA, ID, IL, IN, KS, LA, MA, MD, ME, MN, MO, NC, ND, NE, NH, NM, NV, NY, OH, OR, PA, SC, TN, TX, VA, WA, WI, WV, and WY.

Directions: From Charlottesville, turn north onto Stony Point Road (VA Route 20) at the intersection of U.S. Route 250 and River Bend/Stony Point Roads. Drive 11.6 miles to the winery's drive on the left.

❖ ❖ ❖

Glass House Winery
5898 Free Union Road
Free Union VA 22940

Hours: Th–Su, holiday M 12:00–5:30 (F to 9:00)
Closed New Year's, Thanksgiving, Christmas

434-234-4133
www.glasshousewinery.com
E-mail: info@glasshousewinery.com

Glass House Winery was established by Jeff and Michelle Sanders who moved to Virginia after having spent five years in Honduras where

Jeff operated a plant nursery. Glass House's six-acre vineyard is currently planted to eight varieties of grapes. The winery features a glass-enclosed tropical greenhouse that may be rented for weddings and private events. Michelle's hand-crafted gourmet chocolates are also on sale at the winery which hosts special events, such as live music on weekends, and offers a five-bedroom B&B for overnight stays. Leashed dogs are welcome.

White Wines: Chardonnay, Pinot Gris, Vino Signora, Viognier.

Rosé Wines: Eville Pink Drink.

Red Wines: Barbera, Cabernet Franc, C-Villian, Estratto, Twenty-First.

Sweet/Dessert Wines: Meglio Del Sesso.

Fortified Wines: Bellezza *(port-style)*.

Price Range: $18–$34

Tastings: $8 per person.

Groups: Reservations required for groups of 10 or more.

Purchasing: Online ordering available to AK, DC, FL, MN, and VA.

Directions: From Charlottesville and U.S. Route 29 North, take Barracks Road West (becomes Garth Road) and drive about 4 miles. Turn right onto Free Union Road (Route 601) at the Hunt Country Market. Continue on Free Union Road for 7.9 miles. Turn left onto the winery's drive.

❖ ❖ ❖

Grace Estate Winery
5273 Mount Juliet Farm
Crozet VA 22932

Hours: W–M 11:00–5:30 (F to 9:00, Sa to 8:00 in summer)   434-823-1486
Closed New Year's, Thanksgiving, Christmas   www.graceestatewinery.com
E-mail: info@graceestatewinery.com

Owned by the John Grace family, Grace Estate originally sold fourteen different varieties of grapes from their 60-acre vineyards to other Virginia wineries. The tasting room has ample indoor and outdoor seating, free Wi-Fi, and a large stone fireplace and windows with a view of the 550-acre property. The winery also offers gas grills for use as well as bread, cheeses, and cold cuts for purchase. Grace Estate sponsors live music on Friday evenings in summer and may be rented for weddings and private events. Leashed dogs are welcome.

Sparkling Wines: Herleve (*Chardonnay*).

White Wines: Chardonnay, Le Gras Cuve, Petit Manseng, Viognier.

Rosé Wines: Le Gras Rosé.

Red Wines: Cabernet Franc, Cabernet Sauvignon, Merlot, Petit Verdot, Tannat.

Sweet/Dessert Wines: Adeliza *(Petit Manseng)*.

Price Range: $19–$39

Tastings: $9 per person for white, red, or classic flight.

Groups: Reservations required for groups of 8 or more, $12 per person.

Wheelchair accessible.

Purchasing: Online via VinoShipper to AK, AL, AZ, CA, CO, DC, FL,

GA, HI, IA, ID, IL, IN, KS, LA, MA, MD, ME, MN, MO, NC, ND, NE, NH, NM, NV, NY, OH, OR, PA, SC, TN, TX, VA, WA, WI, WV, and WY.

Directions: From Charlottesville, take Barracks Road West (becomes Garth Road). Continue about 9 miles. Turn left on Browns Gap Turnpike (Route 614) at the Wyant Store. After 0.3 miles, keep straight to stay on White Hall Road (VA Route 789), then make the first right for the winery.

❖ ❖ ❖

Honah Lee Vineyard
13443 Honah Lee Farm
Gordonsville VA 22942

Hours: M–Sa 11:00–6:00, Su 12:00–5:00 (Apr–Dec)   540-406-1313
M–Sa 11:00–5:00 (Jan–Mar)   www.honahleevineyard.com
Closed New Year's, Easter, Thanksgiving, Christmas   info@.honahleevineyard.com

Wayne and Vera Preddy have long been a fixture in Virginia's wine-growing community for their renowned Honah Lee vineyard, whose name came from the song *Puff the Magic Dragon*. The Preddys produced their first wines under their own label in late 2014, using the BerryWood Crafters store as a tasting room. In addition to its own wines, Honah Lee also serves wines from other local wineries, such as Gabriele Rausse Winery and Well Hung Vineyard. Military personnel receive a discount on purchases.

White Wines: Chardonnay, ENJoy, Petit Manseng, Viognier.

Red Wines: De la Merce *(Merlot, Chambourcin).*

Tastings: $6 per person.

Groups: Reservations requested for groups of 10 or more.

Directions: From Orange, drive south on U.S. Route 15 for 5 miles. Turn right onto Honah Lee Farm and the BerryWood Farm store. From

Gordonsville, drive north on U.S. Route 15 for 4 miles and turn left onto Honah Lee Farm Road and the BerryWood Farm store.

❖ ❖ ❖

Horton Vineyards
6399 Spotswood Trail
Gordonsville VA 22942

Hours: Daily 10:00–5:00
Closed New Year's, Thanksgiving, Christmas

800-829-4633
www.hortonwine.com
E-mail: vawinee@aol.com

Horton Vineyards had its origins in a home vineyard started by Dennis Horton who ultimately purchased fifty-five acres in Orange County in 1988. Horton was the first in Virginia to plant the Viognier grape and also was key in reviving the Norton grape, first cultivated in Virginia and widely planted in Horton's home town of Hermann, Missouri. Horton plants the widest range of grape varieties in the state, including lesser-known grapes such as Rkatsiteli and Pinotage. The winery sponsors many events, such as a Mardi Gras festival, annual pig roasts, and a Thanksgiving weekend open house.

Fruit Wines: Blackberry *(with Petit Verdot)*, Blueberry *(Petit Verdot)*, Cranberry *(Cabernet Franc)*, Peach *(Viognier)*, Pear *(Viognier)*, Pomegranate *(Syrah)*, Raspberry *(Cabernet Franc)*, Strawberry *(Grenache)*.

Sparkling Wines: Viognier.

White Wines: Albariño, Chardonnay, Petit Manseng, Rkatsiteli, Stonecastle White, Vidal Blanc, Viognier.

Blush Wines: Stonecastle Blush.

Red Wines: Cabernet Franc, Côtes d'Orange, Malbec, Nebbiolo, Norton, Pinotage, Route 33 Red, South Ridge, Stonecastle Red, Tannat.

Sweet/Dessert Wines: Eden, Eclipse Red, Eclipse White, Late Harvest Rkatsiteli, Niagara, Sweet Concord, Blanco XOCO, Rojo XOCO.

Fortified Wines: Pear, Vintage Port.

Price Range: $14–$25

Tastings: $6 for 10 wines.

Wheelchair accessible

Purchasing: Online via VinoShipper to AK, AL, AZ, CA, CO, DC, FL, GA, HI, IA, ID, IL, IN, KS, LA, MA, MD, ME, MN, MO, NC, ND, NE, NH, NM, NV, NY, OH, OR, PA, SC, TN, TX, VA, WA, WI, WV, and WY.

Directions: From U.S. Route 29, turn east onto U.S. Route 33 East at Ruckersville. Drive 8 miles to the winery entrance on the left.

❖ ❖ ❖

Keswick Vineyards
1575 Keswick Winery Drive
Keswick VA 22947

Hours: Daily 9:00–5:00 (Sa to 6:00, F to 8:00 in summer)   434-244-3341
Closed New Year's, Easter, Thanksgiving, Christmas   www.keswickvineyards.com
E-mail: info@keswickvineyards.com

Al and Cindy Schornberg have owned Keswick Vineyards, located at the historic Edgewood estate just outside Charlottesville, since 2000. South African native Stephen Barnard serves as winemaker, focusing on small-batch production. Keswick's Bordeaux-style blend, Consensus, is so named because wine club members meet each year on successive weekends to test different blends and vote on the one they think is best. The winery patio offers ample outdoor seating for lingering over a bottle with cheese, bread, and crackers are available for purchase. Keswick's events include Sunday afternoon Yappy Hour for dogs and SPCA fundraisers. The facility may be rented for weddings and private events. Children and pets are welcome.

White Wines: Chardonnay, Trevillian White, Viognier.

Rosé Wines: Rosé.

Red Wines: Cabernet Franc, Cabernet Sauvignon, Consensus, Petit Verdot, Red Trevillian *(Bordeaux-style blend).*

Price Range: $23–$65

Tastings: $5 per person for regular tasting.

Groups: Reservations required for groups of 10 or more.

Restrictions: Limos and bus groups Sa–Su from 9:00–1:00 only.

Wheelchair accessible

Purchasing: Online purchasing for AK, CA, CO, DC, FL, GA, MD, MA, MI, MN, MO, NH, NY, NC, OH, PA, SC, TX, VA, and WA.

Directions: From I-64, take Exit 124 onto U.S. Route 250 East (Shadwell). Drive 2 miles and turn onto Louisa Road (Route 22 East). After 5.4 miles, stay straight to go onto Gordonsville Road (Route 231). Continue 2.2 miles to Keswick Winery Drive and the winery on the right.

❖ ❖ ❖

Kilaurwen Vineyards
1543 Evergreen Church Road
Stanardsville VA 22973

Hours: F–Su, holiday M 12:00–5:00 (Apr–Nov) 434-985-2535
Closed Dec–Mar www.kilaurwenwinery.com
E-mail: info@kilaurwenwinery.com

Bob and Dorien Steeves opened Kilaurwen to the public after spending over fifteen years growing and supplying grapes to several other Virginia wineries. Kilaurwen is named after their three daughters, Kimberlee, Laura, and Wendy, who actively assist with winery operations. Light snacks are available in the tasting room. All their wines are from Virginia-grown grapes, most from their own vineyards. Children and pets are welcome.

White Wines: Fiesta White, Kilaurwen White, Riesling.

Rosé Wines: Dry Rosé.

Red Wines: Cabernet Franc, Cabernet Sauvignon, Chambourcin, Fiesta Red, Kilaurwen Red, Three Sisters Red *(Bordeaux-style blend)*.

Price Range: $18–$30

Tastings: $5 per person.

Directions: Take U.S. Route 29 to Ruckersville and turn onto U.S. 33 West to Stanardsville. Turn left onto Dyke Road (Route 810) and drive 5.1 miles. Turn right onto Evergreen Church Road. The winery entrance will be ⅓ mile on the right.

❖ ❖ ❖

Knight's Gambit Vineyards
2218 Lake Albemarle Road
Charlottesville VA 22901

Hours: F 2:00–6:00, Sa–Su 12:00–6:00 (Apr–Oct)   434-566-1168
(Sa to 8:00 in summer)   www.knightsgambitvineyard.com
Closed Nov–Mar   E-mail: info@knightsgambitvineyard.com

Paul and Jill Faulkner Summers first planted a small vineyard on their 400-acre farm west of Charlottesville at the encouragement of their son, Paul, who has worked at several wineries in the greater Albemarle area, including Barboursville and Blenheim. The winery's name is both a chess move and the title of a short story by Jill's father, renowned American author William Faulkner. The winery offers outdoor yoga sessions, a picnic area, croquet field, and beanbag pitch overlooking the vines and horse pastures, where the winery dogs are often on hand to greet visitors.

White Wines: Chardonnay, Pinot Grigio.

Rosé Wines: Rosé.

Red Wines: Meritage, Petit Verdot.

Price Range: $23–$28

Tastings: $7 per person.

Groups: Reservations requested for groups of 8 or more.

Restrictions: No buses.

Directions: From Charlottesville and U.S. Route 29 North, take Barracks Road West, which becomes Garth Road after 2 miles. Continue another 7.5 miles and turn left onto Lake Albemarle Road. Drive 2 miles and stay straight at a sharp right-hand curve to enter the winery driveway.

❖ ❖ ❖

Moss Vineyards
1849 Simmons Gap Road
Nortonsville VA 22935

Hours: F–Su , holiday M 11:00–5:00 (mid-Mar–Dec) 434-990-0111
Closed Thanksgiving, Christmas Eve–New Year's www.mossvineyards.net
E-mail: mossvineyards@gmail.com

Barry Moss opened Moss Vineyards to the public in 2012, three years after first planting the winery's vineyards. Visitors can enjoy scenic views of the winery's vineyards and the hills beyond from the tasting room, which was designed by Barry, an architect in the Norfolk area. A fireplace inside helps warm chilly autumn afternoons, and the tasting room deck offers ample outdoor seating. Moss Vineyards hosts occasional special events and live music. Children and leashed dogs are welcome.

White Wines: Viognier.

Rosé Wines: Rosé.

Red Wines: Archittetura, Cabernet Franc, Vino Rosso *(Bordeaux-style blend)*.

Price Range: $22–$38

Tastings: $8 per person.

Groups: Reservations required for groups of 9 or more.

Purchasing: Online ordering for DC, FL, MA, MD, NC, NY, and VA.

Directions: Take U.S. Route 29 to Ruckersville and turn onto U.S. 33 West to Stanardsville. Turn left onto Dyke Road (Route 810) and drive 8 miles. Turn right onto Simmons Gap Road. The winery entrance will be about ⅓ mile on the left.

❖ ❖ ❖

Reynard Florence Vineyard
16109 Burnley Road
Barboursville VA   22973

Hours: F 12:00–5:00, Sa–Su, holiday M 11:00–5:00   540-832-3895
Closed New Year's, Christmas   www.reynardflorence.com
E-mail: info@reynardflorence.com

Reynard Florence was established by Roe and Dee Allison, who planted their first vines in 2006 and produced their first vintage three years later, working with Michael Shaps. The winery's name combines the old French spelling for "fox" (Reynard) with Dee's first name (Florence). The Allisons' flagship white variety is Petit Manseng, which they use both as a pure varietal and in blending with other grapes. The tasting room overlooks the production facility, which Roe often uses for informal jam sessions with friends on weekends. Children and pets are welcome.

White Wines: Chardonnay, Petit Manseng, Reynard Blanc, Viognier.

Red Wines: Cabernet Franc, Grenache, Merlot, NMA IV, Petit Verdot, Recherché *(Bordeaux-style blend)*.

Price Range: $19–$28

Tastings: $8 per person.

Groups: Reservations required for groups of 8 or more.

Directions: From U.S. Route 29, take U.S. Route 33 East at Ruckersville. Continue 3.6 miles and turn right onto Burnley Road. The winery entrance will be 1.6 miles on the left.

·:·:· ·:·:· ·:·:·

Stinson Vineyards
4744 Sugar Hollow Road
Crozet VA   22932

Hours: Th–Su, hol M 11:00–5:00
Closed New Year's, Easter,
Thanksgiving, Christmas

434-823-7300
www.stinsonvineyards.com
E-mail: info@stinsonvineyards.com

Scott and Martha Stinson opened Stinson Vineyards in 2011 on the grounds of the historic Piedmont House, which dates from 1796. Scott is an architect who purchased the property with the intent of renovating it and became intrigued at the idea of making wine when he discovered an abandoned vineyard on the grounds; he and daughter Rachel Stinson Vrooman are the winemakers. The tasting room offers sandwiches and food platters for purchase, or guests may bring their own for a picnic on the patio.

White Wines: Chardonnay, Petit Manseng, Sauvignon Blanc, Sugar Hollow White, Wild Kat (*Rkatsiteli*).

Rosé Wines: Rosé.

Red Wines: Cabernet Franc, Merlot, Meritage, Sugar Hollow Red.

Fortified Wines: Imperialis *(port-style)*.

Price Range: $16–$32

Tastings: $10 per person.

Groups: Reservations required for groups of 8 or more, $10 per person.

Purchasing: Online to many states; contact the winery for details.

Directions: From Charlottesville and U.S. Route 29 North, take Barracks Road, which becomes Garth Road. Drive 9 miles to the village of White Hall; stay straight in order to go onto Sugar Hollow Road when the main road bends to the right. The winery will be immediately on the right.

❖ ❖ ❖

Stone Mountain Vineyards
1376 Wyatt Mountain Road
Dyke VA 22935

Hours: F–Su, M holidays 11:00–5:00, mid-Mar– mid-Dec   434-990-9463 (WINE)
Closed Easter, mid-Dec–mid-Mar   www.stonemountainvineyards.com
E-mail: info@stonemountainvineyards.com

Stone Mountain, founded in 1986 by Al Breiner, is now owned by Jim and Deanna Gephart, Stone Mountain has twenty acres of vines with noted Virginia vintner Gabriele Rausse serving as a consultant. The tasting room includes an observation deck that offers sweeping views of the valley beneath its 1,700-foot elevation. Visitors are welcome to picnic on the grounds, either with snacks purchased at the winery or their own picnic lunches from home. Leashed well-behaved dogs are welcome.

White Wines: Bacon Hollow Revenuer's Select, Chardonnay, Pinot Grigio.

Rosé Wines: Rosé.

Red Wines: Bacon Hollow Sunset *(Cabernet Franc)*, Cabernet Franc, Malbec, Merlot, Petit Verdot.

Price Range: $19–$48

Purchasing: Online to AK, FL, MD, MN, and VA.

Directions: From U.S. Route 29 at Ruckersville, take U.S. Route 33 West to Stanardsville. Turn left onto Dyke Road (Route 810) to the village of Dyke, then right onto Bacon Hollow Road (Route 627). Drive 3.6 miles. Turn left onto Wyatt Mountain Road (Route 632) (unpaved). Drive up the winding and narrow gravel mountain road 2 miles to the winery entrance on left. (Winery advises **not** using a GPS unit.)

❖ ❖ ❖

White Hall Vineyards
5184 Sugar Ridge Road
White Hall VA 22987

Hours: W–Su 11:00–5:00
Closed New Year's, Easter, Thanksgiving,
Christmas Eve & Day

434-823-8615
www.whitehallvineyards.com
E-mail: tastingroom@whitehallvineyards.com

Tony and Edie Champ established White Hall in 1992 with the planting of their six-acre vineyard. Now expanded to forty-five acres, White Hall's production is supervised by winemaker Michael Panczak, who got his start in the California wine industry. The winery tasting room includes ample seating and a large fireplace that invite visitors to linger after their tastings. The facilities include a large banquet room on the second floor with expansive views of the Blue Ridge that is available for private parties or weddings. Children are welcome.

White Wines: Chardonnay, Gewurztraminer, Pinot Gris, Viognier.

Red Wines: Cabernet Franc, Cabernet Sauvignon, Cuvée des Champs, Merlot, Petit Verdot.

Sweet/Dessert Wines: Edichi.

Price Range: $18–$30

Tastings: $5 per person, $10 per person for groups of 10 or more.

Groups: Reservations required for groups of 7 or more.

Wheelchair accessible.

Restrictions: No vehicles holding 14 or more occupants after noon.

Purchasing: Online available for AK, DC, FL, IA, MN, NM, and VA.

Directions: From Charlottesville and U.S. Route 29 North, take Barracks Road West, which becomes Garth Road. Continue to the village of White Hall, where the road curves to the right at the Piedmont Store and becomes Browns Gap Turnpike (Route 614). Take the first left onto Sugar Ridge Road (portions unpaved). The winery will be 1.5 miles on the right.

SWEET WINES

Sweet wines can range widely from lightly sweet, or "off dry," wines—enjoyed on their own or with food—to rich, almost voluptuous wines that are an exquisite finish to a fine meal.

While the sweetness of a wine is technically defined by its residual sugar (the percentage of sugar per liter of liquid), a wine's perceived sweetness depends on its acidity, tannins, alcohol strength, and serving temperature. This means that wines with as little as 1.5% residual sugar can taste quite sweet.

Sweet wines are made by stopping fermentation before all the natural sugars have been consumed, by adding grape sugar (called "sweet reserve") after fermentation, or by concentrating the grapes' sweetness before fermentation.

While the first two methods are done after the process of making wine from grapes has begun, concentrating the fruit's natural sweetness takes place in advance. The three main ways of concentrating sweetness are by freezing the grapes, drying the grapes, or delaying harvest.

Ice wines are just what they sound like. Grapes are either allowed to freeze on the vine or are frozen through mechanical means after being harvested. Depending on the altitude of a vineyard and the climate of a given year, some Virginia wineries are occasionally able to make true "frozen on the vine" ice wines.

Sweet wine may be made from grapes that have been spread on trays or mats and allowed to dry or "raisin" before the winemaking process begins. Potomac Point Winery, for instance, offers a Vin de Paille as part of its selection of wines; *paille* means "straw" in French and refers to the straw mats traditionally used to dry grapes.

Late-harvest wines use grapes that have been left on the vine to the point of ultra-ripeness or even raisining before they are harvested. This concentrates the natural sugars of the grapes and gives their juice an added richness of flavor.

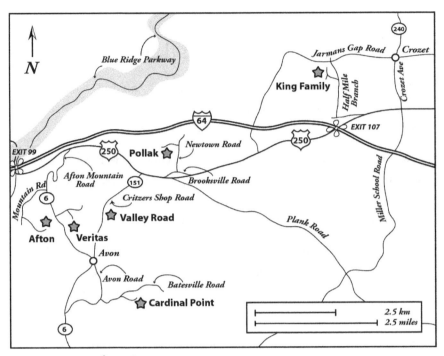

Map 7.7. Afton-Crozet

AFTON-CROZET

Afton Mountain Vineyards
234 Vineyard Lane
Afton VA 22920

Hours: Th–M 11:00–5:30 (summer), F–M 11:00–5:00 (Dec–Feb)   540-456-8667
Closed New Year's, Easter, Thanksgiving,   www.aftonmountainvineyards.com
Christmas Eve & Day   E-mail: finewines@aftonmountainvineyards.com

Nestled at the base of its namesake mountain, Afton Mountain Vineyards is located on the site of the former Bacchanal Vineyards, one of the pioneer vineyards of Virginia. Owned by Tony and Elizabeth Smith since 2009, Afton Mountain produces a dozen wines—from a sparkling méthode champenoise to an ice wine—under the guidance of winemaker Lucien Dimani. Afton's picnic area offers a lovely view of the Virginia countryside and of Afton Mountain itself. Picnic foods are available from the tasting room. The winery is available for weddings and private events. Dogs are welcome.

Sparkling Wines: Bollicine.

White Wines: Chardonnay, Gewurztraminer, Mountain White.

Rosé Wines: Rosé.

Red Wines: Cabernet Franc, Cabernet Sauvignon, Festa di Bacco *(Super Tuscan-style)*, Merlot, Mountain Red *(Sangiovese, Cabernet Franc)*, Petit Verdot.

Fortified Wines: Port-Style VDN.

Price Range: $20–$42

Tastings: $10 per person.

Groups: Reservations required for groups of 7 or more, $12 per person, as well as for all buses, campers, and RVs.

Wheelchair accessible.

Directions: From I-64 Westbound, take Exit 107 onto U.S. Route 250 West. Drive 6.7 miles and turn left onto Afton Mountain Road (Route 6). **From I-64 Eastbound,** take Exit 99 onto U.S. Route 250 East; drive 1.9 miles and turn right onto Afton Mountain Road (Route 6). Descend 1.6 miles and turn right onto Mountain Road (Route 631). Drive 1.2 miles to the winery's long driveway on the left.

❖ ❖ ❖

Cardinal Point Vineyard & Winery
9423 Batesville Road
Afton VA 22920

Hours: Daily 11:00–5:30 (Mar–Dec),
F–M 11:00–5:30 (Jan–Feb)
Closed New Year's, Easter,
Thanksgiving, Christmas

540-456-8400
www.cardinalpointwinery.com
E-mail: info@cardinalpointwinery.com

Cardinal Point was founded by Paul and Ruth Gorman, whose son Tim now serves as the vineyard manager and winemaker. Cardinal Point offers visitors a video tour of the winemaking process from the tasting room, which also includes a small gift area. The winery sponsors a number of special events, including an annual oyster roast which features live music on the outdoor deck. The facilities may be rented for private events. Children and pets are welcome.

Guests may stay overnight at Cardinal Point's restored 19th-century farmhouse; see the website for details and reservations.

White Wines: A6, Chardonnay, IPC Hopped Chardonnay, Quattro.

Rosé Wines: Frai Rosé, Rosé *(Cabernet Franc).*

Red Wines: Cab F+Vio *(Cabernet Franc, Viognier)*, Clay Hill Cabernet Franc, Petit Verdot, Rockfish Red, Union.

Price Range: $20–$30

Tastings: $10 per person; fee waived for teachers and military personnel with valid ID.

Groups: Reservations required for groups of 10 or more; no groups after 1:00.

Wheelchair accessible

Purchasing: Online purchasing is available for CO, DC, FL, MD, MN, NC, and VA.

Directions: **From I-64 Eastbound,** take Exit 99 onto U.S. Route 250 East, and drive 3.8 miles to a right onto Critzers Shop Road (Route 151). **From I-64 Westbound,** take Exit 107 onto U.S. Route 250 West; drive 4.8 miles and make a left onto Critzers Shop Road (Route 151). Once on Route 151, drive 2.5 miles and make a left onto Avon Road. Drive one mile and turn left onto Batesville Road. The winery will be ½ mile on the right.

❖ ❖ ❖

King Family Vineyards & Roseland Polo Farm
6550 Roseland Farm
Crozet VA 22932

Hours: Daily 10:00–5:30 (W to 8:30, summer/fall)   434-823-7800
Closed New Year's Eve & Day, Easter,   www.kingfamilyvineyards.com
Thanksgiving, Christmas Eve & Day   E-mail: info@kingfamilyvineyards.com

King Family Vineyards was founded in 1998 by Texas natives David and Ellen King. The winery's tasting room features a fireplace and a number of small tables at which visitors may sit after over a glass or bottle of wine. The covered veranda and grassy lawn in front of the tasting room offer a spot to relax over a picnic lunch which may be brought from home or purchased at the winery. King Family hosts a range of special events, including Sunday afternoon polo matches (summers only), harvest dinners, and art exhibits. The facility may also be rented for private events and weddings. Mathieu Finot, a native of Crozes-Hermitage in France's Rhone Valley, serves as the winemaker. Chocolates, cheeses, salamis, spreads, and French bread are available for purchase. Children and pets are welcome. Last tastings start at 5:00.

Sparkling Wines: Brut.

White Wines: Chardonnay, Roseland, Viognier.

Rosé Wines: Crosé.

Red Wines: Cabernet Franc, Meritage, Merlot, Petit Verdot.

Sweet/Dessert Wines: Loreley 'Late Harvest' *(Viognier, Petit Manseng)*.

Fortified Wines: Seven *(Merlot, aged in bourbon barrels)*.

Price Range: $22–$35

Tastings: $10 per person.

Groups: Reservations required for groups of 8 or more.

Wheelchair accessible

Purchasing: Online purchasing available for AL, CA, CO, DC, FL, GA, MD, MO, NC, NY, OH, OR, PA, SC, VA, WA, and WY.

Directions: From I-64, take Exit 107 (Crozet) and turn onto U.S. Route 250 East. Drive ½ mile and make a left onto Hillsboro Lane (Route 797). Make the first right onto Half Mile Branch (Route 684) and drive one mile to the winery entrance on left.

❖ ❖ ❖

Pollak Vineyards
330 Newtown Road
Greenwood VA 22943

Hours: Daily 11:00–5:00 (Apr–Oct);
W–Su 11:00–5:00 (Nov–Mar)
Closed New Year's, Thanksgiving, Christmas

540-456-8844
www.pollakvineyards.com
E-mail: info@pollakvineyards.com

Cincinnati residents Margo and David Pollak launched their winery in 2003 in fulfilment of their longstanding dream of having a winery of their own. The ninety-eight-acre farm produces about four thousand cases of estate-grown wine each year, with twenty-five acres currently under vine. The tasting room opened in 2008 and offers visitors scenic views of the vineyards, pond, and adjacent hills from its veranda and tasting area. Hot baguettes and cheese plates are available for purchase to enjoy over a glass or bottle of wine. The winery may be rented for private events, dinners, and weddings. Well-behaved children and pets are welcome.

White Wines: Chardonnay, Pinot Gris, Viognier.

Rosé Wines: Rosé.

Red Wines: Cabernet Franc, Cabernet Sauvignon, Meritage, Merlot, Petit Verdot.

Fortified Wine: Mille Fleurs *(Viognier, eau-de-vie)*.

Price Range: $20–$35

Tastings: $10 per person.

Groups: Reservations required for groups of 6 to 12 (no groups over 12) and for limos; $14 per person.

Wheelchair accessible.

Purchasing: Ordering via VinoShipper for AK, AL, DC, FL, ID, IL, LA, MN, MO, NC, ND, NE, NH, NM, NF, OH, OR, VA, WV, and WY.

Directions: From I-64, take Exit 107 (Crozet) and turn onto U.S. Route 250 West. Drive about 3 miles. Just past Ridgeley Estate, turn right onto Brooksville Road (Route 796) and drive ½ mile. Turn right again onto Newtown Road. The winery drive will be ½ mile on left.

❖ ❖ ❖

Valley Road Vineyards
9264 Critzers Shop Road
Afton VA 22920

Hours: W–Sa 10:30–6:00, Su–M 10:30–5:30   540-456-6350
Closed New Year's, Thanksgiving, Christmas   www.valleyroadwines.com
E-mail: info@valleyroadwines.com

Valley Road Vineyards officially opened its doors in August 2016, founded by Stan Joynes who joined forces with several friends after a long and successful career as a Richmond lawyer. Winemaking is done under the guidance of Mathieu Finot (*King Family Vineyards*), who is using fruit from other Virginia vineyards while Valley Road's own vines mature. The winery sponsors live music on weekends and offers a range of artisanal cheeses, breads, and spreads for purchase. Leashed pets are welcome.

Sparkling Wines: Fête (*Viognier*), Joie (*rosé*).

White Wines: Chardonnay, Destana, Pinot Gris, Viognier.

Rosé Wines: Rosé (*Merlot*).

Red Wines: Meritage, Merlot, Petit Verdot, Torn Curtain.

Sweet/Dessert Wines: Trillium.

Price Range: $22–$35

Tastings: $8 per person for classic, $15 for wine and cheese pairing.

Groups: Reservations required for groups over 8 and for buses.

Directions: **From I-64 Westbound,** take Exit 107 (Crozet) and turn onto U.S. Route 250 West. Drive about 4.8 miles and turn left onto Critzers Shop Road (Route 151). Continue one mile to the winery on the left.

From I-64 Eastbound, take Exit 99 (Afton Mountain) and turn onto U.S. Route 250 East. Drive 3.2 miles and turn right onto Critzers Shop Road (Route 151). Continue one mile to the winery on the left.

❖ ❖ ❖

Veritas Vineyards & Winery
151 Veritas Lane
(GPS address: 145 Saddleback Farm)
Afton VA 22920

Hours: M–F 9:30–5:30, Sa–Su 11:00–5:00

Closed New Year's, Thanksgiving, Christmas

540-456-8000

www.veritaswines.com

E-mail: contact@veritaswines.com

Veritas is owned by Andrew and Patricia Hodson, who opened the winery to the public in 2002; daughter Emily Pelton serves as the winemaker. The spacious tasting room has a long tasting bar as well as armchairs and small sofas for visitors. The veranda offers a view of Veritas's vineyards as well as the Blue Ridge beyond. The facility is available for private events and weddings, and sponsors a variety of special events, including summertime "Starry Nights" and winter winemaker's dinners and festivities. Light fare is available for purchase; picnic foods brought by customers must be consumed outside. Children and pets are welcome, although no pets are allowed for "Starry Nights."

Guests may stay overnight in one of the six suites at The Farmhouse, a restored farmstead originally built in 1836.

Sparkling Wines: Scintilla *(Chardonnay)*, Mousseux *(Merlot)*.

White Wines: Chardonnay, Sauvignon Blanc, Viognier, White Star.

Rosé Wines: Rosé.

Red Wines: Cabernet Franc, Claret, Merlot, Petit Verdot, Red Star, Vintner's Reserve *(Bordeaux-style blend)*.

Sweet/Dessert Wines: Kenmar, Petit Manseng.

Fortified Wines: Othello.

Price Range: $18–$40

Tastings: $10 per person.

Groups: Reservations required for groups of 8 or more, $15 per person. Cellar tours are offered on weekends at 11:00, 12:00, 1:00 and 2:00.

Wheelchair accessible.

Purchasing: Online ordering for AL, AK, AZ, AR, CA, CO, CT, DC, DE, FL, GA, HI, ID, IL, IN, KS, KY, LA, MA, MD, ME, MI, MN, MS, MO, MT, NC, NE, NM, NV, OH, OK, OR, PA, RI, SC, SD, TN, TX, VT, VA, WA, WI, and WY.

Directions: **From I-64 Westbound,** take Exit 107 onto U.S. Route 250 West; drive 6.7 miles and turn left onto Afton Mountain Road (Route 6). **From I-64 Eastbound,** take Exit 99 onto U.S. Route 250 East; drive 1.9 miles and turn right onto Afton Mountain Road (Route 6). Drive 2 miles and turn left onto Saddleback Trail. Continue to the parking lot on the right.

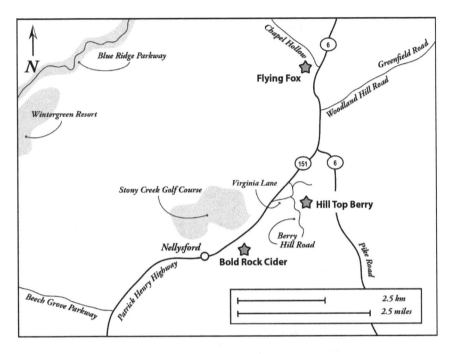

Map 7.8. Rockfish Valley

ROCKFISH VALLEY

Bold Rock Cider
1020 Rockfish Valley Highway
Nellysford VA 22958

Hours: Daily 11:00–6:00 (F, Sa to 8:00 in summer)   434-361-1030
Closed New Year's, Easter, Thanksgiving, Christmas   www.boldrock.com
E-mail: info@boldrock.com

John and Robin Washburn open their cidery upon returning to the U.S. after many years overseas. Cidermaster Brian Shanks brings extensive experience in the field from his native New Zealand and other countries. The tasting room features a large glass wall where visitors can observe the bottling process as it happens. The interior features the longest beam from a single tree in the state, a 50-foot Douglas Fir. Bold Rock offers an rotating menu of dishes for visitors to enjoy either in the spacious indoor fireplace room or the decks and patios, where they may enjoy lovely views of the Rockfish Valley. The upstairs features a small cider history display from an observation deck that looks down onto the bottling floor. Children are welcome, while leashed dogs must remain outside.

Bold Rock ciders can also be found at Chiles Peach Orchard (1351 Greenwood Road, Crozet, open Apr–Nov only) as well as at Carter Mountain Orchard (1435 Carter Mountain Trail, Charlottesville).

Ciders: Crimson Ridge Vat No. 1, Crimson Ridge Vintage Dry, IPA (India Pressed Apple), Pear Cider, Premium Dry, Virginia Apple, Virginia Draft.

Price Range: $9–$10

Directions: From I-64 Eastbound, take Exit 99 onto U.S. Route 250 East; drive 3.8 miles and turn right onto Critzers Shop Road (Route 151).

From I-64 Westbound, take Exit 107 onto U.S. Route 250 West; drive 4.8 miles and turn left onto Critzers Shop Road (Route 151). Once on Route 151, continue 12.5 miles to the cidery parking lot on the left.

❖ ❖ ❖

Flying Fox Vineyard
27 Chapel Hollow Road
Afton VA 22920

Hours: Daily 11:00–5:30 (Apr–Dec),   434-361-1692
F–M 11:00–5:00 (Jan–Mar)   www.flyingfoxvineyard.com
Closed New Year's, Easter, Thanksgiving, Christmas   E-mail: info@flyingfoxvineyard.com

Flying Fox Vineyard is located in the heart of scenic Nelson County. Launched by Rich Evans and Lynn Davis who planted the first vines in 2000, it is now owned by the Hodson family (*Veritas Vineyards*). Most of the winery's production is estate-grown; Flying Fox supplements its own grape production from local vineyards. The tasting room is located next to the Bleu Ridge Bed and Breakfast and is housed in the former stable of this 1840-era inn. The building has a wood-burning fireplace for chilly autumn days and a small pet-friendly picnic area. The tasting room includes art and photography exhibits by local artists. Pets are welcome.

White Wines: Chardonnay, Pinot Gris, Table White, Viognier.

Rosé Wines: Rosé.

Red Wines: Cabernet Franc, Merlot, Petit Verdot, Table Red, Trio *(Bordeaux-style blend)*.

Fortified Wines: Vermouth.

Price Range: $17–$35

Tastings: $5 per person.

Groups: Reservations requested for groups of 6 or more.

Purchasing: Online ordering is available for DC, FL, MD, MN, NC, and VA.

Directions: **From I-64 Eastbound,** take Exit 99 onto U.S. Route 250 East; drive 3.8 miles and turn right onto Critzers Shop Road (Route 151). **From I-64 Westbound,** take Exit 107 onto U.S. Route 250 West; drive 4.8 miles and turn left onto Critzers Shop Road (Route 151). Once on Route 151, continue 7 miles to Chapel Hollow Road and the winery on right.

❖ ❖ ❖

Hill Top Berry Farm & Winery
2800 Berry Hill Road
Nellysford VA 22958

Hours: Daily 11:00–5:00 (summer), W–Su 11:00–5:00 (winter)   434-361-1266
Closed New Year's, Easter, Thanksgiving,   www.hilltopberrywine.com
Christmas Eve & Day   E-mail: hilltop1@ntelos.net

Hill Top Berry has its roots in a pick-your-own blackberry farm begun by Marlyn and Sue Allen. Over the years, their interest in winemaking grew, with a special focus on "true to the fruit" wines and meads. The winery is now owned and operated by the Allens' daughters, Kimberly Allen Pugh, Crystal Allen Brennan, and Marlo Gayle Allen. Because Hill Top's production is seasonal, offerings in the tasting room vary. The winery offers a covered deck with a view of the farm and Rockfish Valley. Special events include a May Day celebration, a blackberry harvest festival, a fall foliage open house, and a holiday open house. Children and dogs are welcome.

Fruit Wines: Blackberry Delight, Blue Heeler *(blueberry)*, Cranberry, Little Heeler *(blueberry)*, Madison Peach Sangria, Mountain Apple, Pear, Plum Crazy, Sweet Melon, Sweet Vixen *(strawberry)*, Three Sisters Elderberry, Virginia Blackberry, Virginia Peach, Virginia Raspberry, Watermelon.

Meads: Dragon's Blood *(pomegranate, honey)*, Dragon's Breath *(smoked hot pepper)*, Eden, Gladius *(pyment)*, Hunter's Moon Melomel *(pumpkin)*, Lavender Metheglin, Nectarine Melomel, Oracle *(rose petal)*, Perry *(pear, honey)*, Pounding Branch Persimmon Melomel, Rockfish River Cyser, Tiger's Eye *(hibiscus)*, Voyage *(honey mead)*.

Red Wines: Raven's Roost Red.

Price Range: $16–$25

Tastings: $5 per person.

Groups: Please call ahead for groups of 6 or more.

Purchasing: Online via VinoShipper to AK, AL, AZ, CA, CO, DC, FL, GA, HI, IA, ID, IL, IN, KS, LA, MA, MD, ME, MN, MO, NC, ND, NE, NH, NM, NV, NY, OH, OR, PA, SC, TN, TX, VA, WA, WI, WV, and WY.

Directions: **From I-64 Eastbound,** take Exit 99 onto U.S. Route 250 East; drive 3.8 miles and turn right onto Critzers Shop Road (Route 151). **From I-64 Westbound,** take Exit 107 onto U.S. Route 250 West; drive 4.8 miles and turn left onto Critzers Shop Road (Route 151). Once on Route 151, continue 10 miles and turn left onto Virginia Lane (Route 612). After 0.4 miles, turn right onto Berry Hill Road. Continue ⅓ mile across the bridge and up the hill to the winery on left.

❖ ❖ ❖

FRUIT WINES, CIDERS, AND MEADS

While most wine is made from grapes, wine can also be made from many types of fruits, most often from apples, berries, and stone fruits such as pears or peaches. These wines may be made entirely from fruit or may contain a mixture of grape-based wine along with the fruit wine. Because many fruits lack enough natural sugars for fermentation to occur, the winemaker often must add sugar to the juice, and fruit wines can be slightly sweet as a result.

Like apple wine, hard cider is fermented apple juice but is lower in total alcohol strength than wine. Ciders range from 2% to 8.5% alcohol strength, while apple wines are higher in alcohol. Ciders may be either still or sparkling, depending on the cidermaker's wish. Cidermaking was brought to the United States by colonists from England, where hard cider is a traditional brew. Hard cider is considered to have been the most popular alcoholic beverage available in colonial America into the nineteenth-century and was consumed by people from all levels of society. Presidents John Adams and Thomas Jefferson, for instance, both regularly drank and served cider.

Mead is a fermented beverage made from honey and has been produced since ancient times in Europe, the Middle East, Africa, and parts of Asia. Mead is often associated with the history of old Germany and Scandinavia, where it was often drunk from horns. Key scenes in the great Anglo-Saxon epic *Beowulf* are set in the king's mead-hall, a large public room in the palace where warriors met to drink their mead in the evenings. Meads made solely from honey may also be called hydromels, the name by which mead is known in France. Meads blended with fruit juice are known as melomels, while metheglin is mead flavored with herbs or spices.

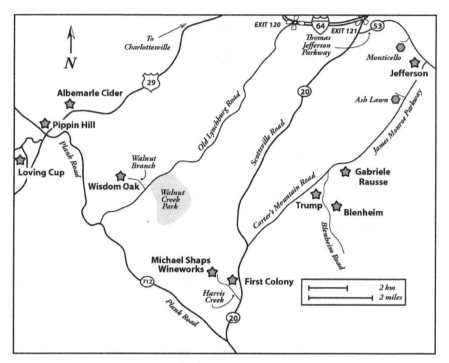

Map 7.9. Lower Monticello (North Garden)

LOWER MONTICELLO

Albemarle Cider Works
2545 Rural Ridge Lane
North Garden VA 22959

Hours: W–Su 11:00–5:00 (Jan–Jun);
Daily 11:00–5:00 (Jul–Dec)
Closed New Year's, Thanksgiving, Christmas

434-979-1663
www.albemarleciderworks.com
E-mail: fruit@albemarleciderworks.com

Chuck and Charlotte Shelton opened Albemarle Cider Works in 2009 as a collateral line to their family's Rural Ridge Orchard. All the Sheltons' ciders are made from classic and heirloom apple varieties, such as Albemarle Pippin, Black Twig, Grimes Golden, and Virginia Crab, among others. The cidery sponsors an apple festival as well as various workshops on apple growing and cider making. Live music is featured on summertime Second Sunday Ciders. Guests may bring their own food or purchase locally-made cheese and charcuterie at the tasting room. Albemarle Cider Works's Rural Ridge Cottage can be booked for overnight stays through the Crossroads Inn website *(www.crossroadsinn.com)*.

Ciders: Arkansas Black, Black Twig, Brut d'Albemarle, GoldRush, Jupiter's Legacy, Old Virginia Winesap, Pomme Mary, Red Hill, Ragged Mountain, Royal Pippin.

Price Range: $16

Tastings: $5–$10 per person, depending on range of ciders available.

Groups: Reservations required for groups of 10 or more.

Directions: From I-64, take Exit 118 onto U.S. Route 29 South. Drive 8 miles and turn right onto Rural Ridge Lane at the Rural Ridge Orchard.

❖ ❖ ❖

Blenheim Vineyards
31 Blenheim Farm
Charlottesville VA 22902

Hours: Daily 11:00–5:30
Closed New Year's Eve & Day, Thanksgiving,
Christmas Eve & Day

434-293-5366
www.blenheimvineyards.com
E-mail: info@blenheimvineyards.com

Blenheim Vineyards was established in 2000 by Dave Matthews on the historic Blenheim estate dating to a 1730 land grant to the famed Carter family and named after a key battle won by England's Duke of Marlborough, an ancestor of Winston Churchill. The tasting area offers a view of the lower-level winemaking facilities through paneled glass floors. Outdoor seating is also available, as are cheeses and snacks for sale in the tasting room. The winery may be rented for private events. Children are welcome.

White Wines: Chardonnay, Painted White, Viognier.

Rosé Wines: Rosé.

Red Wines: Cabernet Franc, Cabernet Sauvignon, Merlot, Painted Red *(Bordeaux-style blend)*, Petit Verdot.

Price Range: $19–$30

Tastings: $6 per person.

Groups: Reservations required for groups of 8 to 15, $10 per person.

Restrictions: No dogs; no groups over 15.

Purchasing: Online to AZ, CA, CO, DC, FL, GA, ID, IL, IN, IA, KS, ME, MD, MI, MN, MO, NE, NV, NH, NM, NJ, NY, NC, ND, OH, OR, SC, TN, TX, VA, VT, WA, WI, WV, and WY.

Directions: From I-64 East, take Exit 121A (Scottsville) onto Route 20 South. Drive ½ mile and turn left onto Thomas Jefferson Parkway (Route 53). After 3.2 miles, make a slight right onto the James Monroe Parkway. Drive 4.8 miles and turn left onto Blenheim Road. The winery entrance will be ½ mile on the right.

❖ ❖ ❖

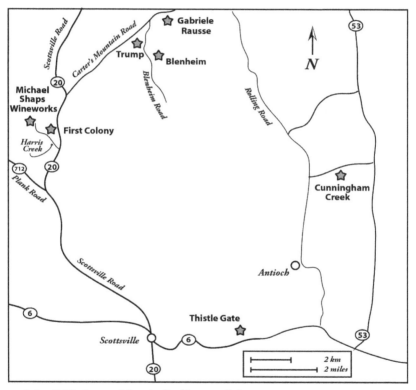

Map 7.10. Lower Monticello (Scottsville)

Brent Manor Vineyards
100 Brent Manor Lane
Faber VA 22938

Hours: F 3:00–6:00, Sa 11:00–5:30, Su 11:30–4:30

Closed New Year's Eve & Day, Thanksgiving,

Christmas Eve & Day

434-826-0722

www.brentmanorvineyards.com

E-mail: wine@brentmanorvineyards.com

Jorge and Tracie Raposo opened Brent Manor in 2016 on a site they had originally planned as a bed-and-breakfast. Tastings are often led by the owners and include both Brent Manor's own wines as well as a selection of wines from Jorge's native Portugal (selections may vary). Seating is available outside overlooking the vines and hills of Virginia's Piedmont. Children are welcome.

White Wines: Sauvignon Blanc, Trio, Viognier.

Rosé Wines: Rosado.

Red Wines: Chambourcin, Patio Red, Tintâo.

Price Range: $17–$30

Tastings: $9 per person with souvenir glass.

Purchasing: Online via VinoShipper to AK, AL, DC, FL, ID, IL, LA, MN, MO, ND, NE, NH, NM, NV, OH, OR, WV, and WY.

Directions: From Charlottesville, take U.S. Route 29 South for 18 miles. At Route 6 (Irish Road), make a U-turn. Drive north 0.7 miles to the winery entrance on the right.

❖ ❖ ❖

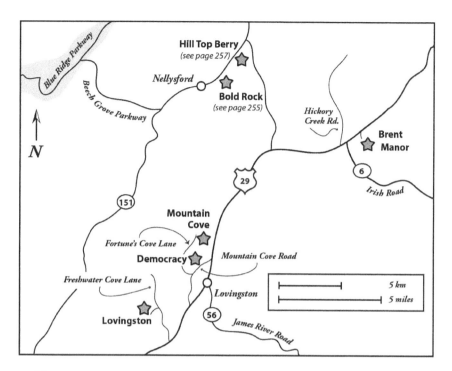

Map 7.11. Lower Monticello (Lovingston)

Cunningham Creek Winery & Farm Store
3304 Ruritan Lake Road
Palmyra VA 22963

Hours: M, Th–Sa 11:00–6:00 (Sa to 9:00 in summer), 434-207-3907
Su 1:00–6:00 http://cunninghamcreek.wine
Closed New Year's, Thanksgiving, Christmas E-mail: info@cunninghamcreek.wine

Bruce and Debby Deal partnered with friends Rick and Sara Hernandez to open Cunningham Creek in 2016, five years after purchasing the property. They work with winemaker Mathieu Finot (King Family) to produce all Virginia-grown wines, either from their own 11-acre vineyard or others nearby. The winery features free Wi-Fi, live music on weekends, locally produced and grown products, including cheeses and crackers. The facilities may be rented for special events. Children are welcome.

Fruit Wines: Strawberry.

White Wines: Chardonnay, Petit Manseng, Viognier.

Rosé Wines: Rosé.

Red Wines: Cabernet Sauvignon, Herd Dog Red, Meritage, Merlot, Petit Verdot, Rivanna Red.

Price Range: $17–$30

Tastings: $8 per person.

Groups: Reservation required for groups of 8 or more, $10 per person.

Directions: From I-64 East, take Exit 121A (Scottsville) onto Route 20 South. Drive ½ mile and turn left onto Thomas Jefferson Parkway (Route 53). After 15 miles, turn right at the village of Cunningham onto Ruritan Lake Road (Route 619). Continue 2 miles to the winery entrance..

❖ ❖ ❖

Democracy Vineyards
585 Mountain Cove Road
Lovingston VA   22949

Hours: Sa–M 12:00–6:00   434-263-8463
Closed mid-Dec–Jan,   www.democracyvineyards.com
Easter, Thanksgiving   E-mail: info@democracyvineyards.com

Susan Prokop and Jim Turpin launched their winery in 2009 on the grounds of an old apple orchard and opened their tasting room to the public three years later. The couple has a long background in politics, a professional interest that is reflected in the choice of names for their wines as well as in the political memorabilia that decorates the tasting room.

Winemaker Ben Margulies uses all Virginia grapes for the wines, either from Democracy's own vines or other Virginia vineyards.

Fruit Wines: Village View Gold *(apple)*.

White Wines: Constitution, Unum.

Rosé Wines: Dawn's Light.

Red Wines: Freedom, Magna Carta, Suffrage, Velvet Revolution.

Sweet/Dessert Wines: Campaign, Parliament, Republic.

Price Range: $16–$23

Tastings: $5 per person regular, $8 for full.

Purchasing: Online purchasing is available for AK, AZ, CA, CO, CT, DC, FL, GA, HI, ID, IL, IN, IA, KS, LA, ME, MD, MI, MN, MO, NE, NV, NH, NM, NY, NC, ND, OH, OR, PA, SC, TN, TX, VA, WA, WV, WI, and WY.

Directions: From I-64, take Exit 118 onto U.S. Route 29 South and drive 28 miles. Turn right onto Mountain Cove Road (Route 718) and drive one mile to the winery on the right.

❖ ❖ ❖

First Colony Winery
1650 Harris Creek Road
Charlottesville VA 22902

Hours: M–F 10:00–6:00, Sa,Su 11:00–6:00   434-979-7105
Closed New Year's, Thanksgiving, Christmas   www.firstcolonywinery.com
E-mail: info@firstcolonywinery.com

Founded in 2000 by Randy McElroy, First Colony Winery is now owned by Bruce and Heather Spiess and Jeff Miller, with winemaking under the guidance of Jason Hayman. The tasting room offers seating at several tables indoors, with a wood stove to provide winter warmth; outdoor decks are also available under the trees that surround the building. Guests may purchase crackers and cheese for a snack on the grounds; groups under ten may also bring their own food from home for a picnic. In addition, First Colony sponsors a number of events and may be rented for private events, parties, and weddings. Children and pets are welcome.

White Wines: Chardonnay, Petit Manseng, Riesling, Totier Creek White, Viognier, Zephyr.

Rosé Wines: Rosé.

Red Wines: Cabernet Franc, Cabernet Sauvignon, Claret, Meritage, Merlot, Petit Verdot, Silver Doctor.

Fortified Wines: Thatch *(port-style)*.

Price Range: $20–$35

Tastings: $5 per person.

Groups: Reservations required for groups of 10 or more.

Purchasing: Online purchasing is available for CA, DC, FL, MN, NC, NY, OH, OR, PA, VA, and WA.

Directions: From I-64, take Exit 121A and merge onto Route 20 South. Drive 10.4 miles and turn right onto Harris Creek Road (portions unpaved). The winery will be on the right in ¾ mile.

❖ ❖ ❖

Gabriele Rausse Winery
3247 Carter's Mountain Road
Charlottesville VA 22902

Hours: Th–F 11:00–5:00, Su 10–4:00   434-977-3042
Closed New Year's, Easter, Thanksgiving, Christmas   www.gabrieleraussewinery.com

Iconic winemaker Gabriele Rausse has been a fixture in the Virginia wine industry since first arriving from Italy to help start Barboursville Vineyards in the 1970s. He went on to play a leading role in establishing vineyards at Jefferson, Kluge (now Trump), Afton Mountain, Blenheim, First Colony, and White Hall, among many others. Rausse founded his own winery in Albemarle County in 1997, ultimately opening a tasting room to the public in 2015. Rausse and son Tim make all Virginia-grown wines using their own vines as well as fruit from established vineyards around the state. There are several tables for seating in the light-filled tasting room as well as outside.

White Wines: Chardonnay, Roussanne, Vin Gris de Pinot Noir.

Rosé Wines: Dry Rosé.

Red Wines: Cabernet Franc, Cabernet Sauvignon, Grenache, Nebbiolo.

Price Range: $16–$35

Tastings: $6 per person for a half-tasting, $12 for full.

Groups: Reservations required for groups of 8 or more.

Wheelchair accessible.

Restrictions: No tour buses.

Directions: From I-64 East, take Exit 121A (Scottsville) onto Route 20

South. Drive ½ mile and turn left onto Thomas Jefferson Parkway (Route 53). After 3.2 miles, make a slight right onto the James Monroe Parkway. Drive 1.1 miles and turn left into the winery's gravel drive.

❖ ❖ ❖

Jefferson Vineyards

1353 Thomas Jefferson Parkway
Charlottesville VA 22902

Hours: Daily 10:00–6:00 (Apr–Nov), 10:00–5:00 (Dec–Mar) 434-977-3042
Closed New Year's, Easter, Thanksgiving, Christmas www.jeffersonvineyards.com
E-mail: info@jeffersonvineyards.com

Jefferson Vineyards is located midway between Thomas Jefferson's Monticello and James Monroe's Ash Lawn on the site of the vineyard originally planted by Filippo Mazzei for Jefferson. Owner Stanley Woodward decided in 1981 to resurrect the vineyard which now includes twenty acres of vines, with Christopher Ritzcowan serving as winemaker. Both outdoor and indoor seating is available either on the grounds overlooking the vines or in the adjacent guest lounge. All the winery's production is from Virginia-grown grapes. Jefferson Vineyards occasionally hosts formal winemaker dinners, including an annual Fête de la Bastille (14 July).

White Wines: Chardonnay, Riesling, Vin Blanc, Viognier.

Rosé Wines: Rosé.

Red Wines: Cabernet Franc, Meritage, Merlot, Petit Verdot, Vin Rouge.

Price Range: $17–$30

Tastings: $12 per person, with souvenir glass.

Groups: Reservations required for groups of 6 or more; no groups on weekends.

Wheelchair accessible.

Restrictions: No tour buses or vans; groups of 6 or more on weekdays only.

Directions: From I-64, take Exit 121A and turn onto Route 20 South. After ½ mile, turn left at the traffic light onto Thomas Jefferson Parkway (Route 53) and drive 3.3 miles to the winery entrance on the right.

❖ ❖ ❖

Loving Cup Vineyard & Winery
3340 Sutherland Road
North Garden VA 22959

Hours: F–Su 11:00–5:00 (Apr–Dec)   434-984-0774
Closed Jan–Mar, Easter, Thanksgiving, Christmas   www.lovingcupwine.com
E-mail: info@lovingcupwine.com

Loving Cup was founded by Karl Hambsch on his family's 150-acre farm as an all-organic operation, using French-American hybrids that are more resistant to bugs and blight. Karl's interest in winemaking was sparked by making crabapple wine with his father; he later honed his skills at Prince Michel Vineyards. Visitors are welcome to linger at one of the tables on the wrap-around deck to enjoy the view of the vines and hills. Part of the proceeds from their Dudley Nose Rosé go to support the Almost Home Pet Adoption Center in Nelson County, a no-kill shelter committed to finding forever homes for abandoned pets. Children and leashed dogs are welcome.

White Wines: Loving Cup White *(Cayuga, Traminette)*.

Rosé Wines: Dudley Nose Rosé *(Corot Noir)*.

Red Wines: Loving Cup Red *(Marquette, Corot Noir)*, Sweet Red Reserve, Tellurian Red.

Price Range: $18–$25

Tastings: $5 per person

Groups: Advance notice requested for groups of 6 or more, $15 per person

Purchasing: Online shipping available to AK, DC, FL, MN, VA, and WA.

Directions: From I-64, take Exit 118 and turn onto U.S. Route 29 South. Drive 9.2 miles and turn right onto Sutherland Road, just after passing Plank Road. Continue 2.1 miles to the winery entrance on the right.

❖ ❖ ❖

Lovingston Winery
885 Freshwater Cove Lane
Lovingston VA 22949

Hours: W–Th 10:00–4:00, F–Su 11:00–5:00 (Apr–Nov)   434-263-8467
Sa only 11:00–5:00 (Jan–Mar)   www.lovingstonwinery.com
Closed New Year's, Thanksgiving, Christmas   E-mail: info@lovingstonwinery.com

Lovingston Winery, located just outside the old village of Lovingston, was opened to the public in 2010 by Ed and Janet Puckett. The couple had cultivated a vineyard in Georgia for several years before moving to Virginia when their daughter enrolled at the University of Virginia. Their tasting room is housed in the winery's production facility, allowing visitors a good view of the winemaking process in action from the second-floor level. Winemaker Riaan Rossouw, a South African native, currently oversees Lovingston's 8.5 acres of vines and wine production.

White Wines: Chardonnay, Petit Manseng, Seyval Blanc.

Red Wines: Cabernet Franc, Merlot, Pinotage, Rotunda Red *(Bordeaux-style blend)*.

Price Range: $16–$30

Restrictions: No pets.

Purchasing: Online to AK, CA, DC, FL, MA, MN, NY, NC, OH, PA, TX, and VA.

Directions: From I-64, take Exit 118 onto U.S. Route 29 South. Drive 32.6 miles and turn right onto Freshwater Cove Lane (Route 653). The winery entrance will be on the left in 1 mile.

❖ ❖ ❖

Michael Shaps Wineworks
1781 Harris Creek Way
Charlottesville VA 22902

Hours: Daily 11:00–5:00
Closed New Year's, Thanksgiving, Christmas

434-296-3438
www.michaelshapswines.com
E-mail: info@virginiawineworks.com

Michael Shaps Wineworks was established by Virginia vintner Michael Shaps after he had spent several years working at both Jefferson Vineyards and King Family Vineyards as well as wineries in France where he has vineyards of his own. Located in the former Montdomaine winery, Shaps produces his wine under two labels, Wineworks and Michael Shaps, with all wines sourced only from Virginia vineyards. The winery also provides custom crush production for over 30 other Virginia wineries.

The winery also has a satellite tasting room in Charlottesville at 1585 Avon Street Extended (W–Su 1:00–7:00, 434-529-6848).

Sparkling Wines: Méthode.

White Wines: Chardonnay, Odette, Petit Manseng, Viognier.

Red Wines: Cabernet Franc, L. Scott, Merlot, Meritage, Petit Verdot, Tannat.

Sweet/Dessert Wines: Raisin d'Être Late Harvest.

Price Range: $25–$58

Tastings: $10 per person.

Groups: Please call ahead for groups of 6 or more.

Purchasing: Online ordering for CA, DC, FL, MD, NC, NY, and VA only.

Directions: From I-64, take Exit 121A and merge onto Route 20 South. Drive 10.4 miles and turn right onto Harris Creek Road (portions unpaved). Continue 1 mile to the winery at the end of the road.

❖ ❖ ❖

Mountain Cove Vineyards
1362 Fortune's Cove Lane
Lovingston VA 22949

Hours: W–Su 12:00–5:00 (Mar–Dec) 434-263-5392
Closed Jan–Feb, Thanksgiving, Christmas www.mountaincovevineyards.com
E-mail: aweed1@juno.com

Founded in 1973 by Al and Emily Weed, Mountain Cove is the oldest winery still operating in Virginia. The vineyards and winery are located in the heart of Nelson County in a scenic valley next to Fortune's Cove, a Nature Conservancy property with numerous hiking trails. As a small family-operated winery, one of the owners is likely to be on hand to greet visitors. Mountain Cove's wines are all vegan and, with the exception of its Chardonnay, all estate grown. While the tasting room has no indoor seating, the winery grounds include a pavilion. The facilities may be rented for private events and weddings. Discounts offered for active or retired military personnel (with I.D.).

Fruit Wines: Apple, Blackberry, Peach.

White Wines: Chardonnay, Skyline White *(Villard Blanc, Vidal Blanc)*, Traminette, Vidal Blanc.

Rosé Wines: Skyline Rosé.

Red Wines: Cabernet Franc, Cabernet Sauvignon, Chambourcin, Tinto.

Price Range: $12–$15

Wheelchair accessible.

Directions: From I-64, take Exit 118 onto U.S. Route 29 South and drive 28 miles. Turn right onto Mountain Cove Road (Route 718) and drive 1.6 miles. Turn right onto Fortune's Cove Lane. The winery will be 1.4 miles on the right.

❖ ❖ ❖

Pippin Hill Farm & Vineyards
5022 Plank Road
North Garden VA 22959

Hours: Tu–Su 11:00–5:00
Closed Thanksgiving, Christmas Eve & Day, 1–15 Jan

434-202-8063
www.pippinhillfarm.com
E-mail: info@pippinhillfarm.com

Lynn and Dean Andrews opened Pippin Hill Farm to the public in 2011 with a focus on sustainable agriculture and eco-friendly practices. Seating is available both indoors and out, with light fare offered for purchase in the tasting room.. Pippin Hill sources its wines from its own vineyards as well as from others in Albemarle County and elsewhere in Virginia. The winery is available for rental for private parties and weddings. Children and pets are welcome.

Sparkling Wines: Blanc de Blanc, Sparkling Rosé.

White Wines: Chardonnay, Petit Manseng, Sauvignon Blanc, Viognier, Zero White.

Rosé Wines: Summer Farm Rosé *(Cabernet Franc)*.

Red Wines: Cabernet Franc, Cabernet Sauvignon, Cannon Red, Clay Hill Petit Verdot, Meritage, Merlot.

Fortified Wines: Bin 21 *(port-style)*.

Price Range: $25–$38

Tastings: $10 per person.

Groups: Reservations required for groups of 10 or more.

Purchasing: Online for CA, DC, FL, NC, and VA.

Directions: From I-64, take Exit 118 and turn onto U.S. Route 29 South. Drive 9 miles and turn right onto Plank Road. The winery entrance will be on the right in ¼ mile.

❖ ❖ ❖

Thistle Gate Winery
5199 West River Road
Scottsville VA 24590

Hours: F–Sa 12:00–5:30, Su 1:00–5:30 (Mar–Dec)
Closed Jan–Feb, Good Friday, Easter,
Thanksgiving, Christmas

434-286-7781
www.thistlegatevineyard.com
E-mail: george@caiweb.com

George and Leslie Cushnie planted their vines in 2008 after moving to the area from Fairfax County, ultimately opening their winery in 2012; they work with winemaker Kirsty Harman (Blenheim Vineyards) to make their all-Virginia-grown wines. The names of their wines often have a local inspiration, drawing especially from Scottsville's riverine past. Guests may linger at one of the tables in the tasting room or on the wraparound deck with a lovely view of the vineyards. Children and leashed dogs are welcome.

White Wines: Chardonnay, Scott's Landing, Thistle White, Traminette, Viognier.

Rosé Wines: Thistle Blush.

Red Wines: Merlot, Petit Verdot, St. George Red, Thistle Red.

Fortified Wines: Highland Red *(port-style)*, Tartan Red *(port-style)*.

Price Range: $16–$27

Tastings: $5 per person for standard, $7 for reserve.

Groups: Reservations required for groups of 10 or more.

Directions: From Charlottesville, take Route 20 south for 19 miles. At Scottsville, turn east onto Main Street (VA 6) and drive ½ mile. Turn left onto West River Road. Drive 5 miles to the winery entrance on the left.

❖ ❖ ❖

Trump Winery
3550 Blenheim Road
Charlottesville VA   22902

Hours: W–M 11:00–4:00

Closed New Year's Eve & Day, Easter,

Thanksgiving, Christmas Eve & Day

434-984-4855

www.trumpwinery.com

E-mail: cstrong@trumpwinery.com

Trump Winery is located on the slopes of Carter's Mountain in the Blue Ridge; purchased by the Trumps in 2011, the winery was formerly known as Kluge Estate. Gourmet sandwiches, small plates, and salads are available for consumption on site, including on the patio where visitors can enjoy the sweeping views of vines and hillsides. The facilities are available for rental for special events, weddings, and dinners. The winery has two hundred acres under vine, the most in the state, and is well known for its range of sparkling wines made in the classic *méthode champenoise*. Last pours for tastings begin thirty minutes before closing.

Guests may stay at the luxury 45-room Albemarle Estate Hotel, visible across the valley and vineyards from the tasting room patio.

Sparkling Wines: Blanc de Blanc, Blanc de Noir, Rosé.

White Wines: Chardonnay, Sauvignon Blanc, Viognier.

Rosé Wines: Rosé.

Red Wines: Cabernet Sauvignon, Meritage, New World Reserve *(Bordeaux-style blend)*, Pinot Noir.

Fortified Wines: CRU *(Chardonnay, brandy)*.

Price Range: $18–$54

Tastings: $12 per person.

Groups: Reservations required for groups of 8 to 12, $200 per group for private seated tasting.

Purchasing: Online ordering for CA, CO, DC, FL, GA, IA, IL, LA, MA, MD, MI, MN, MO, NC, NH, NJ, NV, NY, OH, OR, PA, SC, TX, VA, WA, and WI.

Directions: From I-64 East, take Exit 121A (Scottsville) onto Route 20 South and drive ½ mile. Turn left onto Thomas Jefferson Parkway (Route 53). After 3.2 miles, bend right onto James Monroe Parkway and drive 4.8 miles. Turn left onto Blenheim Road and the entrance ¼ mile on the right.

❖ ❖ ❖

Wisdom Oak Winery
3613 Walnut Branch Lane
North Garden VA 22959

Hours: Th 3:00–7:00, F 12:00–5:30,
Sa 11:00–5:30, Su 11:00–5:00 (Mar–Dec)
Closed New Year's, Easter,
Thanksgiving, Christmas

434-984-4272
www.wisdomoakwinery.com
E-mail: info@wisdomoakwinery.com

Wisdom Oak Winery, originally founded by Jerry Bias, is now owned by Jason and Laura Lavallee on a farm several miles south of Charlottesville. The tasting room includes indoor and outdoor seating that offers a good vantage point of the vineyards and surrounding hills. A selection of cheeses and crackers is available for purchase at the winery. The facilities may be rented for private parties and weddings. Leashed dogs are welcome.

White Wines: Chardonnay, Cloche, North Garden White, Petit Manseng, Vidal Blanc.

Rosé Wines: Rosé, Rosewood.

Red Wines: Meritage, Merlot, North Garden Red, Petit Verdot.

Sweet/Dessert Wines: Savona (*late-harvest Vidal Blanc*).

Fortified Wines: Tinto (*port-style*).

Price Range: $17–$27

Tastings: $8 per person with souvenir glass.

Groups: Reservations required for groups of 8 or more, $10 per person.

Purchasing: Online via VinoShipper to AK, AL, AZ, CA, CO, DC, FL, GA, HI, IA, ID, IL, IN, KS, LA, MA, MD, ME, MN, MO, NC, ND, NE, NH, NM, NV, NY, OH, OR, PA, SC, TN, TX, VA, WA, WI, WV, and WY.

Directions: From I-64, take Exit 120 and turn onto Fifth Street Southwest, which eventually becomes Old Lynchburg Road. Continue on Old Lynchburg Road for about 7.5 miles. Turn right onto Walnut Branch Lane (narrow, portions unpaved) and drive 1.5 miles to the winery.

❧

TASTING ROOM ETIQUETTE

Visiting wineries and trying their wines can be a pleasant and enjoyable way to spend an afternoon. If you have never before gone to a tasting room, here are a few suggestions to help make your visit a fun experience for all:

1. Bring your I.D. along, especially if you are under forty. You'll need to prove you're old enough to consume alcohol.

2. If the tasting bar is crowded, don't force your way in. Make eye contact with the pourer to make sure you've been spotted, then wait. And if you're at the tasting bar and see new arrivals, make space for them if possible.

3. By all means, ask questions about the wine or chat with your tasting bar neighbors, but try to do so at a lower decibel level. And wearing perfumes or colognes can make it hard to really detect the aroma of a wine.

4. Wines are tasted in a particular order. The usual progression is sparkling to still, white to red, and dry to sweet. Dessert wines will always be served last, with fortified wines (if available) closing out the tasting.

5. Skip a wine by placing your hand over the top of the glass. And if you don't like a wine, pour it into the dump bucket without comment, especially negative remarks. After all, the winery owner may be standing right there!

6. Even small pours add up to a lot of wine. Consider this: ten wines on a tasting list, with half-ounce pours for each, will add up to five ounces or one full glass of wine. Pace yourself. Even better, have a designated driver.

7. Keep in mind that many wineries do not deduct the tasting fee when you purchase a bottle or more of wine. If the one you're visiting does, great; if not, accept it and move on.

8. Most important of all, remember to enjoy yourself! Trying different wines is the best way to figure out the kinds of wines you like best.

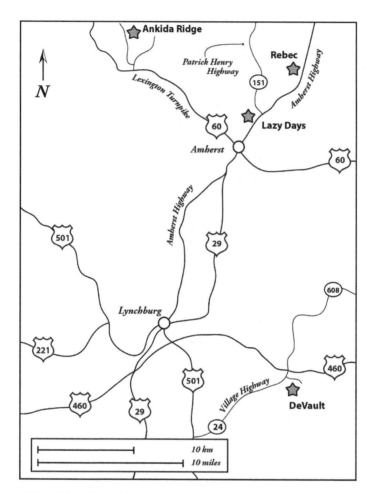

Map 7.12. Lynchburg

LYNCHBURG

Ankida Ridge Vineyards
1304 Franklin Creek Road
Amherst VA 24521

Hours: Sa 1:00–5:00 (spring–fall)
Closed New Year's, Christmas

434-922-7678
www.ankidaridge.com
E-mail: contact@ankidaridge.com

Named for a ancient Sumerian word that means "where the heavens and earth meet," Ankida Ridge Vineyards was founded by Dennis and Christine Vrooman on a mountainside property that reaches 1,800 feet in elevation. Christine serves as the vineyard manager, while son Nathan and daughter-in-law Rachel Stinson Vrooman are the winemakers. In addition to estate-grown Pinot Noir and Chardonnay, Nathan also produces wines under the Rockgarden label using grapes from nearby vineyards. Ankida Ridge sponsors quarterly events (in lieu of first Sunday hours) to celebrate the seasons, including occasional wine tastings.

White Wines: Ankida Ridge Chardonnay, Rockgarden Vert.

Red Wines: Ankida Ridge Pinot Noir, Rockgarden Rouge.

Sweet/Dessert Wines: Rockgarden Vin Doux.

Price Range: $18–$45

Tastings: $10 per person.

Purchasing: Online via VinoShipper to AK, AL, AZ, CA, CO, DC, FL, GA, HI, IA, ID, IL, IN, KS, LA, MA, MD, ME, MO, NC, ND, NE, NH, NM, NV, NY, OH, OR, PA, SC, TN, TX, WA, WI, WV, and WY.

Directions: From Amherst, take U.S. Route 60 West for about 9 miles. Turn right onto Mount Pleasant Road (VA 631). Take the first left onto Franklin Creek Road just after the Liberty gas station and drive 3 miles. Past the sign indicating the end of state maintenance, drive through the gate and continue 0.2 miles to the gray winery building on the left.

❖ ❖ ❖

DeVault Family Vineyards
247 Station Lane
Concord VA 24538

Hours: W–Sa 11:00–5:00 (Apr–Dec),   434-993-0722
Sa only 11:00–5:00 (Jan–Mar)   www.devaultvineyards.com
Closed January, Thanksgiving, Christmas   E-mail: devaultvineyards@hotmail.com

Terry and Sharon DeVault established their boutique winery on a thirty-two-acre farm midway between Appomattox Court House and Lynchburg, with the wood-panelled tasting room housed in a restored barn. The winery sponsors an annual holiday open house in December as well as live music and special events throughout the year. In addition to wine tastings, DeVault offers visitors a tennis court, basketball goal, stocked fishing pond, and an indoor pool. The facilities, including the pool, may be rented for parties and weddings. Children and pets are welcome.

Fruit Wines: Old Time Watermelon.

White Wines: Sweet Autumn Mist, Virginia Niagara.

Blush Wines: Lover's Blush.

Red Wines: Darien's Reserve *(Norton)*, Mr. D's Blend, Norton.

Price Range: $15–$24

Tastings: $5 per person.

Wheelchair accessible.

Purchasing: Online via VinoShipper for AK, AL, AZ, CA, CO, DC, FL, GA, IA, ID, IL, KS, LA, MA, MD, ME, MN, MO, NC, ND, NE, NH, NM, NV, NY, OH, OR, SC, TN, TX, VA, WA, WI, WV, and WY.

Directions: From Lynchburg, take U.S. Route 460 East for 10 miles and turn right onto Village Highway (Route 24). Take the second left onto Station Lane (Route 741). Drive ⅓ mile and bear right to stay on Station Road. The winery entrance will be 0.2 miles on the right.

❖ ❖ ❖

Lazy Days Winery
1351 North Amherst Highway
Amherst VA 24521

Hours: W–Su, 11:00–5:00
Closed New Year's, Thanksgiving, Christmas

434-381-6088
www.lazydayswinery.com
E-mail: events@lazydayswinery.com

Bill and Marianne Fitzhugh established Lazy Days in 2007 when they planted the first vines in their three-acre vineyard; the winery opened to the public in 2010. The tasting room is a renovated livestock pavilion, which offers views of the vineyard from its covered patio. Visitors are welcome to bring a picnic lunch to enjoy on the grounds. Lazy Days sponsors several special events throughout the year, including a summer solstice festival and live music on select weekends. The facilities are available for private events and weddings. Children and pets are welcome.

Fruit Wines: Bill's Wild Blackberry, Sweet Peaches.

White Wines: Capuchin White *(Petit Manseng)*, Chardonnay, Sweet Lazy Days White.

Rosé Wines: Rosé.

Red Wines: Cabernet Sauvignon, Malbec, Merlot, Petit Verdot, Vintner's Reserve.

Sweet/Dessert Wines: Sweet Lazy Days Red, Sweet Nights.

Price Range: $18–$42

Directions: From Lynchburg, take U.S. Route 29 North and drive 5 miles in the direction of Charlottesville. Make a U-turn at the intersection with Route 151 North to circle back onto U.S. Route 29 South. The winery will be on the right.

❖ ❖ ❖

Rebec Vineyards
2229 North Amherst Highway
Amherst VA 24521

Hours: Daily 10:00–5:00
Closed New Year's, Thanksgiving, Christmas

434-946-5168
www.rebecwinery.com
E-mail: winery@rebecwinery.com

Richard and Lynn Hanson founded Rebec on their seventy-acre farm at the edge of the Blue Ridge and began selling wines to the public in 1988. The winery was designed and built by Richard and son-in-law Mark Magruder, who used wood salvaged from old outbuildings on the property, including a two-hundred-year-old tobacco barn. Rebec is now owned by its longstanding winemaker Svetlozar Kanev who makes a Bulgarian-style herbal sweet wine, Sweet Sofia, in honor of his home country. Visitors are welcome to picnic on the grounds or sit on the deck behind the tasting room. On the second weekend in October, Rebec hosts the annual Virginia Wine and Garlic Festival. The winery also sponsors a Summer Cooler festival (proceeds are donated to the American Cancer Society) and Third Thursday live music performances. Children and pets are welcome.

Fruit Wines: Cherry, Pear.

White Wines: Chardonnay, Gewurztraminer, Landmark White, Pinot Grigio, Riesling, Viognier.

Rosé Wines: Sweet Briar Rose.

Red Wines: Cabernet Franc, Cabernet Sauvignon, Landmark, Merlot, Pinot Noir.

Sweet/Dessert Wines: Autumn Glow, Landmark, Sweet Sofia.

Price Range: $12–$23

Tastings: $7 per person.

Groups: Please call ahead for groups of 8 or more.

Purchasing: Online ordering to many states; contact winery for details.

Directions: From I-64, take Exit 118 onto U.S. Route 29 South and drive 40.3 miles to the winery entrance on the right. From the town of Amherst, drive 5 miles north on U.S. Route 29 to the winery on the left.

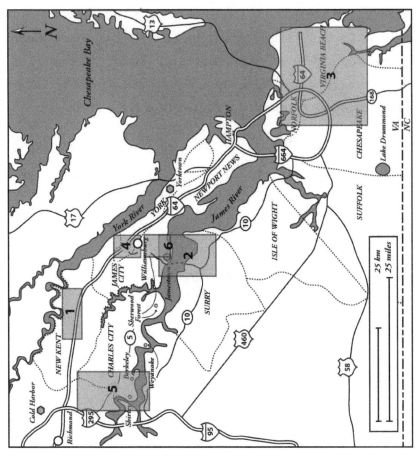

Map 8.1. Hampton Roads Region: (1) New Kent;
(2) Hampton Roads Winery; (3) Norfolk-Virginia Beach; (4) Silver
Hand; (5) Upper Shirley; (6) Williamsburg Winery

8. HAMPTON ROADS REGION

Located in the Tidewater of Virginia, this region is one of gentle, low hills and terrain crisscrossed with small creeks that flow into the James and York Rivers. The climate on the Virginia Peninsula and southeastern Virginia is the warmest in the state. Summers are hot and humid, while temperatures rarely dip below freezing in the winter. Soils in the region range from rich and loamy to downright swampy; indeed, the region is home to the Great Dismal Swamp which straddles the Virginia-North Carolina line. It also is the site of Lake Drummond, one of Virginia's only two natural lakes.

❖ ❖ ❖

Things to see and do: Virginia's Hampton Roads Region is, in many ways, the heart of historic Virginia. It was here that English colonists first settled in 1607 at Jamestown and, after a shaky start, gradually began expanding their presence further into Virginia. This is also where Virginia's four original counties as an English colony were established in 1617: Henrico, James City, Bermuda Hundred, and Kecoughtan (the latter two no longer exist). Williamsburg was the colonial capital of Virginia from 1704 until 1799 and is just northwest of the site of the decisive Revolutionary War battle at Yorktown, where American forces defeated British troops and won America's struggle for independence.

Just across the James River from Williamsburg and Jamestown is Bacon's Castle, built in 1665 by Arthur Allen. The property is best known for its role in Bacon's Rebellion, a 1676 uprising led by Nathaniel Bacon against Royal Governor William Berkeley.

The John Tyler Memorial Highway (Route 5) is a scenic road that winds along the James River from Williamsburg to Richmond. There are a number of historic homes along its path for visitors to explore, including President John Tyler's Sherwood Forest, the Harrison family's Berkeley Plantation, and the Carter family's Shirley Plantation. More details are available at the James River Plantation website (http://www.jamesriverplantations.org).

Civil War history abounds here as well. McClellan's peninsula campaign of 1862 started at Fort Monroe, at the tip of Hampton Roads, and the army moved up the peninsula toward Richmond, where the Seven Days' Battles occurred. In 1864, General Ulysses Grant moved down from Spotsylvania in pursuit of General Robert E. Lee. The battlefield at Cold Harbor, where Grant's army launched a headlong assault on Lee's fortified position, offers a vivid and moving glimpse into what soldiers faced on the field of war. Grant then moved his army across the James at Weyanoke, starting the final campaign that ultimately ended in Lee's surrender at Appomattox Court House in 1865.

Visitors may also explore the numerous black history sites in the area. Hampton University's museum is the oldest African-American museum in the United States, featuring art and artifacts from Africa and of Native American origins. The Virginia War Museum, the Casemate Museum at Fort Monroe, and the Virginia Air & Space Center all include exhibits on the role of black Americans in the history of our country.

Nature lovers and biking enthusiasts will enjoy the Virginia Capital Trail, a 52-mile-long paved jogging and biking trail stretching from Richmond to Williamsburg alongside Route 5. The interactive trail map includes key features, including restaurants, bike rental and repair facilities, lodging, convenience stores, and picnic areas; see the website at http://virginiacapi-taltrail.org for more details.

The Virginia Beach-Hampton Roads area offers numerous attractions for visitors, including the Virginia Aquarium and Marine Science Center, the Mariner's Museum, and Nauticus. Those interested in spending time on the beach and boardwalk will find ample opportunity for food and fun at Virginia Beach.

❖ ❖ ❖

<u>Wine Trails</u>: The wineries in the Hampton Roads Region are included in the Williamsburg Tasting Trail which focuses on wineries, breweries, and a meadery in and around Williamsburg See the Appendix for more details.

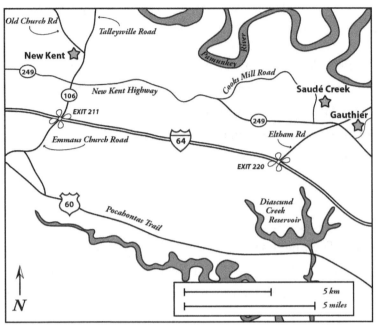

Map 8.2. New Kent

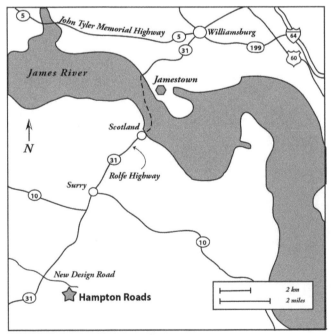

Map 8.3. Hampton Roads Winery

HAMPTON ROADS

Gauthier Vineyard
5000 Farmers Drive
Barhamsville VA 23011

Hours: F 4:00–8:00, Sa–Su 11:00–5:00 (6:00 in summer)   757-634-7527
Closed New Year's, Easter, Christmas   www.gauthiervineyard.com
E-mail: sandigauthier@aol.com

Maurice ("Mo") and Sandi Gauthier were inspired to start their own vineyard after visiting Cave Ridge Winery in the Shenandoah Valley. Working under the mentorship of Cave Ridge's owner Randy Phillips, the Gauthiers planted their first vines in 2012 on the 110-acre farm that they purchased after retiring from the Navy. After sampling their Virginia-grown wines, visitors are welcome to linger inside the tasting room or outside on the wraparound veranda overlooking the winery pond. Gauthier Vineyards sponsors occasional live music on weekends as well as charitable events to benefit first responders and wounded warriors. There is a 15% discount on purchases for active-duty or retired military.

White Wines: Chardonnay, Riesling, Traminette, Viognier.

Red Wines: Brick House Red, Cabernet Franc, Chambourcin, Petit Verdot.

Fortified Wines: Lafayette's Reserve, Rochambeau's Starboard.

Price Range: $18–$30

Tastings: $10 per person, $12 for reserve, both with souvenir glass.

Groups: Reservations requested for groups of 8 or more.

Directions: From I-64 East, take Exit 220 and turn onto Eltham Road (Route 33 East). Drive 3 miles and turn right onto New Kent Highway (VA 249/VA 30). Drive 3.4 miles and turn left onto Farmers Drive (VA 273). Continue 0.8 miles to the winery entrance on the left.

❖ ❖ ❖

Hampton Roads Winery
6074 New Design Road
Elberon VA 23846

Hours: Daily 12:00–6:00 (May–Dec)   757-899-0203
Th–M 12:00–6:00 (Jan–Apr)   www.hamptonroadswinery.com
Closed New Year's, Easter, Thanksgiving, Christmas

Hampton Roads is the dream project of David and Diane Shelton who opened their winery on the grounds of a lovely 1898 house just south of the James River. The large tasting room, built in the style of a horse barn, features a gift shop and, just outside, a paved patio and a goat tower for baby goats, inspired by the goat towers they saw during a trip to Portugal. Hampton Roads offers yoga classes in summer and live music on weekends. The facilities are available for rental for private parties and events.

White Wines: Chardonnay, Seyval Blanc, Simply Seyval, White Oak White.

Red Wines: Cabernet Franc, Petit Verdot.

Sweet/Dessert Wines: Hog Island Sweet Red, Hog Island Sweet White.

Price Range: $18–$24

Tastings: $7 per person with souvenir glass.

Groups: Reservations requested for groups of 8 or more.

Purchasing: Online via VinoShipper to AL, AK, DC, FL, ID, IL, LA, MN, MO, ND, NE, NH, NM, NV, OH, OR, VA, WV, and WY.

Directions: From Williamsburg, cross the James River on the Jamestown-Scotland free ferry. After landing, continue straight on Rolfe Highway (VA 31 South) for 10 miles. At the hamlet of Elberon, turn left at the Dendron Fire Department onto New Design Road. The winery's gravel drive will be 0.4 miles on the right.

❖ ❖ ❖

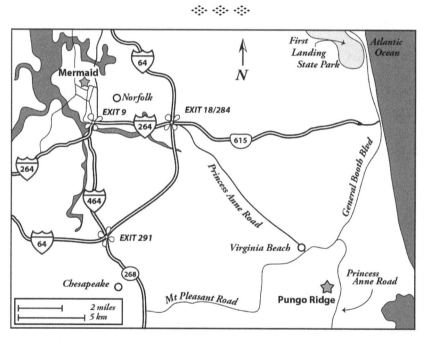

Map 8.4. Norfolk-Virginia Beach

Mermaid Winery
330 West 22nd Street, #106
Norfolk VA 23517

Hours: Su–Th 11:00–11:00, F–Sa 11:00–midnight
Closed Thanksgiving, Christmas, New Year's

757-233-4155
www.mermaidwinery.com
E-mail: info@mermaidwinery.com

Mermaid Winery is owned by Jennifer Doumar, who opened her urban winery in 2012 in Norfolk's Ghent neighborhood. The wines are currently made by Dean Gruenburg and are sourced from vineyards in Virginia as well as from other regions. The winery hosts various events, including wine pairing dinners, and offers eleven other tasting flights of wines in addition to its own production. Mermaid offers appetizers and light dishes to enjoy, as well as a list of over 450 different wines from around the world.

Fruit Wines: My Beach Peach *(Viognier, peach),* Riverview Raspberry *(Zinfandel, raspberry).*

White Wines: Chardonnay, Siren's White.

Red Wines: Cabernet Franc, Cabernet Sauvignon, Malbec, Merlot, Norfolk Express Red, Pinot Noir.

Price Range: $20–$40

Tastings: $6.50 per person.

Groups: Reservations required for groups of 10 or more.

Wheelchair accessible.

Purchasing: Online for CA, DC, MD, NC, and VA.

Directions: From I-264, take Exit 9 (Waterside Drive/St. Paul's Boulevard) onto St. Paul's Boulevard (U.S. Route 460 Alt East). Drive 1.5 miles and turn left onto East Princess Anne Road. Take the third right onto Llewellyn Avenue. After ½ mile, turn left onto 22nd Avenue. The winery is ¾ mile on the right at the Palace Station Shops.

❖ ❖ ❖

New Kent Winery
8400 Old Church Road
New Kent VA 23124

Hours: Daily 10:00–5:00 (6:00 in summer)
Closed New Year's, Thanksgiving, Christmas

1-804-932-8240
www.newkentwinery.com
E-mail: info@newkentwinery.com

New Kent Winery opened in 2008 on the grounds of the Viniterra residential community just east of Richmond. Winemaker Tom Payette oversees the production of New Kent's mostly estate-grown wines at the 17,000-square-foot winery, which is owned by the Dombroski family. After tasting, visitors are welcome to stay for light snacks and wine either in the two-story tasting room or on one of the shaded patios with views of the vineyards. The winery sponsors a range of special events and may be rented for private parties and weddings.

White Wines: Chardonnay, Vidal Blanc.

Rosé Wines: White Merlot, White Norton.

Red Wines: Merlot, Meritage, Norton.

Sweet/Dessert Wines: Sweet Virginia.

Price Range: $20–$42

Tastings: $10 per person.

Groups: Reservations required for groups of 10 or more.

Wheelchair accessible.

Purchasing: Online ordering for many states; check the website for details.

Directions: From I-64, take Exit 211 (Talleysville/Roxbury) north onto Emmaus Church Road (VA 106 North). At the third roundabout, take the second exit onto Old Church Road. The winery will be ⅓ mile on the left.

⋄ ⋄ ⋄

Pungo Ridge Winery
1665 Princess Anne Road
Virginia Beach VA 23456

Hours: F–Su 12:00–4:30 (Jun–Nov)
Closed Dec–May

757-426-1665
www.pungoridgewinery.com
E-mail: fred@fredhavens.com

Photographer Fred Havens opened Pungo Ridge Winery in 2011 after making blackberry wine as a hobby for some years. Fred runs the winery with brother Eugene and produces his wines using much of the Havens' own fruit grown on their five-acre farm in the Pungo region of Virginia Beach with the balance coming from other Virginia farms. In addition to sampling Pungo Ridge wines in the tasting room in the family home, visitors may be able to get a guided tour of the small production building where Fred makes, bottles, and labels his true-to-the-fruit wines.

Fruit Wines: Apple, Blackberry, Blueberry, Blueberry-Honey, Chocolate-Blueberry, Mint-Honey, Muscadine, Pear, Plum, Pumpkin, Strawberry, Tomato.

Meads: Clove Mead.

Price Range: $21–$32

Tastings: $7 per person.

Directions: From I-64, take Exit 286B onto Indian River Road East. Continue following Indian River Road for 12.5 miles and turn right onto Princess Anne Road (VA 615). Drive ¾ mile to the winery on the right.

❖ ❖ ❖

Saudé Creek Vineyards
16230 Cooks Mill Road
Lanexa VA 23089

Hours: W–M 11:00–6:00 (F to 9:00) (summer)
W–M 11:00–5:00 (winter)
Closed New Year's, Thanksgiving, Christmas

804-966-5896
www.saudecreek.com
E-mail: info@saudecreek.com

Jason Knight and John Britt opened Saudé [*SAW-dee*] Creek Vineyards in 2011 after selling their wines for several years at wine festivals and other events. The winery is located on the grounds of Frank's Tavern, a colonial-era inn (now no longer standing) that counted George Washington and French General Rochambeau among its clientele; the winery's name is from a creek that ran behind the Alabama home of Jason's grandmother. The wines are all from Virginia-grown fruit, much of it from the owners' forty-acre vineyard in Halifax County. Saudé Creek offers ample seating indoors in its spacious two-story tasting room as well as outside on the decks and covered porches, which provide a scenic view of the grounds and the Pamunkey River. The facilities are available for private parties or events, with several outdoor areas ideal for weddings.

Fruit Wines: Saudé Creek White.

White Wines: Chardonnay, Pamunkey Fall, Riesling, Tavern White, Traminette, Vidal Blanc, Viognier.

Rosé Wines: Squire's Blend *(Chambourcin, Muscadine).*

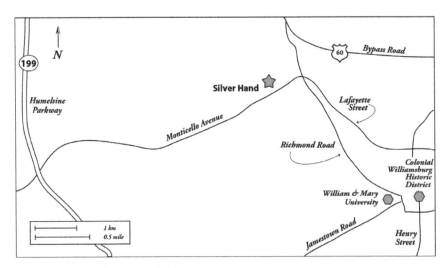

Map 8.5. Silver Hand Meadery

Red Wines: 1791, Barrel 76, Cabernet Franc, Meritage, Merlot, Saudé Creek Red, Sweet Rebellion, Syrah, Tavern Red.

Sweet/Dessert Wines: Sweet Rebellion, Traminette.

Price Range: $15–$35

Tastings: $10 per person, $17 for premium, both with souvenir glass.

Groups: Reservations required for groups of 8 or more, $17 per person fee.

Wheelchair accessible.

Directions: From I-64 East, take Exit 220 and turn onto Eltham Road (Route 33 East). Drive 2.9 miles and turn left onto New Kent Highway (Route 249). After a mile, turn right onto Cooks Mill Road (Route 623). The winery entrance will be on the right after another mile.

❖ ❖ ❖

Silver Hand Meadery
224 Monticello Avenue, Suite C
Williamsburg VA 23185

Hours: W–Th 1:00–6:00, F 1:00–8:00,
Sa 11:00–8:00, Su 1:00–5:00
Closed New Year's, Easter, Memorial Day,
Independence Day, Labor Day, Thanksgiving, Christmas

757-378-2225
www.silverhandmeadery.com
E-mail: info@silverhandmeadery.com

Glenn and Sherri Lavender decided to start a meadery inspired in part by Glenn's interest in the historical Celtic novels of Stephen Lawhead which frequently cited mead as a common drink. Indeed, the meadery's name comes from Lawhead's novel, *The Silver Hand*. Glenn uses honeys from Virginia and other states as well as a range of herbs and fruits in fermenting his meads, all of which have music-themed names in honor of his previous career as a musician in a band. Silver Hand also features honey tastings, including many of the honeys used to produce their meads. Please note, no sales by the glass are permitted except on eight Mead-Up weekends per year.

Meads: All Blues *(blueberry blossom honey, blueberries)*; Dream by the Fire *(apple cider, spices)*; Scarborough Fair *(star thistle honey, rosemary, thyme)*, Soak Up the Sun *(orange blossom honey)*, Strawberry Swing, Terres Brûlées *(bochet-style, cooked clover honey)*, Virginia Moon *(Virginia wildflower honey)*.

Price Range: $18–$24

Tastings: Complimentary for meads, $5 for honeys.

Groups: Reservations required for groups of 6 or more.

Purchasing: Online via VinoShipper to AK, AL, AZ, CA, CO, DC, FL, GA, HI, IA, ID, IL, IN, KS, LA, MA, MD, ME, MN, MO, NC, ND, NE, NH, NM, NV, NY, OH, OR, PA, SC, TN, TX, VA, WA, WI, WV, and WY.

Directions: From Richmond, take I-64 East to Exit 234 (Humelsine Parkway). Drive south for six miles and take the exit onto Monticello Road (VA 321 East). Continue two miles and turn left into the parking lot.

From Hampton Roads, take I-64 west to Exit 242 (Humelsine Parkway). Drive 1.4 miles and turn onto U.S. Route 60 West (Pocahontas Trail) which will become Lafayette Street. Drive four miles in all and cross Richmond Road. Turn right into the parking lot after 0.2 miles.

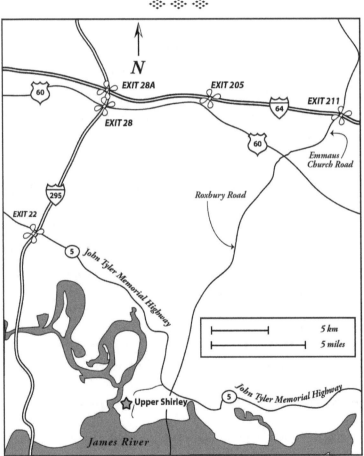

Map 8.6. Upper Shirley

Upper Shirley Vineyards
600 Shirley Plantation Road
Charles City VA 23030

Hours: W–M 11:00–5:00
Closed New Year's, Thanksgiving, Christmas

804-829-9463
www.uppershirley.com
E-mail: info@uppershirley.com

Tayloe and Suzy Dameron opened Upper Shirley Vineyards adjacent to the historic Shirley Plantation, high on the north bank of the James River. After sampling Upper Shirley's all Virginia-grown wines, guests may linger on the shaded front porch looking out onto the vines or on the wide back veranda offering sweeping views of the James River and the Presquile National Wildlife Refuge. The winery also includes an onsite restaurant providing seated service (indoors only) for lunch and dinner and featuring locavore dishes. Winemaking is by Michael Shaps (*Michael Shaps Wineworks*).

Sparkling Wines: Blanc de Blancs, Sparkling Rosé.

White Wines: #2 White Blend, Chardonnay, Sauvignon Blanc, Viognier.

Rosé Wines: Rosé.

Red Wines: #1 Red Wine Blend, Cabernet Franc, Petit Verdot, Tannat.

Price Range: $22–$65

Tastings: $10 per person.

Groups: Reservations requested for groups of 5 or more.

Wheelchair accessible.

Directions: From I-295 around Richmond, take Exit 22 onto John Tyler Highway (Route 5). Drive east toward Williamsburg for 10 miles and turn right onto Shirley Plantation Road. Drive 1.5 miles and turn left at the sign for Shirley Plantation. Continue to the winery's parking lot on the right.

❖ ❖ ❖

The Williamsburg Winery
5800 Wessex Hundred
Williamsburg VA 23185

Hours: M–Th 10:00–6:00, F–Su 11:30–6:30 (Apr–Oct)   757-229-0999
M–Th 11:30–4:30, F–Su 11:30–5:30 (Nov–Mar)   www.williamsburgwinery.com
Closed New Year's, Thanksgiving, Christmas   E-mail: wine@wmbgwine.com

Located just minutes from Colonial Williamsburg, Williamsburg Winery is one of Virginia's largest. Founded in 1985 by the Belgian Duffeler family, Williamsburg Winery produces sixty-thousand-plus cases per year from estate-grown fruit or from other Virginia and non-Virginia vineyards. All winemaking is under the guidance of winemaker Matthew Meyer, who trained in California. The winery offers guided tours and an onsite wine museum. Guests may dine at the Gabriel Archer Tavern or the Café Provençal located next to the winery itself. All the facilities are available for private parties, dinners, and weddings.

Williamsburg Winery also offers overnight stays at the twenty-eight-room Wedmore Place hotel on the winery grounds.

White Wines: Acte 12 Chardonnay, Chardonnay, Governor's White, James River White, John Adlum Chardonnay, Midsummer Night's White, Petit Manseng, Sauvignon Blanc, Vidal Blanc, Viognier.

Rosé Wines: Dry Rosé, Plantation Blush.

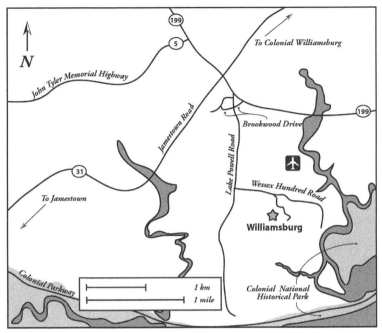

Map 8.7. Williamsburg Winery

Red Wines: Adagio, Cabernet Franc, Cabernet Sauvignon, Gabriel Archer Reserve, J. Andrewes Merlot, Mount Juliet Red, Susan Constant Red, Syrah, Trianon, Virginia Claret, Wessex Hundred Merlot, Wessex Hundred Petit Verdot.

Sweet/Dessert Wines: Licoreux de Framboise *(raspberry)*, Late Harvest Vidal.

Seasonal Wines: Settlers' Spiced Wine.

Price Range: $12–$72

Tastings: $8 per person, $15 for reserve tasting.

Groups: Reservations required for groups of 8 or more.

Wheelchair accessible.

Purchasing: Online purchasing for residents of AK, CA, CO, DC, FL, GA, IL, LA, ME, MD, MI, MN, MO, NH, NJ, NY, NC, OH, OR, SC, TX, VT, VA, and WI; some wines available only to VA residents.

Directions: **From I-64 Eastbound,** take Exit 234 onto Route 199 East and drive 8 miles. Turn right onto Brookwood Drive and make the first left onto Lake Powell Road (Route 617). Drive about 1 mile and turn left onto Wessex Hundred and the winery.

From I-64 Westbound, take Exit 242 onto Route 199 West. Drive 5 miles and turn left onto Brookwood. Turn left onto Brookwood Drive and make the first left onto Lake Powell Road (Route 617). Drive about 1 mile and turn left onto Wessex Hundred and the winery.

TASTING TIPS

Getting the most from what a wine has to offer is a truly sensory experience that fully engages your senses of sight, smell, and taste to appreciate the full range of characteristics of the wine in your glass. Wine tasting can be broken down into five simple steps:

1. Look at the color of the wine by tilting the glass slightly away from you and holding it above a white background. Notice the depth of color and, for reds, whether you can see your fingers through the wine or not. This may give a hint as to the richness or fullness of the wine.

2. Swirl the wine in the glass to help release the aromas.

3. Smell the wine, first about chin level and then by sticking your nose into the glass. Notice whether it is delicately scented or highly aromatic. Does it have a fruity or jammy aroma? Does it smell grassy or spicy? Does it have vanilla or oaky overtones? Is the aroma simple and straightforward, or is it complex, with several different smells?

4. Taste the wine by getting at least a couple of tablespoons of wine in your mouth. Hold it there for at least several seconds. Notice whether the wine is light or full-bodied. Is it sweet, tannic, crisp, or fruity? As with smell, is the taste simple and straightforward, or is it more complex, with different aspects to the flavor?

5. Reflect on the overall taste and balance of the wine, once you have swallowed it (or spit it out into a tasting bucket, if you're tasting many different wines). How long do the flavors last in your mouth? Does one flavor stand out or is the wine balanced? Does the taste seem to evolve and change?

While wineries include their own descriptions on tasting sheets, try not to be influenced by them. Rather, think about what the wine smells and tastes like to you, and jot down your own comments on the page.

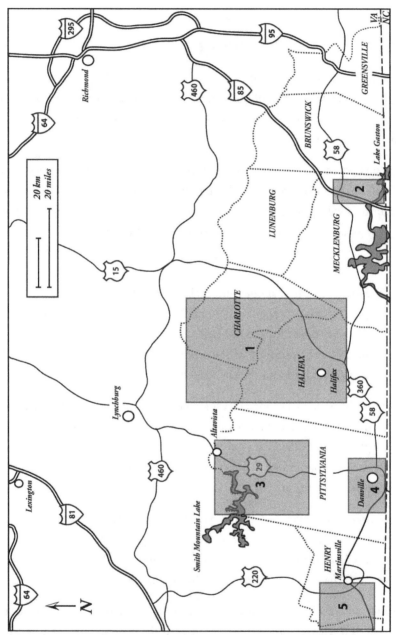

Map 9.1. South Virginia Region: (1) Halifax; (2) Rosemont;
(3) Danville-Alta Vista; (4) Danville City; (5) Martinsville.

9. SOUTHERN VIRGINIA REGION

Centered on the Virginia-North Carolina border, the Southern Virginia region is farm country, dotted with lakes, state parks, and small towns. Sometimes called the Southside of Virginia or Southern Piedmont, the area features a rolling landscape, a long growing season, and mild winters, with 43 inches of precipitation annually, the second highest in the state. The wineries in this region are all family-run farm wineries that offer guests a slower pace and a chance to explore sites that are a little off the beaten path.

<u>Things to see and do</u>: Many of the region's towns offer driving and walking tours that highlight historic homes and sites. Nature lovers will appreciate the Staunton River, a popular canoeing and tubing venue, and Lake Gaston's ample boating and sport fishing possibilities. History buffs may be interested in Red Hill, the home of Patrick Henry of "Give me liberty or give me death!" fame. Historic Noland Village near Nathalie is a restored mid-19th century village that recaptures life in rural Virginia.

The area is also home to a growing number of Old Order Amish families that began settling in the Nathalie area around 2005. Several have established several small businesses offering fresh-baked goods, furniture, and plants. Visitors may also encounter Amish horse-drawn buggies on roadways, so slow down and keep an eye open!

❖ ❖ ❖

<u>Winery Trails</u>: The SoVA Wine Trail includes most of the region's wineries.

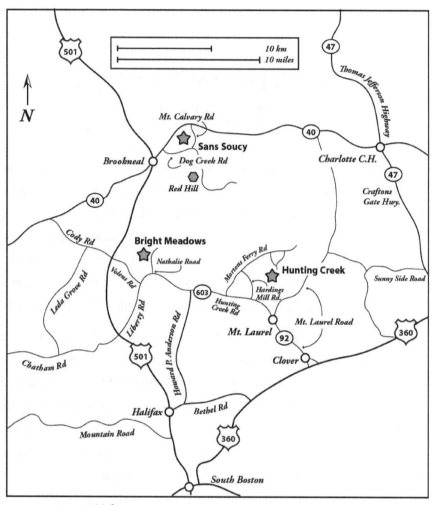

Map 9.2. Halifax

HALIFAX

Bright Meadows Farm Vineyard & Winery
1181 Nathalie Road
Nathalie VA 24577

Hours: W–Sa 11:00–6:00, Su 1:00–6:00 (Apr–Dec)   434-349-9463
Closed Jan–Mar, Thanksgiving, Christmas   www.brightmeadowsfarm
E-mail: BrightMeadowsFarm@yahoo.com

Boyd and Shirley Archer first opened their family-operated winery to the public in 2005. Located on the grounds of a nineteenth-century tobacco plantation, Bright Meadows' winery production facility and tasting room are in a restored 117-year-old barn. Visitors are welcome to enjoy the walking paths and picnic areas on the property after their tastings. The facilities are available for private parties and weddings. Children and pets are welcome.

Fruit Wines: Apple, BAG *(blackberry, apple, grape)*, Blackberry.

White Wines: Bright Leaf White, Bright Meadows White *(Niagara)*.

Rosé Wines: Sunrise Surrender.

Red Wines: Bright Meadows Red *(Concord)*, Burley Red *(Chambourcin)*, Dan River Noir *(Chambourcin)*, Halifax Red *(Concord)*, Rebellion Red *(Norton)*.

Price Range: $12–$17

Purchasing: To VA or via VinoShipper to AK, AL, CA, DC, FL, ID, IL, LA, MN, MO, NE, NV, NH, NM, NC, ND, OH, OR, WV, and WY.

Directions: From Halifax, take U.S. Route 360 East. Turn left onto Howard P. Anderson Road. Drive 8.7 miles and turn left onto Lennig Road (Route 603). Continue 3.7 miles and turn right onto Nathalie Road. The winery will be on the left in ¾ mile.

❖ ❖ ❖

Hunting Creek Vineyards
2000 Addie Williams Trail
Clover VA 24534

Hours: Sa 11:00–5:00 (mid-Apr–mid-Dec) (always call ahead)   434-454-9219
Closed Thanksgiving, mid-Dec–mid-Apr   www.hcvwines.com
E-mail: info@huntingcreekvineyards.com

Hunting Creek Vineyards is owned by Milt and Sandy McPherson, who started a three-acre vineyard in 2002 intending to sell grapes to others while keeping enough to make their own wine. Their son Jimmy serves as the winemaker. The tasting room is in a log cabin that offers seating both indoors and out, with works by local artists adorning its walls. Hunting Creek has an annual harvest party for volunteers who help harvest grapes. Always call ahead, especially on weekdays or the off-season to double-check that the tasting room is open. Children and leashed pets are welcome.

White Wines: Pure Luck *(Viognier).*

Red Wines: Decadence, Envy, Indulgence, Repentance, Temptation.

Other: Dare *(jalapeño).*

Price Range: $15

Purchasing: Online to CO, NC, and VA, and via VinoShipper to AK, DC, FL, ID, LA, MN, MO, NE, NV, NH, NM, ND, OH, OR, WV, and WY.

Directions: From U.S. Route 360, drive north on Moseley Ferry or Clover Road; they merge to become Main Street and then Mt. Laurel Road (Route 92). After 4 miles, turn left onto Hunting Creek Road (Route 603). Drive 2 miles and turn right onto Hardings Mill Road. Continue 2 miles and turn right again onto Mortons Ferry Road. Drive 3 miles and turn right onto Addie Williams Trail (portions unpaved). The winery is 1 mile on the right.

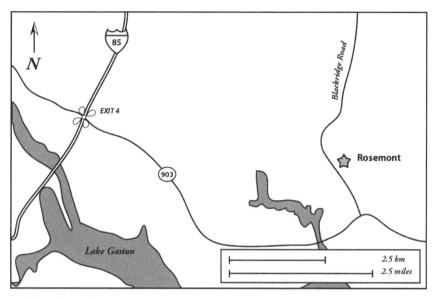

Map 9.3. Rosemont

❖ ❖ ❖

Rosemont Vineyards & Winery
1050 Blackridge Road
LaCrosse VA 23950

Hours: M–Sa 11:00–6:00, Su 1:00–6:00   434-636-9463

Closed New Year's, Thanksgiving, Christmas   www.rosemontofvirginia.com

E-mail: sales@rosemontofvirginia.com

Rosemont Vineyards & Winery is located on the 450-acre Rosemont Estate, a working farm that has been in the Rose family since 1858. The family first began planting the vineyard in 2003 and produced their first vintage five years later. All Rosemont's wines are from estate-grown fruit. The winery features special tasting menus on the weekends and also hosts an annual Harvest Festival, the Wine and Art Festival, and occasional live music and barbecues. Tours of the production area and barrel room are available. The winery may be rented for special events and weddings. Children and leashed pets are welcome.

White Wines: Pinot Grigio, Traminette, Vidal Blanc, Virginia White.

Rosé Wines: Rosé.

Red Wines: Cabernet Franc, Kilravock, Merlot, Syrah, Virginia Red.

Sweet/Dessert Wines: Blackridge Red, , Lake Country Sunset.

Fortified Wines: Milis Or, Tartan *(port-style)*.

Price Range: $14–$28

Tastings: $10 per person.

Groups: Reservations required for groups of 6 or more.

Purchasing: Online ordering for CA, DC, FL, MD, NC, and VA, and also via VinoShipper for AK, AL, CA, DC, FL, ID, IL, LA, MD, MN, MO, NC, ND, NE, NH, NM, NV, OH, OR, VA, WV, and WY.

Directions: From I-85, take Exit 4 (Bracey/Lake Gaston) onto Route 903 East. Drive about 7.5 miles and turn left onto Blackridge Road. The winery will be on the right after 1 mile.

❖ ❖ ❖

Sans Soucy Vineyards & Winery
1571 Mount Calvary Road
Brookneal VA 24528

Hours: M–Sa 11:00–5:00 (Mar–Dec);
Sa only 1:00–5:00 (Jan–Feb)
Closed Thanksgiving, Christmas

434-376-9463
www.sanssoucyvineyards.com
E-mail: tastingroom@sanssoucyvineyards.com

Owner-winemaker Paul Anctil and his wife, Jackie, started their winery in 2004 on a farm near Patrick Henry's Red Hill estate and Appomattox Court House. Paul oversees the 5.5-acre vineyard and wine production with son Paul. Sans Soucy's winery and tasting room are in a hundred-year-old barn with seating indoors as well as outdoors. Cheeses and sausages are available for purchase in the tasting room. Sans Soucy sponsors a monthly outdoor concert series, as well as Bark & Wine benefits for the All-American Mutt Rescue. The winery can be rented for private parties and weddings, and offers free Wi-Fi. Children and leashed dogs are welcome.

Fruit Wines: Blackberry, Oak N'Berry *(Petit Verdot, blackberry).*

White Wines: Chato-O White, Traminette, Viognier.

Red Wines: Cabernet Franc, Petit Verdot.

Sweet/Dessert Wines: Ginger.

Price Range: $17–$30

Tastings: $5 per person.

Groups: Reservations requested for groups of 8 or more for tastings and pairings.

Wheelchair accessible.

Purchasing: Online via VinoShipper for AK, AL, AZ, CA, CO, DC, FL, GA, IA, ID, IL, KS, LA, MA, MD, ME, MN, MO, NC, ND, NE, NH, NM, NV, NY, OH, OR, SC, TN, TX, VA, WA, WI, WV, and WY.

Directions: From U.S. Route 501, turn east in Brookneal onto Lynchburg Avenue (Route 40) which bends to the left and becomes Wickliffe Road. After about 1 mile, turn right onto Dog Creek Road and continue 2.3 miles. Make a left onto Mount Calvary Road. The winery will be ⅓ mile on the left.

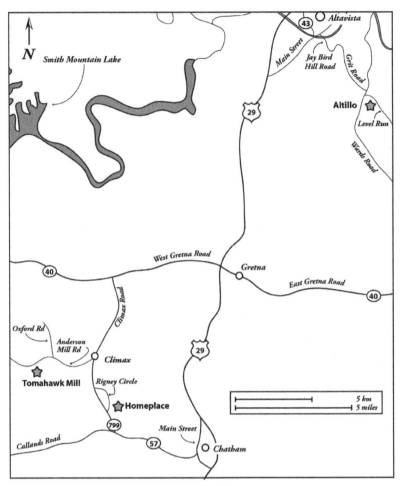

Map 9.4. Danville (Altavista section)

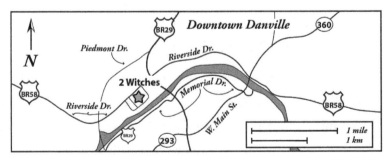

Map 9.5. Danville (Danville City)

DANVILLE

2 Witches Winery & Brewing
209 Trade Street
Danville VA 24541

Hours: Th, F 5:00–9:00, Sa 12:00–9:00, Su 1:00–6:00   434-549-2739
Closed New Year's, Thanksgiving, Christmas   www.2witcheswinebrew.com
E-mail: 2witcheswinery@gmail.com

Virginia's first collocated winery and brew pub, 2 Witches was started by Julie and Ethan Brown, who were inspired to open their combination winery and brewery after a visit to North Carolina. Their nearby vineyards are planted to Cabernet Sauvignon and Traminette, with three wines now on offer. Most of their production is currently in the form of various craft beers. 2 Witches also features hot food vendors, live music, and special events, including yoga classes.

Fruit Wines: 2 Witches Magic Apple.

White Wines: Traminette.

Red Wines: Cabernet Franc.

Tastings: $3 per person.

Directions: From U.S. Route 29 Business South, merge onto Riverside Drive (U.S. 58 Business West). Turn left onto Barter Street, then right onto Trade Street. The brewpub-winery will be on the left.

❖ ❖ ❖

Altillo Vineyards
620 Level Run Road
Hurt VA 24533

Hours: Sa 12:00–6:00
Closed New Year's, Christmas

434-324-4160
www.altillovineyards.com
E-mail: altillovineyards@yahoo.com

Altillo Winery is a small family-owned and operated vineyard that opened its doors to the public in 2010. Originally named Altavista, Altillo was launched by Bob and Eric Schenkel, who bought the property in 2000 and produced their first vintage in 2009. Altavista produces all Virginia-grown wine using both fruit from their own vineyards and from other nearby growers. The winery sponsors occasional live music and special events. Dogs are welcome.

White Wines: Chardonnay, Viognier, Vista Blanca.

Rosé Wines: Vista Rosa.

Red Wines: Cabernet Franc, Meritage, Shiraz.

Price Range: $15–$20

Tastings: $10 per person.

Directions: From U.S. Route 29, take the Route 43 exit onto Bedford Avenue into Altavista. Turn left onto Main Street (U.S. Route 29 Business) and take the third right onto Pittsylvania Avenue (Route 668) which becomes Ricky van Shelton Drive after crossing the Roanoke River, then Jay Bird Hill Road and finally Grit Road, driving 4 miles in all. Turn left onto Level Run Road. Continue about ½ mile to the winery entrance on the right.

❖ ❖ ❖

Hamlet Vineyards
405 Riverside Drive
Bassett VA 24055

Hours: Su 1:00–5:00
Closed New Year's, Easter, Christmas

276-629-2121
www.hamletvineyards.com
E-mail: va@hamletvineyards.com

Virginia and Butch Hamlet opened their winery on the grounds of Eltham Manor, their historic three-hundred-acre farm in the foothills of the Blue Ridge. They use Virginia-grown grapes for their wines, either from their own vines or from other vineyards in the state. Winemaking is done under the guidance of Michael Shaps Wineworks.

Sparkling Wines: VaVino *(Viognier).*

White Wines: Bottled Blonde, Pinot Gris, Viognier.

Rosé Wines: Cardinal Rosé.

Red Wines: Cabernet Sauvignon, Eltham (*Bordeaux-style blend*), Old Virginia Red, Petit Verdot.

Price Range: $17–$30

Directions: From Martinsville, take VA Route 57 north, turning onto North River Road after crossing the Smith River. Drive 2.9 miles to the winery driveway on the left.

❖ ❖ ❖

Homeplace Vineyard
568 Rigney Circle
Chatham VA 24531

Hours: M–Sa 11:00–5:00 (Mar–Nov)   434-432-9463 (WINE)
Closed Jan–Feb, Thanksgiving, Christmas   www.thehomeplacevineyard.com
E-mail: thehomeplacevineyard@yahoo.com

Joe and Brenda Williams established Homeplace Vineyard in 2005 on a farm that has been in the Williams family for four generations. After converting the tobacco fields into a vineyard, the couple began selling grapes to other wineries in the area before opening their own in 2010. The tasting room was built on the site of the original family homestead, using timbers from the old tobacco barns from the property. Homeplace sponsors Flip Flop Fridays in the summer that feature live music and sangria and wine tastings. The facility may be rented for weddings and private parties.

Fruit Wines: Cabin Sunset *(strawberry)*.

White Wines: Vidal Blanc, Viognier.

Red Wines: Cabernet Franc, Cabernet Sauvignon, Chambourcin.

Price Range: $10–$15

Tastings: $5 per person.

Directions: From Chatham, take Route 57 west for 4.5 miles. Turn right onto Climax Road (Route 799) and drive 1.4 miles. Turn right onto Rigney Circle and drive ½ mile. The winery entrance will be on the right.

❖ ❖ ❖

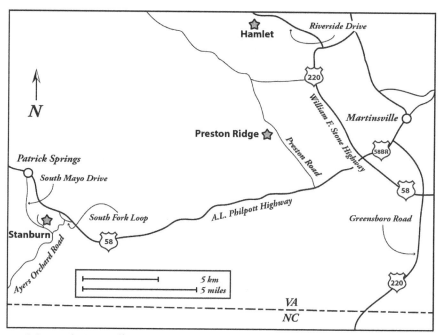

Map 9.6. Danville (Martinsville sections)

Preston Ridge Winery

4105 Preston Road

Martinsville VA 24112

Hours: Sa 10:00–6:00 (Apr–Sep);
Closed Oct–Mar

276-957-3844
www.prestonridgewinery.com
E-mail: PrestonRidge@comcast.net

Preston Ridge was established by Lawrence and Lois Penn, who opened their small winery to the public in March 2010. After spending several years honing his skills as a home winemaker, Lawrence decided to open a tasting room featuring wines made from locally grown fruit. Visitors may bring a picnic lunch to enjoy on the grounds. The winery gift shop includes a range of winemaking supplies for purchase.

Fruit Wines: Apple, Blueberry.

White Wines: Chardonnay, Riesling, Vidal Blanc.

Rosé Wines: Blushing Katie.

Red Wines: Cabernet Franc, Chambourcin, Rosie Ryan.

Price Range: $14–$16

Tastings: $5 per person.

Purchasing: Online ordering to many states; contact winery for details.

Directions: From Martinsville, take the A.L. Philpott Highway (U.S. Route 58 Business) south for about 5 miles. Turn right onto Preston Road and drive 4 miles. The winery driveway will be on the left.

❖ ❖ ❖

Stanburn Winery
158 Conner Drive
Stuart VA 24171

Hours: Sa 12:00–6:00, Su 1:00–5:00 (Apr–mid-Dec)
Closed mid-Dec–Mar

276-694-7074
www.stanburnwinery.com
E-mail: info@stanburnwinery.com

Nelson and Elsie Stanley began operations in 1999 when they planted a ten-acre vineyard on their hundred-acre property. After selling their grapes to other wineries for over a decade, they opted to open their own winery, whose name combines Stanley with Elsie's maiden name of Burnette. The family converted an old farmhouse on their Patrick County property to serve as a tasting facility. Stanburn offers live music and dancing on summertime Saturdays. Son David and daughter Dawn Stanley Osborne oversee the vineyards, working with winemaker Jocelyn Kuzelka.

White Wines: Chardonnay, Highfly, Meadow Breeze, Traminette, Vidal Blanc.

Blush Wines: Bull's Blush.

Red Wines: Barbera, Big A Red, Cabernet Franc, Chambourcin, Poorhouse.

Price Range: $12–$16

Tastings: $6 per person, with souvenir glass.

Purchasing: Online via VinoShipper to AK, AZ, CO, DC, FL, GA, HI, IA, ID, IL, IN, KS, LA, MA, MD, ME, MN, MO, NC, ND, NE, NH, NM, NV, NY, OH, OR, PA, SC, TN, TX, WA, WI, WV, and WY.

Directions: From U.S. Route 58, turn south onto the South Fork loop **and** then south again onto Ayers Orchard Road. Drive 2.2 miles and turn right onto South Mayo Drive. After ¾ mile, turn right onto Conner Drive. The winery entrance will be on the right.

❖ ❖ ❖

Tomahawk Mill Winery
9221 Anderson Mill Road
Chatham VA 24531

Hours: Tu–Sa 11:00–5:00, Su 1:00–5:00 (15 Mar–15 Dec)   434-432-1063
Closed Thanksgiving, 15 Dec–15 Mar   www.tomahawkmill.com
                                      E-mail: info@tomahawkmill.com

Tomahawk Mill is housed in a grist mill founded in 1888 by James Anderson and operated continuously by the same family until 1988, when they closed the mill and planted a vineyard. Now owned by Corky and Nancy Medaglia, Tomahawk Mill offers tastings in the restored mill; guests may also picnic on the grounds. Special events include a summer festival, Halloween in the Gristmill, and a Holiday Open House in December.

Fruit Wines: Apple.

White Wines: Chardonnay, Riesling, Vidal Blanc.

Blush Wines: Country Blush.

Red Wines: Sergeant Anderson's Red *(Concord)*, Tobacco Road Blues.

Sweet/Dessert Wines: Earl of Chatham Mead, Sweet Concord.

Price Range: $11–$20

Purchasing: Online for VA or via VinoShipper for AK, AL, CA, DC, FL, ID, IL, LA, MN, MO, NE, NV, NH, NM, NC, ND, OH, OR, WV, and WY.

Directions: From Chatham, turn west on Depot Street (Route 57) and drive 4.5 miles. Turn right onto Climax Road (Route 799) and drive 3.5 miles. Make a sharp left onto Anderson Mill Road (Route 649) and continue 3 miles to the winery on the left.

༯

SERVING TEMPERATURES

A commonly held rule of thumb is that sparkling, white, and rosé wines should be served chilled, while red wines are served at room temperature. But what do "chilled" and "room temperature" really mean? And how much does temperature really matter?

To test the effect of temperature on wine flavor for yourself, pour equal amounts of a white wine and a red wine into glasses, cover them with plastic wrap, and refrigerate the glasses for at least one hour. Have a friend blindfold you so that you cannot see the wine. Can you tell which is the red and which is the white?

According to many wine experts, the ideal serving temperatures for white and rosé wines range from about 45 to 55 degrees Fahrenheit, and reds from 50 to 65 degrees Fahrenheit. In general, that means whites and rosés are often served much too cold, while reds could be slightly cooler than they often are.

Colder serving temperatures tend to reduce the aroma of a wine, while warmer temperatures let it blossom. Cooler temperatures also tend to bring out the acidity and tannins in a wine, while warmer serving temperatures reduce them.

To test this, pour a glass of a tannic red, such as Cabernet Sauvignon, cover with plastic wrap, and let it chill in the refrigerator for an hour. You'll probably find that the chilled Cabernet is so astringent as to be barely drinkable. Let it warm to room temperature, however, and the tannins will soften.

Similarly, chilling a very fruity white wine will add crispness to balance out the fruit and give it better structure. Pour two glasses, cover both with plastic wrap, and put one in the refrigerator while leaving the other on the counter. After an hour, compare them. The colder wine will have a bit more acidic crispness to it.

For sparkling wines, serving temperature is also important. Colder temperatures help reduce the release of the carbon dioxide bubbles in sparkling wines, helping them keep their bubbliness longer.

༯

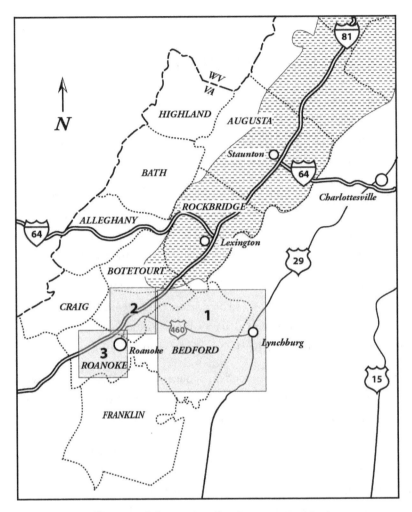

Map 10.1. Virginia Mountains Region (1) Bedford;
(2) Roanoke (north); (3) Roanoke (south).

10. VIRGINIA MOUNTAINS REGION

The Virginia Mountains Region is very rural and very mountainous. Craig and Alleghany Counties have but one traffic light between them, and Highland County is more alpine than southern, with the highest mean elevation of any county in the United States east of the Mississippi River. If you are looking to escape, this is a good place to go.

Things to see and do: This is an outdoor enthusiast's delight, with lakes and rivers, mountains and hiking trails at every turn. Near Roanoke, visitors can hike to McAfee Knob, featured in the 2015 film, *A Walk in the Woods*, Bill Bryson's humorous memoir of his hike along the Appalachian Trail. Other attractions include Franklin County, the "Moonshine Capital of the World," where visitors may sample Twin Creeks' Sweet Mash Corn, the first legal moonshine in the county since Prohibition.

It is also an area where history abounds. The Jefferson Pools in Bath date from the early 1800s and were named after President Thomas Jefferson who "took the waters" for his health there in 1818. Jefferson's retreat, Poplar Forest, is also nearby. More modern historical markers include the National D-Day Memorial at Bedford, the American town with the highest per capita losses at that pivotal event during World War II.

❖ ❖ ❖

Winery Trails: The region includes the Bedford County Wine Trail and the Wine Trail of Botetourt County. Please see Appendix I for details.

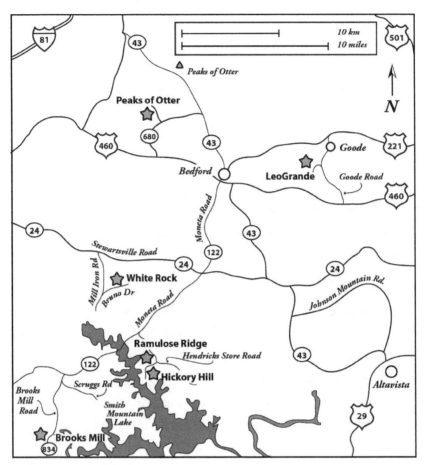

Map 10.2. Bedford

BEDFORD

Brooks Mill Winery
6221 Brooks Mill Road
Wirtz VA 24184

Hours: Th–M 11:00–5:00 (April–Labor Day)

Closed Sep–Mar, Easter

540-721-5215

www.brooksmillwine.com

E-mail: taste@brooksmillwine.com

H.T. and Rhonda Page started making fruit wine for family and friends over a dozen years before deciding to open to the public in 2008, first by appointment only and then on weekends. They offer their semi-dry to sweet wines in a tasting room housed in a converted garage on their property. With five acres of land, the Pages are able to grow their own blackberries, blueberries, and other fruit for their production, supplementing it as needed with produce from other Virginia farmers. Children and pets are welcome.

Fruit Wines: Black & Blue, Blackberry, Dry Blackberry, Blueberry, Cherry, Peach, Pear, Plum, Sweet Blackberry, Sweet Blueberry.

Price Range: $12–$14

Purchasing: Online via VinoShipper for AK, AL, CA, DC, FL, ID, IL, LA, MN, MO, NE, NV, NH, NM, NC, ND, OH, OR, VA, WV, and WY.

Directions: From Bedford, drive south for 20 miles on Moneta Road (VA 122), which will become Booker T. Washington Highway after crossing Smith Mountain Lake. Turn left onto Scruggs Road (VA 616) and drive 0.8 miles. Turn right onto Brooks Mill Road (VA 834). Drive another 4 miles to the winery entrance on the right.

❖ ❖ ❖

Hickory Hill Vineyards & Winery
1722 Hickory Cove Lane
Moneta VA 24121

Hours: W–Su 12:00–5:00 (Apr–Oct); 540-296-1393
Sa 12:00–5:00 (Nov–Mar) www.smlwine.com
Closed mid-Dec–mid-Jan E-mail: info@hickoryhillvineyards.com

Hickory Hill Vineyard was founded by Roger and Judy Furrow, long-time home winemakers who opened their renovated 1923 farmhouse to the public in 2001. Hickory Hill is located on scenic Smith Mountain Lake, best known for standing in for Lake Winnipesaukee in the 1991 movie, *What About Bob?* The winery does not sell food, but guests may bring their own picnics. Hickory Hill includes a small gift shop with crafts from local artisans and offers live music performances. Children and dogs are welcome.

White Wines: Chardonnay, Smith Mountain Lake Mist, Vidal Blanc.

Red Wines: Cabernet Franc, Cabernet Sauvignon, Merlot, Smith Mountain Lake Country Red.

Sweet/Dessert Wines: Smith Mountain Lake Redbud *(Chardonnay, Vidal Blanc, Merlot)*, Smith Mountain Lake Sunset *(Chardonnay)*, Sweet Red Sail *(Cabernet Franc, Cabernet Sauvignon)*.

Price Range: $10–$20

Groups: Reservations required for groups of 10 or more.

Wheelchair accessible.

Purchasing: Online for VA and via VinoShipper to AK, AL, CA, DC, ID, IL, LA, MN, MO, NE, NV, NH, NM, NC, ND, OH, OR, WV, and WY.

Directions: From U.S. Route 460, take Route 122 south onto Burks Hill Road. After 14.4 miles, turn left on Hendricks Store Road. Drive 2 miles and turn right on Hickory Cove Lane. The winery is 1 mile on the left.

❖ ❖ ❖

LeoGrande Vineyards & Winery
1343 Wingfield Drive
Goode VA 24556

Hours: W–Su 11:00–6:00 (Mar–Dec)   540-586-4066
Closed Jan–Feb,   www.facebook.com/leogrande-vineyard-and-winery.com
Thanksgiving, Christmas   E-mail: cmleogrande@gmail.com

Norman LeoGrande launched his small boutique winery on his four-hundred-acre working farm, where he also raises Black Angus cattle and American Saddlebred horses. A renovated farmhouse serves as the tasting room, which also includes a porch from which to appreciate the view of the winery's vines and a splendid view of the surrounding mountains. The winery dogs may be on hand to greet you, or you may spot them on patrol, walking through the vines. Nearly all LeoGrande's wines are estate-grown; as a small-lot producer, the specific wines available for tasting may vary greatly from month to month. Children and pets are welcome.

White Wines: Chardonnay, Roaring White *(Niagara, Sauvignon Blanc)*, Sauvignon Blanc.

Rosé Wines: Roaring Rosé.

Red Wines: Barbera, Nebbiolo, Roaring Red *(Sangiovese)*, Sangiovese, Syrah.

Sweet/Dessert Wines: Autumn Kiss *(Sangiovese, Barbera ice wine)*.

Price Range: $10–$25

Tastings: $4 per person with souvenir glass.

Groups: Please call ahead for groups of 6 or more.

Directions: From Lynchburg, take U.S. Route 221 South about 9 miles. Turn left onto Goode Station Road (Route 668) into the town of Goode.

331

Turn right onto Goode Road and drive 1.3 miles. Make another right onto Wingfield Drive. The winery will be on the right in ½ mile.

❖ ❖ ❖

Peaks of Otter Winery & Orchards
2122 Sheep Creek Road
Bedford VA 24523

Hours: Daily 12:00–5:00 (Apr–Dec),   540-586-3707
Sa–Su 12:00–5:00 (Jan–Mar)   www.peaksofotterwinery.com
Closed New Year's, Thanksgiving, Christmas   E-mail: appleseed@earthlink.net

Peaks of Otter Winery is owned and operated by Danny and Nancy Johnson, who opened the winery in 1995 on the grounds of their fifth-generation apple orchard. The winery offers its own jams, jellies, relishes, and sauces. Be sure to try the winery's pepper wines. Chili Dawg is paired with Cheez Whiz for tasting, while trying the winery's Kiss The Devil wine will earn an "I kissed the devil" sticker. Facebook fans receive a 5% discount on purchases. Children and dogs are welcome. A four-bedroom guest house, Elmo's Rest, is available for weekly rental.

Fruit Wines: Apple Blueridge, Apple Truffle, Blackberry Cobbler, Blackberry Jammed, Blueberry Muffin, Café Vino *(apple, coffee)*, Cherry Cheese Cake, Cinfulicious *(apple, cinnamon)*, Light Peach, Light Pear, Mango Tango, Mojo, Plumalicious, Puff *(apple, dragonfruit)*, Pumpkin Pie, Pure Passion, Ras Ma Tas Raspberry, Strawberry Shortcake, Sweetheart *(apple, pomegranate)*, Vino Colado, Virginia Apple Lovers Dry Apple.

Grape Wines: Blue Ridge Mountain Grape *(Concord)*, Frosty Morn, Sangria.

Other: Chili Dawg *(apple, chili pepper)*, Kiss The Devil *(30 chili peppers)*.

Price Range: $10–$25 ($30 for specialty bottles)

Wheelchair accessible.

Purchasing: Online via VinoShipper to AK, AL, AZ, CA, CO, DC, FL, GA, IA, ID, IL, IN, KS, LA, MA, MD, ME, MN, MO, NC, ND, NE, NH, NM, NV, NY, OH, OR, PA, SC, TN, TX, VA, WA, WI, WV, and WY.

Directions: From U.S. Route 460, go north onto Patterson Mill Road, which becomes Sheep Creek Road (Route 680). Drive 5.5 miles to winery entrance on left.

❖ ❖ ❖

Ramulose Ridge Vineyards
3061 Hendricks Store Road
Moneta VA 24121

Hours: Daily 1:00–6:00   540-314-2696
Closed New Year's, Thanksgiving, Christmas   www.ramuloseridgevineyards.com
                                                                      E-mail: ramuloseridge@msn.com

Jim and Sandy Ramaker drew on their long-standing interest in wine in founding Ramulose Ridge on the grounds of their 100-acre property near Smith Mountain Lake. Sandy serves as the winemaker for their Virginia-grown production. The tasting room offers ample seating indoors with a fireplace for winter warmth or outdoors on the partially covered patio which offers a view of the estate's vineyards. The facilities may be rented for private events and parties. Ramulose Ridge also offers cigars for sale in the tasting room, along with suggested wine pairings to go with them.

White Wines: Chardonel, Traminette, Vidal Blanc, Viognier.

Red Wines: Cabernet Franc, Chambourcin, Robusto, Syrah.

Sweet/Dessert Wines: Blackwater, Blush, Muscat, Sweetwater, Tendril.

Price Range: $12–$18

Directions: From U.S. Route 460 at Bedford, take Route 122 south onto Burks Hill Road (Route 122), which becomes Moneta Road. After 14.4 miles, turn left on Hendricks Store Road and drive 2 miles to the winery.

❖ ❖ ❖

White Rock Vineyards, Winery, & Brew Haus
2117 Bruno Drive
Goodview VA 24095

Hours: Th–M 12:00–5:00 (Apr–Nov)   540-890-3359
Closed Thanksgiving   www.whiterockwines.com
E-mail: whiterockwines@gmail.com

Fred and Drema Sylvester planted their first vines in 2000, opening to the public five years later. Their certified Virginia Green tasting room offers a covered veranda where visitors may sit and enjoy the view over White Rock's estate-grown wines. The winery sponsors festivals, including a West Virginia Heritage Festival in the fall and a Fork and Cork festival in the spring. White Rock also now includes a farm brewery on the premises with a range of craft beers made in the German and Belgian style.

White Wines: Chardonnay, Moon Glow, White Mojo.

Red Wines: Cabernet Franc, Scarlet Sunrise, Tangled Trio, Velvet Sky.

Price Range: $14–$22

Directions: From U.S. Route 460, take the Route 122 ramp at Bedford and turn south onto Burks Hill Road (Route 122), which becomes Moneta Road, and drive 7 miles. Turn right onto Stewartsville Road (Route 24) and drive 9 miles. Turn left onto Mill Iron Road (Route 653). After 2 miles, turn left on Bruno Drive. The winery is 1 mile on the left.

ॐॐ

WINE AROMAS

One of the most important elements of appreciating wine comes from the fragrance of the wine. Indeed, our sense of smell is so critical that we can perceive very little flavor from food or beverages without it.

Most wineries use tasting sheets to describe the aromas and tastes of the wines they present. These descriptions can be a helpful way to build our wine vocabulary, but it is important to also think about what the wine smells and tastes like to you. Each of us has distinct preferences in terms of smells and tastes; some people love green peas, for instance, while others loathe them. Wine is no different.

Wine aromas can be sorted into five broad clusters: fruit, floral, vegetal and spice, animal, and roasted.

Fruit aromas include citrus (orange or grapefruit, for instance), tropical (banana or pineapple), red berry (strawberry, raspberry), black berry (blackberry, blueberry, black currant), and stone fruit (apricot, peach). Floral tones include flowers (rose, violet), trees (hawthorn or linden), and even honey.

Vegetal and spice aromas encompass green pepper, earthy smells (mushroom or truffle), spicy tones (cedar or licorice), herbs (thyme, clove), and even vanilla. A wine may have a leathery or buttery smell; these, along with musk, are in the animal group. The roasted category includes toast, roasted nuts (hazelnut or almond), coffee, chocolate, and even smoke.

One way to build an aroma vocabulary is to start by identifying which broader category best categorizes the wine, then a subcategory, and finally a specific aroma. For example, if a wine smells fruity, think about whether that fruity aroma is a citrus or berry or stone fruit smell. Then decide which specific flavor you detect, such as peach or raspberry or pineapple. Over time, you'll develop a broader set of terms to describe the wines that you are tasting.

ॐॐ

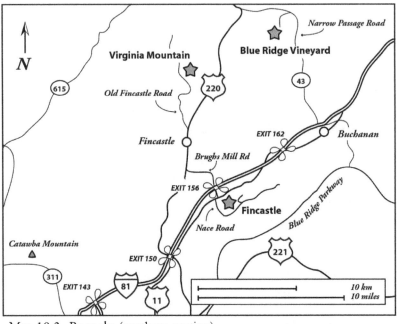

Map 10.3. Roanoke (northern section)

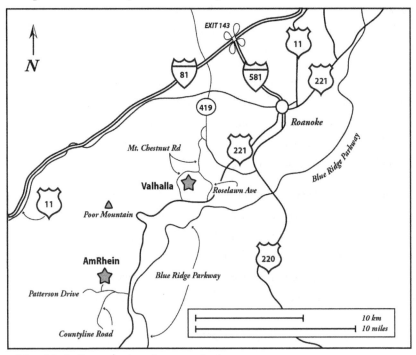

Map 10.4. Roanoke (southern section)

ROANOKE

AmRhein Wine Cellars
9243 Patterson Drive
Bent Mountain VA 24059

Hours: Th–M, 11:00–5:00 (May–Dec); F–Su 11:00–5:00 (Jan–Apr)   540-929-4632
Closed New Year's, Thanksgiving, Christmas   www.amrheins.com
E-mail: info@amrheins.com

Russ and Paula Amrhein have owned and operated AmRhein Wine Cellars since 1995, when they purchased forty acres on Bent Mountain. AmRhein's tasting room offers views of the surrounding hills and vineyards from the tables indoors and on the deck. Light fare is available for purchase, including wraps, cheese, and crackers; for special events, visitors may bring their own picnics. The winery hosts a range of special events, including live music on summer weekends, an annual Oktoberfest, and harvest soup weekends. Weather permitting, winemaker Steve Bolleter produces a true frozen-on-the-vine ice wine from the Vidal Blanc grapes in AmRhein's vineyards, which reach up to 2,500 feet in elevation. The winery is available for weddings and private events. Children are welcome.

Fruit Wines: Vin de Pêche *(peach)*.

White Wines: Chardonnay, Petit Manseng, Pinot Grigio, Traminette, Vidal Blanc.

Red Wines: Aglianico, Cabernet Franc, Cabernet Sauvignon, Chambourcin, Merlot, Petit Verdot.

Sweet/Dessert Wines: Ruby, Seduction.

Price Range: $14–$27

Groups: Reservations required for groups of 8 or more.

Directions: From Roanoke, take U.S. Route 221 South and drive 13.7 miles. Turn right onto Countyline Road and continue 1.2 miles. Bear right at the fork onto Patterson Drive. The winery will be ½ mile on the right.

❖ ❖ ❖

Blue Ridge Vineyard
1027 Shiloh Drive
Eagle Rock VA 24085

Hours: F–M 12:00–5:00 (Mar–Dec)   540-798-7642
Closed Thanksgiving, Christmas, Jan–Feb   www.blueridgevineyard.com
E-mail: wine@blueridgevineyard.com

Jim Holaday and Barbara Kolb first launched Blue Ridge Vineyard in 1985 and opened their winery to the public twenty-one years later. Their tasting room is housed in an old barn; in the summer and during special events, tasting tables are also set up outside. Visitors can appreciate the outstanding views of the Blue Ridge from the picnic tables or outdoor gazebo. The winery sponsors a number of live music events on weekends, ranging from bluegrass to rock to jazz, as well as special donations for the All-American Mutt Rescue. Soup 'n Sip Sundays offer live music, fresh breads, soups, and chili at no charge. Children and dogs are welcome.

White Wines: Big Bear White, Equinox, Gewurztraminer, Riesling, Traminette.

Red Wines: Big Bear Red, Cabernet Franc, Pinot Noir, Solstice, Sweet Shiloh.

Price Range: $14–$25

Wheelchair accessible.

Directions: From I-81, take Exit 162 toward Buchanan and turn onto U.S. Route 11 North. After 4.8 miles, turn left onto 1st Street (Route 43), which will become Narrow Passage Road, and drive for 11.4 miles. Turn left onto Shiloh Drive (portions unpaved). Winery will be on the left in 0.8 miles.

❖ ❖ ❖

Fincastle Vineyard & Winery
203 Maple Ridge Lane
Fincastle VA 24090

Hours: F–Sa, M 11:00–5:00, Su 1:00–5:00
Closed New Year's, Easter, Thanksgiving, Christmas

540-591-9000
www.fincastlewine.com
E-mail: info@fincastlewine.com

Fincastle Vineyard & Winery was first opened to the public in 2003 by David and Georgia Sawyer and their son Richard Classey. Fincastle is located on an eighty-acre farm that had formerly been an apple orchard and a tomato farm at various points before the family purchased the property in 1987. The tasting room is in a small stone building attached to the main farmhouse with a stone patio for guests. The winery building is built into a hillside to allow gravity-fed processing of Fincastle's mostly estate-grown wines. Fincastle sponsors several music festivals in the summer featuring local groups and musicians; guests are welcome to bring their own picnic food to enjoy on the grounds. Dogs are welcome.

The family's renovated 1926 farmhouse is also a bed & breakfast that is perfect for nature lovers who want to explore the hiking, canoeing, and other outdoor activities in the vicinity.

White Wines: Chardonnay, Hybrid Vigor, Traminette, Viognier.

Rosé Wines: Rosé *(Chambourcin, Vidal Blanc)*.

Red Wines: Cabernet Franc, Cabernet Sauvignon, Knight's Tour.

Sweet/Dessert Wines: Traminette.

Price Range: $12–$15

Groups: Reservations required for groups of 6 or more.

Purchasing: Online purchasing only for Virginia residents living within 25 miles of the winery, minimum one case.

Directions: From I-81, take Exit 156 (Troutville) east onto Brughs Mill Road (Route 640). Turn right in ½ mile onto Lee Highway (U.S. Route 11 South). After about ½ mile, turn left onto Nace Road (Route 640). Continue for 1.7 miles. Make a left onto Maple Ridge Lane (portions unpaved); the winery entrance will be on the left.

❖ ❖ ❖

Valhalla Vineyards
6500 Mt. Chestnut Road
Roanoke VA 24018

Hours: Sa 12:00–5:00, Su 1:00–5:00 (Apr–Oct)   540-725-9463
Sa only (12:00–5:00, Nov–Mar)   www.valhallawines.com
Closed New Year's, Easter, Christmas   E-mail: info@valhallawines.com

James and Debra Vascik established their winery and vineyard in 1994 on a two-thousand-foot mountain property overlooking the city of Roanoke. The two opera lovers named their winery after the home of the Norse gods made famous by German composer Richard Wagner. Their winemaking facility and barrel cave were built in 1996, with the barrel cave carved sixty feet underground into the mountainside. The "Cellar Door" tasting room was opened to the public in 2004 and features an arched paneled ceiling and a large stone tasting bar along one wall. Light snacks are available for purchase in the tasting room. In cooler weather, visitors can warm up next to the floor-to-ceiling stone fireplace inside the tasting room or can sit near the large outdoor fireplace on the patio. Valhalla offers winemaker dinners, wine education events, and live music in summers. The facility is available for weddings and private events.

White Wines: Rheingold Chardonnay, Viognier.

Red Wines: Alicante Bouschet, Cabernet Sauvignon, Cabernet/Shiraz, Cornucopia, Götterdämmerung *(Cabernet Franc, Merlot)*, Norton, Sangiovese, Syrah, Valkyrie *(Bordeaux-style blend)*.

Sweet/Dessert Wines: Late Harvest Alicante Bouschet.

Price Range: $15–$30.

Purchasing: Surface mail or fax ordering for VA only.

Directions: From Roanoke, drive south on I-581 until it ends. Exit onto Franklin Road and continue through seven stoplights. Then turn left onto Brambleton Road (U.S. Route 221 South). At the third traffic light, turn right onto Roselawn Road. Continue 2.3 miles and turn left onto Mt. Chestnut Road. The winery will be one mile on the left.

❖ ❖ ❖

Virginia Mountain Vineyards
4204 Old Fincastle Road
Fincastle VA 24090

Hours: W–Su 12:00–6:00 (mid-Mar–mid-Dec)   540-473-2979
Closed Thanksgiving, mid-Dec–mid-Mar   www.vmvines.com
                                          E-mail: info@vmvines.com

David and Marie Gibbs opened Virginia Mountain to the public in 2006 after several years of selling the grapes from their ten-acre vineyard to nearby wineries. The winery hosts monthly summer music evenings with local performers, "Wine, Moon, and Stars" evenings with the Roanoke Astronomy Club, and a Holiday Open House in December. The facility may be rented for private parties or weddings. Children and pets are welcome.

White Wines: Acacia Gold, Chardonnay, Traminette.

Rosé Wines: Rosé.

Red Wines: Cabernet Franc, Merlot, Petit Verdot, Trinity *(Bordeaux-style blend)*.

Sweet/Dessert Wines: Virginia White, Virginia Red, Strawberry Frost.

Price Range: $12–$20

Tastings: $3–$5 per person (amount varies depending on wines available for tasting).

Groups: Reservations required for groups of 8 or more.

Wheelchair accessible.

Purchasing: Online via VinoShipper for AK, AL, AZ, CA, CO, DC, FL, GA, HI, IA, ID, IL, IN, KS, LA, MA, MD, ME, MN, MO, NC, ND,

NE, NE, NH, NM, NV, NY, OH, OR, SC, TN, TX, VA, WA, WI, WV, and WY.

Directions: From I-81, take Exit 150 onto U.S. Route 220 West. Drive 10.7 miles and turn left onto Old Fincastle Road (Route 655) just past the town of Fincastle. The winery will be on the right in 4.3 miles.

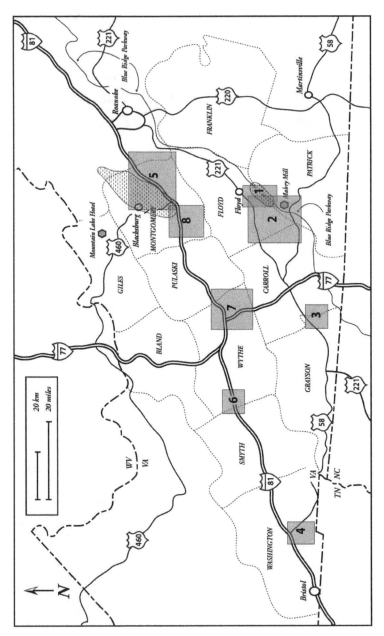

Map 11.1. Blue Ridge Region & Rocky Knob AVA: (1) Mabry Mill;
(2) Floyd; (3) Mt. Vale; (4) Abingdon; (5) Beliveau; (6) Rural Retreat;
(7) West Wind/Iron Heart; (8) Whitebarrel.

11. BLUE RIDGE & ROCKY KNOB AVA

The Blue Ridge Mountains stretch from Virginia's border with Maryland down into North Carolina. The Blue Ridge is the easternmost ridge of the Appalachian Mountain chain, and its southern stretches have some of the highest elevations in the United States east of the Rocky Mountains, with some peaks in North Carolina and Tennessee reaching over six thousand feet above sea level. As one would expect given the elevations, summer temperatures in the Blue Ridge wine region are cooler than elsewhere in the state. Along with the Heart of Appalachia region, this area has the highest precipitation in all Virginia, with just over forty-seven inches per year.

The Blue Ridge's wineries capture the full range of winery sizes and experiences in Virginia. From Chateau Morrisette's expansive grounds and on-site restaurant to the more intimate experiences at Blacksnake Meadery and Foggy Ridge Cider, the Blue Ridge offers something for every visitor's tastes and preferences. Two of its wineries—Chateau Morrisette and Villa Appalaccia—are in the Rocky Knob AVA, which is the smallest AVA in Virginia, while Beliveau Estate is in the North Fork of the Roanoke AVA.

❖ ❖ ❖

<u>Things to see and do</u>: Rich in natural beauty, the Blue Ridge area is perfect for nature lovers, offering multiple trails, camping sites, and fishing spots. The 469-mile Blue Ridge Parkway stretches from Waynesboro down into North Carolina; its northern extension, the Skyline Drive, meanders north-

ward to Front Royal. It is a lovely driving tour that is popular in summer for its access to outdoor activities and in the fall for its colorful foliage displays. The Parkway's website (www.blueridgeparkway.org) lists special events and programs, fishing and hiking information, and weather closures.

Mabry Mill in Floyd County at Blue Ridge Milepost (MP) 176 is one of the most picturesque and photographed structures in the area. In addition, there are several living history sites along the Parkway in the summer, including the mid-19th century Johnson Farm and Aunt Polly's Ordinary at MP 85 in the Peaks of Otter. The Blue Ridge region is also home to one of Virginia's only two natural lakes, Mountain Lake, whose size can vary considerably due to leakage from a natural crevice in the lake bottom. The Mountain Lake Conservancy Hotel was featured in the 1987 film *Dirty Dancing* and offers special *Dirty Dancing* weekends in the summer for guests.

The Blue Ridge Region is also home to the eastern and southern portions of the Crooked Road Heritage Trail, a scenic trail that winds from Rocky Mount to Floyd, then to Stuart, where it follows U.S. Route 58 westward through Abingdon and Bristol. The trail features numerous events and places highlighting the region's deep bluegrass music history and culture. Downloadable maps and other information can be accessed at www.thecrookedroad.org.

❖ ❖ ❖

<u>Wine Trails</u>: The Mountain Road Wine Experience covers seven wineries in the Blue Ridge and South Virginia regions. More details are included in Appendix 1.

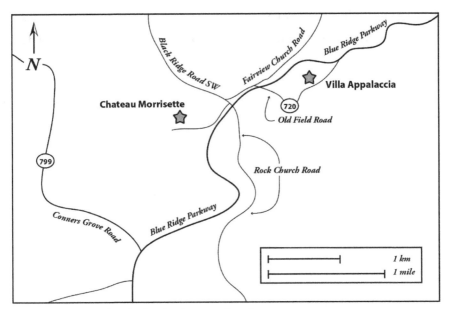

Map 11.2. Blue Ridge Parkway (Floyd)

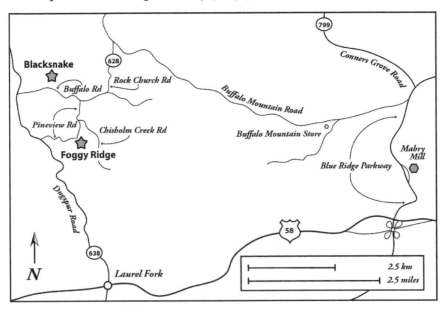

Map 11.3. Blue Ridge Parkway (Mabry Mill)

BLUE RIDGE PARKWAY

Blacksnake Meadery
605 Buffalo Road
Dugspur VA 24325

Hours: 11:00–5:00 Sa–Su (May–Nov, always call first to confirm)   540-834-6172
Closed Dec–Apr   www.blacksnakemead.com
E-mail: blacksnake@blacksnakemead.com

Teachers Steve and Joanne Villers started their meadery after spending several years making their own home brews. Honeybees on their Blue Ridge property now supply about half of the honey used in their production. Their meads include traditional mead as well as cyser (pressed apple cider and honey), melomel (mead with fruit), and hydromel (light mead). Blacksnake offers honey tastings and Thanksgiving and Holiday (December) open houses. Children are welcome.

Blacksnake's meads may also be sampled at The Hive, a satellite tasting room in Roanoke (1116A Main Street SW, Th–F, 5:00–8:00, Sa 1:00–8:00, Su 1:00–6:00).

Meads: Ginny Raz *(raspberry, honey)*, Meloluna, Summer Lea, Sweet Virginia, Wildflower Honey Wine.

Hydromel: Hoppy Bee Brew, Lime Bee Brew.

Price Range: $12–$18

Purchasing: Online via VinoShipper to Al, AK, AZ, CA, CO, DC, FL, GA, ID, IL, IN, IA, KS, LA, ME, MD, MA, MN, MO, NE, NV, NH, NM, NY, NC, ND, OH, OR, SC, TN, TX, VA, WA, WV, WI, and WY.

Directions: From the Blue Ridge Parkway, turn between Milepost 174 and 175 onto Buffalo Mountain Road (Route 628) and drive 7 miles, staying straight at the Buffalo Mountain Store. Turn left onto Rock Church Road. which becomes Buffalo Road at the Buffalo Presbyterian Church. Continue ½ mile and bear right to stay on Buffalo Road. Turn in 0.8 miles into the driveway on the right.

❖ ❖ ❖

Chateau Morrisette Winery
287 Winery Road SW
Floyd VA 24091

Hours: M–Th 10:00–5:00, F–Sa 10:00–6:00, Su 11:00–5:00   540-593-3647
Closed Thanksgiving Eve & Day, Christmas Eve & Day   www.thedogs.com
E-mail: info@thedogs.com

Chateau Morrisette was established in 1978 when the Morrisette family planted their first vines. Now selling well over sixty thousand cases of wine annually, the winery is one of the largest in Virginia, producing fifteen different wines from 150 acres of vineyards across Virginia as well as from grapes from other states. Winemaker Brian Cheeseborough joined the winery team in 2015 after working at wineries in California, France, and Argentina.

Chateau Morrisette sponsors live music, food and wine pairing dinners, and festivals. A portion of the proceeds from several special wine label series support various charities, such as a Virginia Tech scholarship fund, medical research into canine EPI disease, and Service Dogs of Virginia and St. Francis Service Dogs. Lunch and dinner are available at the winery restaurant. The facilities may also be rented for private parties and weddings. Children and leashed pets are welcome.

Fruit Wines: Apple, Blackberry, Cherry, Sangria.

White Wines: 4 White Grapes, Chardonnay, Nouveau Chien, Our Dog Blue, Petit Manseng, Vidal Blanc, Viognier.

Rosé Wines: Vin Gris.

Red Wines: 5 Red Grapes, Archival, Black Dog, Cabernet Sauvignon, Chambourcin, Merlot, Petit Verdot, Pinot Noir.

Sweet/Dessert Wines: Frosty Dog, Red Mountain Laurel, Sweet Mountain Laurel.

Fortified Wines: Heritage *(port-style)*.

Price Range: $12–$48

Tastings: $8 per person; $40 per person for elite tasting, reservations required.

Groups: Reservations required for groups of 12 or more.

Wheelchair accessible.

Purchasing: Online purchasing for residents of VA and most other states; contact the winery for specifics.

Directions: From the Blue Ridge Parkway, turn west onto Black Ridge Road between Milepost 171 and 172. Take an immediate left onto Winery Road; the winery will be about ½ mile on right.

❖ ❖ ❖

Foggy Ridge Cider
1328 Pineview Road
Dugspur VA 24325

Hours: Sa 11:00–5:00, Su 12:00–5:00 (Apr–Dec)   276-398-2337
Closed Jan–Mar   www.foggyridgecider.com
                                        E-mail: info@foggyridgecider.com

Chuck and Diane Flynt first began planting their orchard in 1996 and now grow over thirty varieties of apples on two hundred acres on elevations reaching three thousand feet. Their apples include Harrison, Graniwinkle, Roxbury Russet, Virginia Hewe's Crab, Dabinett, Tremlett's Bitter, Muscadet de Berney, and Cox's Orange Pippin. Diane is the original cidermaker, now joined by Jocelyn Kuzelka, and currently produces four sparkling and two fortified ciders. Foggy Ridge's outstanding website offers much interesting information and history about apples and cider.

Sparkling Ciders: First Fruit *(American heirloom apples)*, Handmade *(Newtown Pippin)*, Serious Cider *(Tremlett's Bitter, Dabinett, Ashmead's Kernel, Roxbury Russet)*, Sweet Stayman Cider *(Stayman, Grimes Golden, Cox's Orange Pippin)*.

Fortified Ciders: Pippin Black *(Black Twig, Arkansas Black)*, Pippin Gold *(Newtown Pippin, Apple Brandy)*.

Price Range: $16–$30

Purchasing: Shipping to Virginia residents only.

Directions: From Blue Ridge Parkway, turn west between Milepost 174 and 175 onto Buffalo Mountain Road (Route 758). Drive for 7 miles, staying straight at the Y at Buffalo Mountain Store. Turn left onto Rock Church Road (Route 628). Pass the Buffalo Presbyterian Church and then turn left onto Pineview Road (Route 656) to the cidery ½ mile on left.

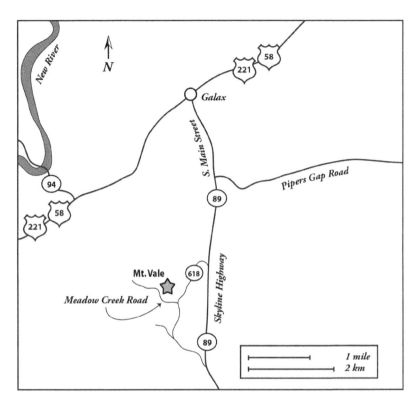

Map 11.4. Blue Ridge Parkway (Mt. Vale)

❖ ❖ ❖

Mt. Vale Vineyards
3222 Meadow Creek Road
Galax VA 24333

Hours: F–Sa 12:00–6:00 (Apr–Dec)   276-238-9946
Su 1:00–5:00 (Jun–Sep only)   www.mtvalevineyard.com
Closed Christmas, Dec–Mar   E-mail: mtvalewine@gmail.com

Mt. Vale Vineyard was opened to the public in late 2011 by Noel and
Peggy Belcher, who decided to establish Mt. Vale to fulfill a long-held
dream after both retired from their construction and nursing professions in

Raleigh, North Carolina. The couple found their ideal property on a scenic setting just off the Blue Ridge Parkway. North Carolina vintner Mary Simmons is serving as Mt. Vale's winemaker. Visitors are welcome to linger in the tasting room or outdoor patios and gazebos. The winery sponsors wine dinners and live music, and may be rented for weddings or special events. Light fare is available for purchase.

Mt. Vale's Guest House and Cottage offer lodging for overnight stays on the property.

Fruit Wines: Blue Ridge Blackberry, Cranberry Delight *(Chardonnay, cranberry)*.

White Wines: Cellar Door *(Chardonel)*, Chardonnay, Misty Morning.

Red Wines: Cabernet Sauvignon, Table for Two *(Cabernet Franc, Marquette, Frontenac)*, Vale Reserve *(Bordeaux-style blend)*.

Fortified Wines: Rosé *(bourbon barrel aged)*, Vale Reserve *(bourbon barrel aged)*.

Price Range: $15–$26

Tastings: $5 per person.

Purchasing: Online ordering available to all 50 states.

Directions: From U.S. Route 221, turn south onto Main Street (VA 89) at the town of Galax. Drive 3.3 miles and turn right onto Mt. Vale Road. After ½ mile, turn left onto Meadow Creek Road. The winery entrance will be another ½ mile on the right.

❖ ❖ ❖

Villa Appalaccia Winery
752 Rock Castle Gorge
Floyd VA 24091

Hours: F 11:00–5:00, Sa 11:00–6:00, Su 12:00–4:30 (May–Nov)   540-358-0357
Sa 11:00–5:00, Su 12:00–4:30 (Mar–Apr)   www.villaappalaccia.com
Closed Dec–Mar   E-mail: chianti@swva.net

Located just one mile from Chateau Morrisette, Villa Appalaccia opened to the public in 1995, six years after Stephen Haskill and Susanne Becker planted their first two-acre vineyard. The winery specializes in such Italian varietals as Primitivo, Malvasia, Aglianico, Corvina Veronese, and, most recently, Vermentino. Visitors may relax in the music garden or play on the bocce court. Cheeses, meats, and breads are available for purchase.

White Wines: Pinot Grigio, Simpatico, Vermentino.

Red Wines: Aglianico, Cabernet Franc, Rustico, Sangiovese, Toscanello *(Cabernet Franc, Sangiovese, Primitivo)*.

Sweet/Dessert Wines: Corvina Amaro, Raspberry Cab.

Price Range: $18–$22

Tastings: $5 per person.

Restrictions: No groups over 6.

Purchasing: Online to VA residents and via VinoShipper to AK, AL, CA, DC, FL, ID, IL, LA, MN, MO, NC, ND, NE, NH, NM, NV, OH, OR, WV, and WY.

Directions: From the Blue Ridge Parkway, turn east onto Old Field Road (Route 720) between Milepost 170 and 172; there are two entrances to Old Field Road, one between MP 170 and 171, and another between MP 171 and 172. Follow Old Field Road (unpaved) to the winery driveway.

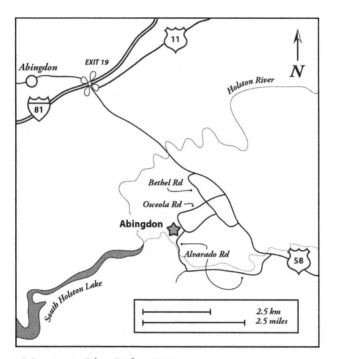

Map 11.5. Blue Ridge/I-81 (Abingdon)

BLUE RIDGE/I-81

Abingdon Vineyard & Winery
20530 Alvarado Road
Abingdon VA 24211

Hours: Tu–Sa 10:00–6:00,
Su 12:00–6:00 (mid-Mar to mid-Dec)
Closed Thanksgiving, mid-Dec to mid-Mar

276-623-1255
www.abingdonwinery.com
E-mail: info@abingdonwinery.com

Abingdon Winery is a small farm winery along the scenic South Holston River. The winery is owned and operated by Ron Carlson and his wife Janet Lee Nordin, who began planting their first vines in 1998 on the fifty-three-acre property. Abingdon is near a number of boating, hiking, and camping sites, with the Virginia Creeper Trail a mere half-mile away and the Appalachian Trail just five miles down the road in Damascus, Virginia. Snacks are available for purchase in the tasting room.

White Wines: Bare Chardonnay, Chardonnay, Chardonel, Misty River, Riesling, Traminette.

Blush Wines: White Pinot Noir.

Red Wines: Bare Chambourcin, Cabernet Franc, Cabernet Sauvignon, Chambourcin, Norton, Red Hawk *(Chambourcin, Chardonel)*, Royal Blend, Special Red *(Cabernet Franc, Chambourcin, Norton)*.

Sweet/Dessert Wines: Alvarado Rouge, Appalachian Autumn, Appalachian Sunset *(Niagara, Cayuga)*, Creekside Blush, Dazzle, Misty River II, Razzle, Triple Duck.

Price Range: $11–$17

Tastings: First six tastes are complimentary; $1 per taste afterwards.

Groups: Reservations required for groups of 15 or more.

Purchasing: Online via VinoShipper to AK, AL, CA, DC, FL, ID, IL, LA, MN, MO, NE, NV, NH, NM, NC, ND, OH, OR, VA, WV, and WY.

Directions: From I-81, take Exit 19 onto U.S. Route 58 East. Turn right after 5 miles onto Osceola Road (Route 722). Drive 2.4 miles and turn right onto Alvarado Road, immediately after a sharp turn; the winery driveway will be on the right.

❖ ❖ ❖

Beliveau Estate

5415 Gallion Ridge Road

Blacksburg VA 24060

Hours: W–Su 12:00–6:00 (W, F to 8:00 in summer) 540-961-0505
Closed New Year's, Easter, Thanksgiving, Christmas www.beliveauestate.com
E-mail: info@beliveauestate.com

Joyce and Yvan Beliveau opened their winery in 2012, three years after planting their first vineyard and five years after establishing their bed & breakfast inn on a 165-acre property located between Roanoke and Blacksburg. Visitors can enjoy scenic views of the hills and ponds from the tasting room's verandas. Beliveau sponsors a Lavender Festival the last Sunday in June, as well as Tapas Nights and other special events.   The facilities are available for weddings and private events.

The Inn at Beliveau Estate offers five guest rooms for overnight stays; special packages are available.

White Wines: Afternoon Delight (*Vidal Blanc, Chardonnay*), Captivate (*Riesling*), Destiny (*Vidal Blanc*), Mystique (*Chardonnay*), Pristine (*Chardonel*), Reflection (*Traminette*).

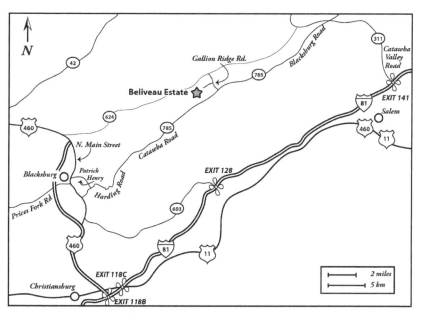

Map 11.6. Blue Ridge/I-81 (Beliveau)

Red Wines: Acapella, Fireside Chat (*Cabernet Franc*), Portal (*Zinfandel*), Soul Singer (*Chambourcin*), Trailblazer (*Merlot*).

Sweet/Dessert Wines: Crown Jewel, Discovery (*Niagara*), Lovers' Quest (*Chardonnay, Vidal Blanc*), Sweet Surrender (*Concord*), Warm Glow (*Chambourcin*).

Price Range: $16–$32

Tastings: $5 per person.

Purchasing: Online via VinoShipper to AK, AL, CA, DC, FL, ID, IL, LA, MN, MO, NE, NV, NH, NM, NC, ND, OH, OR, VA, WV, and WY.

Directions: From I-81 Northbound, take Exit 118B toward Christiansburg/ Blacksburg and merge onto U.S. Route 460 West. Drive 9.4 miles and exit onto Prices Fork Road (VA 412 East) into Blacksburg. Drive 1.5 miles and turn left onto North Main Street (U.S. Route 460 Business). After about one mile, turn right onto Patrick Henry Drive and continue 0.8 miles. Turn left onto Harding Avenue which will become Harding Road and then Catawba Road. Drive 10.9 miles in all and turn left onto Gallion Ridge Road (portions unpaved). Drive 1.2 miles and turn left into the long winery drive; the winery will be ¾ mile ahead.

From I-81 Southbound, take Exit 141 (New Castle) and merge onto Catawba Valley Road (Route 311 North). Drive 7 miles and turn left onto Blacksburg Road (Route 785). Drive 10 miles and turn right onto Gallion Ridge Road (portions unpaved). Continue 1.2 miles and turn left into the long winery drive; the winery will be ¾ mile ahead.

❖ ❖ ❖

Davis Valley Winery & Vineyard
1167 Davis Valley Road
Rural Retreat VA 24368

Hours: M–Sa, 10:00–5:00, Su 12:00–5:00　　　　　276-686-8855
Closed New Year's, Thanksgiving, Christmas　　　www.davisvalleywinery.com
　　　　　　　　　　　　　　　　　　　　E-mail: info@davisvalleywinery.com

After Rusty and Ruth Rhea Cox purchased this scenic hilltop property, they converted the former dairy farm to a vineyard, with plantings that include Maréchal Foch, Norton, Corot Noir, and Steuben. Visitors can sample a flight of wines on a hundred-year-old bar in their tasting room. The winery may be rented for special events, dinners, and weddings.

Davis Valley has now opened a distillery on-site, producing Virginia Frost Vodka and Appalachian Moon moonshine.

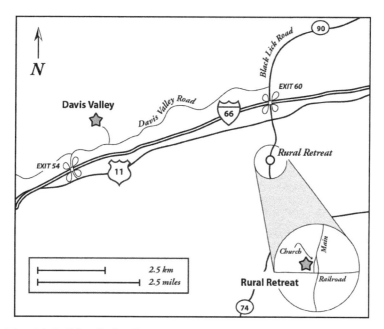

Map 11.7. Blue Ridge/I-81 (Rural Retreat)

White Wines: Appalachian Breeze, Chardonnay, Davis Valley White, Virginia Breeze White.

Red Wines: Autumn Red, Cabernet Franc, Chambourcin, Davis Valley Red *(Maréchal Foch)*, Virginia Breeze Red *(Steuben)*.

Price Range: $14–$21

Tastings: $4 per person.

Directions: From I-81, take Exit 54 (Grose Close). Turn north onto Winsor Road, which will bend right and become Davis Valley Road (portions unpaved). Continue 1.4 miles to the winery on the left.

❖ ❖ ❖

Rural Retreat Winery & Dye's Vineyards
201 Church Street
Rural Retreat VA 24368

Hours: M–Th 11:00–5:30, Fr–Sa 11:00–6:30,   276-686-8300
Su 12:30–5:00 (summer only)   www.ruralretreatwinery.com
Closed New Year's, Thanksgiving, Christmas   E-mail: info@ruralretreatwinery.com

Rural Retreat is owned and operated by Scott and Linda Mecimore, who purchased Dye's Vineyards and Winery in 2007. The tasting room is located in a combination gift shop and eat-in deli, with the tasting bar toward the back. Children are welcome. The winery also offers a two-bedroom suite for overnight stays.

White Wines: Chardonnay, Golden Muscat, Riesling, Rural Retreat Blanc, Sweet Kitty White, Viognier.

Rosé Wines: Chambourcin Rosé, Russell Rosé, Sainte Marie Rosé.

Red Wines: Cabernet Franc, Cardinal Red, Chambourcin, Cripple Creek, Depot Red (*Steuben, Concord*), Sweet Gracie Red.

Price Range: $10–$20

Tastings: $4.50 per person.

Purchasing: Direct to VA residents or via VinoShipper to AK, AL, DC, FL, ID, IL, LA, MN, MO, NE, NV, NH, NM, NC, ND, OH, OR, WV, and WY.

Directions: From I-81 take Exit 60 onto Route 90 South toward Rural Retreat and drive 1.6 miles. Turn right onto Railroad Avenue and make an immediate right onto Church Street and the winery on the left.

❖ ❖ ❖

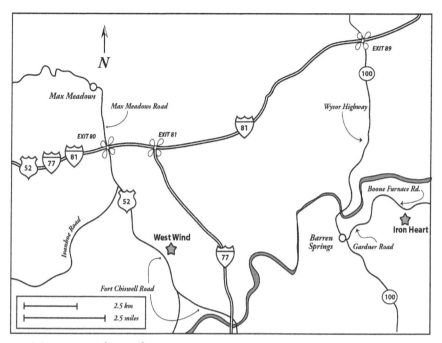

Map 11.8. Blue Ridge/I-81 (West Wind-Iron Heart)

Iron Heart Winery
3742 Boone Furnace Road
Allisonia VA 24347

Hours: Sa 12:00–4:00, Su 1:00–4:00
Closed New Year's, Thanksgiving, Christmas

540-320-0203
www.iheartvirginiawine.com
E-mail: info@ironheartwinery.com

The newest winery in the Blue Ridge Region, Iron Heart was launched by Adam Farriss and his father Dr. Bruce Farris on their fourth-generation family farm. In addition to trying Iron Heart's wines, visitors can enjoy the ample fishing, rafting, and hiking opportunities throughout the scenic New River Valley. The winery also offers several high-end restored cabins that can be rented for overnight stays or private events.

White Wines: Chardonnay, Riesling, Vidal Blanc.

Rosé Wines: Rosé.

Red Wines: Cabernet Franc, Chambourcin.

Price Range: $15–$23

Tastings: $5.00 per person.

Directions: From I-81, take Exit 89A (Draper) onto VA Route 100 South. Drive 6.7 miles and turn left onto Gardner Road (Route 608) which will become Boone Furnace Road after 2 miles. Continue another 0.6 miles to Farris Farms and the winery entrance.

❖ ❖ ❖

West Wind Farm Winery
180 West Wind Drive
(Alternate GPS address: 2228 Fort Chiswell Road)
Max Meadows VA 24360

Hours: M–Sa 11:00–6:00, Su 1:00–6:00   276-699-2020
Closed New Year's, Easter, Thanksgiving, Christmas   www.westwindwine.com
                                                          E-mail: info@westwindwine.com

West Wind is owned and operated by Paul and Brenda Hric on a family farm that has been in Brenda's family for four generations. The Hrics began planting their five-acre vineyard in 2003 and made their first wine in 2005. West Wind's tasting room offers both indoor and outdoor seating for visitors, as well as a gift shop with candles, glassware, and pottery. The winery hosts live music at Summer Saturdays concerts, as well as various festivals, including a fall Wine and Swine barbecue. The facilities may

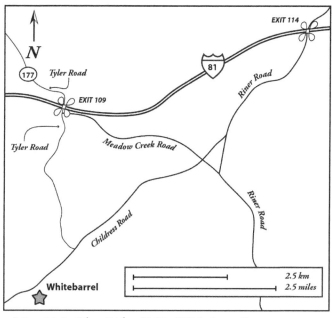

Map 11.9. Blue Ridge/I-81 (Whitebarrel)

be rented for private events and dinners. The winery is certified Virginia Green. Children and leashed dogs are welcome

Fruit Wines: Galena Creek Blackberry, Galena Creek Peach.

White Wines: Galena Creek White, Gewurztraminer, Pinot Gris, Riesling.

Red Wines: Cabernet Sauvignon, Chambourcin, Galena Creek Red, Heritage Reserve, Merlot.

Sweet/Dessert Wines: New River Red *(Concord)*, New River White *(Niagara)*.

Price Range: $13–$19

Tastings: Complimentary tasting of 3 wines, $3 for additional tastes.

Groups: Reservations required for buses, groups of 8 or more, $5 per person.

Directions: From I-80/I-77, take Exit 80 at Fort Chiswell. Follow Fort Chiswell Road (U.S. Route 52) south for 4 miles to the winery entrance on the left, just past Archer Drive.

❖ ❖ ❖

Whitebarrel Winery
4025 Childress Road
Christiansburg VA 24073

Hours: M–Tu 12:00–5:00, W–Th 12:00–7:00,
F–Sa 11:00–8:00, Su 12:00–6:00
Closed New Year's, Thanksgiving, Christmas

540-382-7619
www.whitebarrel.com
E-mail: wine@whitebarrel.com

New Jersey native **Rik Obiso** established Whitebarrel Winery in 2007 after coming back to southwestern Virginia where he had attended Virginia Tech some years earlier. The 16-acre vineyard was first planted that same year, with Whitebarrel's first harvest in 2010. Rik drew on his experience as a biotechnologist in building his knowledge of winemaking, now producing a range of wines. Light snacks and tapas are available for purchase at the tasting room, which offers both indoor and outdoor seating for visitors.

Whitebarrel has now opened a wine and tapas bar in nearby Blacksburg (301 South Main Street, Su–Th 11:00–11:00, F–Sa 11:00–midnight) where visitors can try Whitebarrel's wines.

Fruit Wines: Bin 101 *(apple)*, Bin 127 *(white wine, mango)*.

White Wines: Bin 704, Chardonnay, Vidal Blanc.

Rosé Wines: Bin 997.

Red Wines: Bin 214, Bin 260, Cabernet Franc, Cabernet Sauvignon, Chambourcin.

Fortified Wines: Bin 831 (*port-style*).

Price Range: $20–$49

Tastings: $5 per person; $1 per taste for reserve tasting.

Groups: Reservations requested for groups of 10 or more.

Purchasing: Online via VinoShipper to AK, AL, AZ, CA, CO, DC, FL, GA, HI, IA, ID, IL, IN, KS, LA, MA, MD, ME, MN, MO, ND, NE, NH, NM, NV, NY, OH, OR, PA, SC, TN, TX, VA, WA, WI, WV, and WY.

Directions: From I-81, take Exit 109 (Radford) south onto Tyler Road (Route 177). Drive 3 miles and turn right onto Childress Road. The winery entrance will be 1 mile on the left.

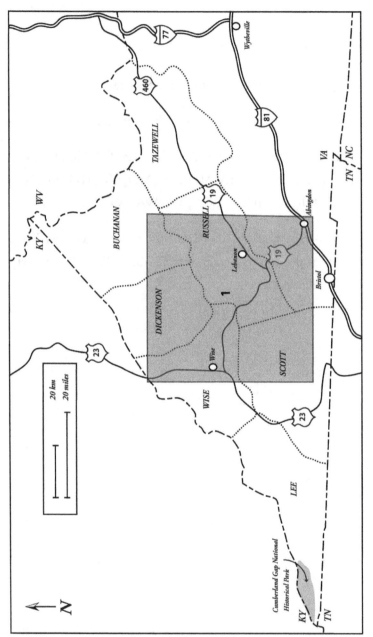

Map 12.1. Heart of Appalachia Region: (1) Heart of Appalachia

12. HEART OF APPALACHIA

The mountainous southwest corner of Virginia is an area of scenic and rugged natural beauty where river gorges cut through spectacular sandstone cliffs and rich coal seams streak through the rock formations. With its high elevations, the region has the coolest summer temperatures and highest precipitation in the state. The region's two wineries offer an intimate experience unique to the region. MountainRose honors the region's long coal-mining history in its wine names, while Vincent's Vineyard is a haven for fly-fishermen (and women).

❖ ❖ ❖

<u>Things to see and do:</u> Multiple scenic drives allow nature lovers to enjoy the region's fall foliage. The area offers many opportunities for hiking, camping, and fishing. The region's coal mining history was depicted in John Fox's *Trail of the Lonesome Pine*, a 1913 novel adapted for film in 1936. The Heart of Appalachia Driving Tour leads visitors through various sites and towns through the region's counties; tour stages can be printed from Virginia's tourism website (www.virginia.org/heartofappalachiadrivingtour/).

The independent-minded people who settled this region brought with them a rich culture that endures in the rhythms and cadences of bluegrass and country music. This is the birthplace of country music legends June Carter Cash and the Carter Family, and Ralph Stanley. Visitors can experience the history and music of the region on the Crooked Road Heritage Trail which winds through ten counties and even more towns with local music festivals and jams; more information, including a map, is available at www.crookedroad.org.

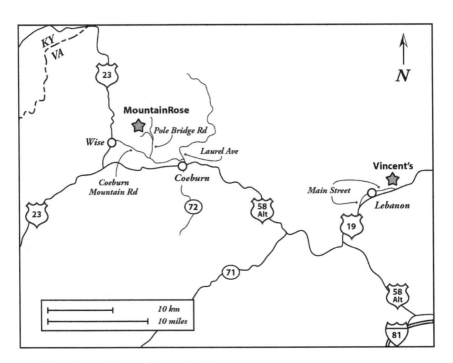

Map 12.2. Heart of Appalachia

HEART OF APPALACHIA

MountainRose Vineyards
10439 North Reservoir Road
Wise VA 24293

Hours: M–Sa 10:00–5:00 (Jan–Feb); until 6:00 (Mar–Dec) 276-328-2013
Closed New Year's, Thanksgiving, Christmas www.mountainrosevineyard.com
E-mail: swlawson@comcast.net

MountainRose got its start in 1996 when David Lawson first rooted one hundred grape vines from an eighty-year-old Concord vine on land his family has owned since the 1850s. The winery vineyard includes plantings of Niagara, Traminette, and Vidal Blanc; the winery also has a vineyard in neighboring Russell County. In honor of the area's long coal history, the Lawsons have named their wines after old coal seams and are active advocates of reclaiming old strip-mined lands through grape and apple cultivation. MountainRose hosts a variety of events at the winery, including festivals, grape stomps, live music, and quilt shows. The winery facilities are available for rental for private parties or weddings. Children are welcome.

White Wines: Blair White, Splashdam White, Sweet MountainRose White *(Niagara)*, Traminette.

Blush Wines: Darby Blush *(Chambourcin)*.

Red Wines: Concord, Dorchester Red *(Chambourcin, Tannat)*, Jawbone Red, Pardee Red *(Chambourcin, Chancellor)*.

Sweet/Dessert Wines: Autumn Gold.

Price Range: $10–$20

Wheelchair accessible.

Purchasing: Online for VA residents or via VinoShipper to AK, AL, AZ, CA, CO, DC, FL, GA, ID, IL, IA, KS, LA, ME, MD, MA, MN, MO, NE, NV, NH, NM, NY, NC, ND, OH, OR, WC, TN, TX, WA, WV, and WY.

Directions: From U.S. Route 23, take Business 23 into the town of Wise. Once in Wise, turn right at the first traffic light onto Main Street. Take a right at the third light onto Darden Drive. Just past the University of Virginia campus, Darden Drive becomes Coeburn Mountain Road (Route 646). Continue for four miles and turn left onto Pole Bridge Road at Hard Rock Contractors. Follow Pole Bridge Road 1.8 miles and turn left onto North Reservoir Road. The winery driveway will be ½ mile on right.

❖ ❖ ❖

Vincent's Vineyard
2313 East Main Street
Lebanon VA 24266

Hours: M–Sa 11:00–6:00 (Apr–Dec)
Closed Jan–Mar, 4th of July,
Thanksgiving, Christmas

276-889-2505
www.vincentsvineyard.com
E-mail: vincentsvineyard@yahoo.com

Vincent and Betsy Gilmer established this small family winery on their sixth-generation family farm in Russell County. The winery's three-acre vineyard and tasting room are located adjacent to Big Cedar Creek, a favorite spot for fly fishing in the foothills of Clinch Mountain. Visitors can sit and enjoy the view of the mountains and the farm's Katahdin sheep from the tasting room, which offers snacks and artisanal crafts for sale. Leashed pets are welcome.

White Wines: Angler's Choice, Shepherd's White, Traminette.

Blush Wines: Make Me Blush *(Chambourcin)*.

Red Wines: Ambrosia *(Steuben)*, Cabernet Franc, Shepherd's Red.

Price Range: $11–$14

Groups: Please call ahead for group tastings.

Purchasing: Online via VinoShipper to AK, AL, CA, DC, FL, ID, IL, LA, MN, MO, NE, NV, NH, NM, NC, ND, OH, OR, VA, WV, and WY.

Directions: From I-81, take Exit 17 (Abingdon/South Holston Dam) onto U.S. Route 19 North/U.S. Route 58 Alt. Stay on U.S. Route 19 North for 21.6 miles into Lebanon. Turn left onto East Main Street (U.S. Route 19 Business) at the first light after Walmart. Drive ½ mile to the winery entrance on right, just past Big Cedar Creek Bridge.

APPENDIX 1
VIRGINIA WINE TRAILS

Virginia has an ever-increasing number of wine trails that offer visitors a nicely packaged way of visiting the state's many wineries. The wine trails have a range of features, including several with passport programs that offer reduced tasting fees for visits to multiple wineries.

Northern Virginia Region:

Fauquier County Wine Trail (www.visitfauquier.com/things-to-do/wineries)
Website offers an events calendar, a printable map, as well as links to restaurants, dining.

Loudoun Wine Country (www.visitloudoun.org/eat-drink; then select "Wineries & Tasting Rooms")
Website has links to touring guide, wineries, wine tour services, local attractions, and passport program.

Vintage Piedmont (http://vintagepiedmont.com)
Website has a map and links to the five wineries along I-66 that are included in the trail.

Shenandoah Valley Region:

Blue Ridge Whiskey Wine Loop (www.discovershenandoah.com/whiskey-wine-loop)

Wineries, one distillery from Front Royal to Luray. Includes a printable driving map and a list of attractions. On Facebook.

Blue Ridge Wine Way (www.blueridgewineway.com)

Website has a printable trail map, e-newsletter sign-up, and an events calendar. Links to restaurants, lodgings, and local attractions.

Shenandoah County Wine Trail (www.visitshenandoahcounty.com—select "Breweries, Wineries, Cideries, Distilleries" under Experience in the top toolbar)

Website has downloadable Google maps of winery locations, links to local attractions, and an online Shenandoah County travel guide.

Shenandoah Valley Wine Trail (http://shenandoahvalleywinetrail.com)

Website includes an events calendar, links to wineries, local attractions, and a printable Google trail map.

Chesapeake Bay/Northern Neck Region:

Chesapeake Bay Wine Trail (www.chesapeakebaywinetrail.com)

Trail centers on Northern Neck wineries. Website includes a printable map, dining, lodging, and local attractions, as well as passport program.

Central Virginia Region

Foothills Scenic Wine Trail (www.foothillsscenicwinetrail.com)

Website has an events calendar and downloadable maps of the two wineries near Old Rag Mountain.

Heart of Virginia Wine Trail (http://hovawinetrail.com)
Passport program includes tastings at six wineries, souvenir glass, entry for prize drawing. Downloadable trail map, events calendar.

Monticello Wine Trail (www.monticellowinetrail.com)
Website has customizable and printable maps that allow visitors to create their own itineraries; also includes an events calendar, restaurants, and lodgings.

Nelson 151 (http://nelson151.com)
Website offers an events calendar, links to wineries, breweries, cideries, restaurants, and lodgings along Route 151, as well as a printable map.

Hampton Roads Region

Williamsburg Tasting Trail (www.visitwilliamsburg.com/trip-idea; select Tasting Trail)
Includes wineries, craft breweries, and a meadery located in the greater Williamsburg. Website offers a map and links to activities.

Southern Virginia Region:

Southern Virginia Wine Trail (www.sovawinetrail.bksites.com)
Website includes a printable passport, a list of bed & breakfast inns, a trail map, and an events calendar.

Virginia Mountains Region:

Bedford County Wine Trail (www.thebedfordwinetrail.com)
Passport program offering a free wine glass for visiting all the county's wineries. Map with links to festivals, attractions, lodgings, and restaurants.

Wine Trail of Botetourt County (www.botetourtwinetrail.com)

Website includes a downloadable trail map, links to wineries, places to stay, and local attractions.

Blue Ridge Region:

Mountain Road Wine Experience (www.mountainroadwineexperience.com)

Two-day ticket program includes tastings at all wineries. Website includes links to wineries and some local lodgings and restaurants.

Heart of Appalachia Region:

Heart of Appalachia (www.heartofappalachia.com/)

Interactive map with customizable itineraries including wineries, hiking and bike trails, scenic attractions, camping, and more.

APPENDIX 2
VIRGINIA WINE BLOGS

Wine blogs seem to come and go, with new ones routinely popping up to replace others that fall by the wayside. The following list represents a quick selection of the most durable blogs that focus predominately on Virginia wines and wineries. These bloggers have a wide range of styles and opinions; try several on for size to see which offers you the best fit.

Charlottesville Uncorked (http://cvilleuncorked.com)
Authored by Tricia Traugott, a realtor and Texas native who focuses on the Charlottesville area, with photos and links. Facebook, Twitter.

Drink What You Like (http://drinkwhatyoulike.wordpress.com)
Frank Morgan blogs about wine and breweries in Virginia (and occasionally other states). Twitter, e-mail updates.

Hagarty on Wine (www.hagarty-on-wine.com)
Produced by John Hagarty, whose blog ranges from interviews with winemakers to tasting notes on various wines.

My Vine Spot (http://vinespot.blogspot.com)
Dezel Quillen reviews wines from around the world, occasionally also including Virginia, with tasting notes. Facebook, Twitter, YouTube.

Richard Leahy's Wine Report (http://www.richardleahy.com/blog)
Author Richard Leahy posts in-depth blogs on the Virginia wine industry as a whole. E-mail updates.

Virginia Pour House (http://virginiapourhouse.com)
Tony Marocco blogs about brewpubs and wineries with personal ratings. Includes photos, interviews, tasting notes. Twitter, e-mail updates.

Virginia Winos (http://virginiawinos.com)
Blog by Alli and Amy about wine, food, and Virginia (mostly northern and central) with photos, videos, and contests. Twitter, Instagram.

Virginia Grape (www.thevirginiagrape.com)
Charlottesville-area resident Bryan Yost covers a multitude of Virginia wineries, including many off the beaten path. Twitter, Instagram.

Virginia Wine Time (www.virginiawinetime.com)
Warren Richard and Paul Armstrong are long-time bloggers, focusing exclusively on Virginia wineries. Facebook, Twitter, RSS feed, YouTube.

Wine About Virginia (http://wineaboutvirginia.blogspot.com)
Written by Kurt Jensen, this blog includes photos of Virginia wineries, with tasting room and wine reviews. E-mail updates.

Wine Trail Traveler (www.winetrailtraveler.com)
Terry and Kathy Sullivan review wineries with photos, wine routes, wine information, search engine. Facebook, Twitter, YouTube.

BIBLIOGRAPHY

Frye, Keith. *Roadside Geology of Virginia.* Missoula: Mountain Press Publishing Company, 2001.
Good introduction to the geologic structure and history of Virginia; includes numerous driving trails and maps.

Halliday, James and Hugh Johnson. *The Art and Science of Wine.* New York: Firefly Books, 2007.
An in-depth exploration of winemaking techniques for a range of noble grape varieties.

Heinemann, Ronald L., et al. *Old Dominion, New Commonwealth: A History of Virginia, 1607-2007.* Charlottesville: University of Virginia Press, 2008.
A good basic overview of the history of Virginia.

James, Victoria. *Drink Pink: A Celebration of Rosé.* New York: Harper-Collins, 2017.
A quick and amusing overview of rosé wines worldwide, with multiple recipes in the second half for dishes that pair well with rosé.

Kliman, Todd. *The Wild Vine: A Forgotten Grape and the Untold Story of American Wine.* New York: Clarkson Potter, 2010.
The dual-track story of Virginia's Norton grape and of Jennifer McCloud of Chrysalis Vineyards, who is perhaps the Norton's strongest champion.

Kramer, Matt. *Making Sense of Wine.* Philadelphia: Running Press, 2003.
Elegantly written essay on wine appreciation; includes a number of good recipes and wine pairings.

Kupperman, Karen Ordahl. *The Jamestown Project.* Cambridge: Belknap Press, 2007.
Very readable study of the origins, challenges, and economic development of the Jamestown Colony.

Leahy, Richard. *Beyond Jefferson's Vines: The Evolution of Quality Wines in Virginia.* CreateSpace, 2014.
Overview of the history of modern winemaking in the state by one of Virginia's experts on wine.

Lukacs, Paul. *American Vintage: The Rise of American Wine.* Boston: Houghton Mifflin, 2000.
Excellent short history of the American wine industry, from its earliest days to the present.

Mapp, Alf J., Jr. *The Virginia Experiment: The Old Dominion's Role in the Making of America, 1607-1781.* Lanham: Madison Books, 1990.
Detailed history of colonial Virginia, from its founding to the American Revolution.

McCusker, John. *The Economy of British America, 1607-1789.* Chapel Hill: University of North Carolina Press, 1991.
Scholarly examination and comparison of the economic development of the original thirteen American colonies and the Caribbean.

Pinney, Thomas, *A History of Wine in America, Volume One: From the Beginnings to Prohibition.* Berkeley: University of California Press, 1999. And *A History of Wine in America, Volume Two: From Prohibition to the Present.* Berkeley: University of California Press, 2005.
An outstanding and highly detailed two-volume history of winemaking in the United States.

Robinson, Jancis. *The 24-Hour Wine Expert.* New York: Abrams Books, 2016.
A quck and entertaining overview of wines and wine tasting from one of the most knowledgeable and informative experts in the world.

Robinson Jancis. *American Wine: The Ultimate Companion to the Wines and Wineries of the United States.* Berkley, Los Angeles: University of California Press, 2012.
Excellent encyclopedia of American wine history and production, including the major wine regions and varieties.

Robinson, Jancis. *How To Taste: A Guide to Enjoying Wine.* New York: Simon & Schuster, 2008.
Very good introduction to wine tasting aimed at helping readers develop good palette pictures of the noble grape varieties.

Robinson, Jancis, ed., *The Oxford Companion to Wine.* Oxford: Oxford University Press, 2015.
A comprehensive wine encyclopedia for the true wine geek.

Rowe, Walker Elliott *A History of Virginia Wines: From Grapes to Glass.* Charleston: History Press, 2009.
A short general overview of Virginia's wine industry, including some wine-maker interviews (no index).

Simonetti-Bryan, Jennifer. *The Everyday Guide to Wine* (DVD). Chantilly: The Great Courses, 2010.
An entertaining and informative video introduction to wine and wine tasting. (Be patient: Great Courses has frequent sales on this!)

Simonetti-Bryan, Jennifer. *Rosé Wine: The Guide to Drinking Pink*. New York: Sterling Epicure, 2017.
A highly readable and informative guide to the production and enjoyment of rosé wines by a wine expert who makes wine and wine appreciation approachable for everyone.

GLOSSARY OF WINE TERMS

Aglianico *(ah-lee-AH-nee-koh)*: A dark-skinned grape variety of Greek origin generally cultivated in the south of Italy, known for its dark ruby color and assertive flavor; the name is a corruption of *Ellenico*, Italian for "Greek."

Albariño *(ahl-bah-REE-nyoh)*: An aromatic white grape variety commonly grown in Spain's Galicia region as well as Portugal's Vinho Verde area.

Alcohol strength: The amount of alcohol in wine as measured in parts per one hundred; the alcohol strength of most wines falls between 9 and 15 percent.

Alicante Bouschet *(ah-lee-cahnt boo-shay)*: A black grape from southern France, generally known simply as Alicante; originally bred in the mid-1800s by Henri Bouschet, who crossed Petit Bouschet and Grenache grapes.

American Viticultural Area (AVA): Since 1983, a geographic designation generally defined by geographic and climatic boundaries; approval for an AVA designation must be granted by the Bureau of Alcohol, Tobacco, and Firearms. At least 85 percent of wine with an AVA designation must originate from grapes grown in that AVA.

Aromella: An aromatic hybrid white grape variety developed by Cornell University, combining Traminette and Ravat 34; highly winter-hardy.

Barbera *(bar-BEAR-ah)*: A late-ripening dark-skinned grape from Italy's Lombardy region; one of that country's most commonly planted varieties.

Blaufränkisch *(blaw [rhymes with "how"] fren-kish)*: One of the most widely planted black grape varieties in Austria, particularly in Burgenland; known in Germany as Limberger and in Washington state as Lemberger.

Blend: Any wine made from two or more different grape varieties.

Blush wine: A very pale pink and often sweet wine, noticeably lighter than rosé, often made from black-skinned grapes.

Bordeaux-style blend: Generally used to designate a dry red wine made from a blend of two or more of five grape varieties: Cabernet Sauvignon, Cabernet Franc, Merlot, Petit Verdot, and Malbec.

Brut: Designation for a sparkling wine made with little or no residual sugars.

Buffalo: A blue-black native American hybrid, often used for making grape juice.

Cabernet Franc *(ca-behr-nay frahn)*: A French black grape with long historic roots in France, lighter in color and tannins than Cabernet Sauvignon; it is one of the five varieties commonly used in Bordeaux blends.

Cabernet Sauvignon *(ca-behr-nay soh-vee-nyon)*: One of the most widely known red wine grapes, determined in 1997 by DNA analysis to be a cross of Cabernet Franc and Sauvignon Blanc; the primary variety used in Bordeaux, it produces wines that are often deep in color with good potential for aging.

Carmine: A cross between Carignan and Cabernet Sauvignon, first produced in California.

Catawba: A pink-skinned hybrid from an unknown native American *la brusca* and European *vinifera* grape, first identified in North Carolina in 1802.

Cayuga: A white hybrid bred from a Seyve-Villard grape and the North American Schuyler grape, first produced in the Finger Lakes region of New York in 1945.

Chambourcin *(shahm-boor-sehn)*: A French-American hybrid grape that produces deep red wine with an aromatic nose; commercially available since 1963.

Chancellor: A red hybrid grape first bred in France where it is known as Seibel 7053; now more commonly grown now in the central and eastern United States.

Chardonel *(shar-doh-nel)*: A cross between Seyval Blanc and Chardonnay, first bred in New York in 1953 and commercially released in 1990.

Chardonnay *(shar-doh-nay)*: A white grape variety originating from the Burgundy region of France; one of the most widely planted white wine grapes in North America.

Cider: Fermented apple juice, ranging from 2 to 8.5 percent alcohol content.

Claret: An English term for red wines from the Bordeaux region in France.

Concord: A highly aromatic native American *labrusca* grape widely grown in the eastern United States and named after the town of Concord, Massachusetts; commonly used in producing grape juice and grape jelly.

Corot Noir *(koh-roh nwahr)*: A red wine hybrid between a European Seyve-Villard and American Steuben grape; first produced in New York in 1970.

Corvina Veronese *(kohr-VEE-nah veh-roh-NAY-zay)*: A red wine grape that is the predominate component of several Italian wines, including Valpolicella, Bardolino, and Amarone; also known simply as Corvina.

Cross: The result of crossing two grapes of the same species; for example, two *Vitis vinifera* grapes.

Cyser: Fermented honey and apple juice.

Dessert wine: In the United States, dessert wines are defined as wines between 14% and 24% alcohol strength; dessert wines may or may not be fortified. In Europe, often defined as sweet wines.

Dornfelder: A red grape that is a cross between the Helfensteiner and Heroldrebe varieties, first propagated in Germany in 1956 by August Herold; known for its deep color and aromatic fruit.

Dry: A wine tasting term meaning a lack of sweetness.

Eau-de-vie *(oh-duh-vee)*: A grape-based distilled spirit, such as brandy.

Fer Servadou *(fair sehr-vah-doo)*: A black grape variety from southwest France; also known simply as Fer. The Fer variety cultivated in Argentina is not related to the French variety.

Filtration: A winemaking process in which sediments and particles are filtered out of the wine; wines that do not undergo filtration are said to be unfiltered.

Fining: A winemaking process intended to clarify and stabilize the wine by use of a fining agent, such as bentonite or egg whites.

Finish: A wine-tasting term signifying how long the wine lingers on the palate after swallowing. Finishes are often said to be short (no lingering taste) or long (taste lingers).

Fortified wine: Wine whose alcohol strength has been increased by the addition of grape spirit; port and sherry are examples of fortified wines.

Frontenac: Red, cold-hardy hybrid propagated by the University of Minnesota, made by crossing Landot Noir and a *Vitis riparia* grape.

Fruit forward: A wine tasting term indicating a noticeable fruitiness with the first taste of a given wine; also called "up-front fruit"; a characteristic of many New World wines.

Fumé Blanc *(foo-may blahn)*: Another name for Sauvignon Blanc, first coined by Robert Mondavi in the 1970s; Fumé Blanc wines often have undergone some oak aging.

Gewurztraminer *(geh-VOOHRTS-trah-mee-ner)*: A pink-skinned aromatic mutation of the Traminer grape, first reported in the Italian Tyrol region around 1000 and widely planted in Alsace and Germany; also spelled Gewürztraminer.

Golden Muscat *(moos-kah)*: A green-golden grape that is a hybrid between Muscat Hamburg and the North American Diamond grape; first bred in New York.

Graciano *(grah-see-AH-noh)*: A black grape variety from the Rioja region in northern Spain; also known as Graciana.

Grauburgunder *(graw [rhymes with "how"]-boor-goon-der)*: The Austrian name for Pinot Gris.

Grenache *(gruh-nahsh)*: A black grape variety most commonly planted in France's southern Rhone Valley and Languedoc-Roussillon region, as well as in Spain where it is known as Garnacha.

Hybrid: The result of crossing two grapes of different species; for example, a *Vitis vinifera* grape with a *Vitis labrusca* grape.

Hydromel: Pure mead, often light or low-alcohol.

Ice wine: Sweet wine made from ripe grapes that are picked when frozen on the vine; also includes wines made by artificially freezing the grapes.

Isabella: An American hybrid of unknown origin, thought to have been first developed in 1816 in South Carolina; also known as Isabelle.

Jeropiga *(zheh-roh-pee-gah)*: Traditional Portuguese-style wine made by adding grape spirits to unfermented grape must.

Kvevri: Large earthenware vessels lined with beeswax and traditionally used in the Republic of Georgia for making wine; also spelled *qvevri*.

Landot Noir *(lan-doh nwahr)*: A red grape variety that is a hybrid of Landal Noir and Seyve Villard; most commonly grown in New York and Ontario, Canada.

Late harvest: Wine made from grapes left on the vine beyond the regular harvest time in order to concentrate the fruit and natural sugars.

Lemberger *(lame-bear-ger)*: The name given in Washington state to the Limberger grape variety, also called Blaufränkisch in Austria.

Library Wines: Wines put aside by a winery to age, generally of higher quality than ordinary vintages; may also refer to a home collection of wine.

Madeira *(mah-DARE-uh)*: A fortified wine originally from the Portuguese island of the same name.

Malbec *(mall-beck)*: A black grape variety grown in the Bordeaux and Loire regions of France, and one of the five varieties used in Bordeaux blends; now commonly associated with wine from Argentina and Chile.

Malolactic fermentation: A secondary fermentation during which malic acid is converted to the smoother tasting lactic acid in both red and white wines; produces greater flavor and smoothness in the final product.

Malvasia *(mall-vah-ZEE-ah)*: An ancient grape varietal family of Greek origin that includes mostly whites and some light-colored reds; wines are often characterized by higher residual sugars and alcohol strength.

Maréchal Foch *(mar-eh-shall fosh)*: A red grape hybrid of uncertain parentage first propagated in France.

Marquette: A relatively new, dark-skinned hybrid cross by the University of Minnesota between Ravat, an offspring of Pinot Noir, and a complex hybrid combining *Vitis riparia* and *Vitis vinifera* grapes; very cold hardy.

Mataro: A synonym for Mourvedre, often used in the United States.

Mead: A fermented drink made from honey and commonly believed to predate either beer or wine.

Melomel: Honey and fruit-based mead.

Metheglen: Mead blended with herbs or spices.

Méthode champenoise *(meh-tode sham-puh-nwahz)*: Sparkling wine made in the style of the Champagne region of France.

Meritage: A term coined in 1981 for American wines made from a Bordeaux-style blend of Cabernet Sauvignon, Cabernet Franc, Merlot, Malbec, and/or Petit Verdot; sometimes also used for white blends of Sauvignon Blanc, Semillon, and/or Muscadelle; rhymes with "heritage."

Merlot *(mehr-loh)*: A black grape variety that is the predominate red wine grape in France's Bordeaux region and widely planted in northern Italy, among other regions.

Montepulciano *(mon-tay-pool-CHA-no)*: A red grape variety widely planted in central Italy.

Moscato: Another name for Muscat.

Mourvedre *(moor-veh-dra)*: The second most planted black grape variety in Spain, where it probably originated near the town of Murviedro near Barcelona; also known as Mataro, particularly in the United States.

Muscat *(moos-kah)*: An ancient grape variety from the Mediterranean region with multiple varieties in different colors; known in Italian as Moscato.

Muscat Blanc *(moos-kah blahn)*: One of the earliest grapes grown in France, dating from ancient Roman times; also known as Muscat Canelli and White Muscat, among other names.

Muscat Canelli: Another name for Muscat Blanc.

Muscat of Alexandria: An ancient Muscat variety unrelated to Muscat Blanc and believed to have been first cultivated in Egypt.

Muscat Orange *(moos-kah oh-rahnzh)*: A white grape variety often used to produce dessert wines; unrelated to Muscat Blanc.

Muscat Ottonel: A white grape variety first bred in 1852 in France from Chasselas and Muscat de Saumur.

Must: The unfermented mixture of grape juice, pulp, skins, stem fragments, and seeds produced after grapes have been crushed at the start of the winemaking process.

Nebbiolo *(neh-bee-OH-loh):* A black grape from the Piedmont region in northwest Italy and the variety used in Italy's Barolo and Barbaresco wines.

Niagara: A green grape that is a cross between the native American Concord grape and the white Cassady hybrid.

Norton: A native American, dark-skinned grape variety bred in the 1820s by Dr. Daniel Norton on his farm near Richmond; the variety was first recognized for its winemaking potential by George Husmann of Hermann, Missouri, in the 1850s.

Orange Muscat: See Muscat Orange.

Orange Wine: Wine made from white grape varieties; it is kept in contact with the grape skins for an extended period, giving the finished product a deeper golden hue.

Petit Manseng *(puh-tee mahn-sang):* A white grape variety from southwest France and the Pyrenees region, noted for its flavor.

Petit Verdot *(puh-tee vehr-doh):* A black grape variety used in Bordeaux and Bordeaux-style blends, noted for its rich color.

Pinotage: A hardy red grape variety first bred in South Africa by A.I. Perold, who crossed Pinot Noir and Cinsaut, the latter also known as Hermitage.

Pinot Grigio *(PEE-noh GREE-joe)*: The Italian name for Pinot Gris.

Pinot Gris *(pee-noh gree)*: A mutation of Pinot Noir with greyish blue to brownish pink berries; known in Germany as either Ruländer when sweet or Grauburgunder when dry.

Pinot Meunier *(pee-noh muh-nee-aye)*: A black grape variety often used to produce classic French champagne.

Pinot Noir *(pee-noh nwahr)*: The classic black grape variety of the Burgundy region of France, noted for lower tannins and a somewhat fruity taste.

Port: A fortified wine originally from the Douro region or Portugal, made by adding brandy to wine; may be either red or white.

Primitivo: A red grape variety grown extensively in southern Italy, principally in Apulia, and confirmed by DNA analysis to very closely related to Zinfandel.

Reserve wines: Generally intended to designate wines of superior quality, although there are few controls on how and when the term may be used.

Residual sugar: The amount of natural grape sugar remaining in wine after fermentation, measured in percent per liter.

Retsina: A resinated wine common in Greece and Cyprus; protected by the EU as a traditional appellation.

Riesling *(reece-ling)*: The classic white wine grape of Germany, known for its aroma and flavor; also called White, Rhine, or Johannisberg Riesling.

Rkatsiteli *(ahr-kat-sah-teh-lee)*: A white grape variety first documented in the country of Georgia; widely planted in Russia and the Caucasus.

Rosé: Pink-colored wine made either by leaving dark grape skins in contact with the juice just long enough to color it, or by pressing the juice from red wine grapes in a process called "saignée."

Roussanne *(roo-sahn):* A reddish-skinned aromatic white grape from the Rhone region in France.

Saignée *(sen-yay):* French term meaning "bled" and designating a process for making rosé wines in which a certain amount of juice is pressed or "bled" from dark-skinned grapes.

Sangiovese *(sahn-joh-VEH-seh):* A red grape that is the most commonly planted variety in Italy, where it is used in producing Chianti's wines.

Sauvignon Blanc *(sew-vee-nyohn blahn):* An aromatic white grape variety, often crisp and sometimes even grassy in taste.

Semillon *(seh-mee-yohn):* A golden grape variety from southwest France, frequently used in blending with other varieties; spelled Sémillon in French.

Seyval Blanc *(say-vahl blahn):* A white grape Seyve-Villard hybrid often producing crisp wines and popular in Canada and the United States.

Sherry: A dry fortified wine from Spain, ranging in style from the pale *fino* to darker *oloroso.*

Shiraz *(shih-RAZZ):* Name given in Australia and South Africa to the Syrah grape; Shiraz-style designates a wine that is somewhat sweeter and riper than French Syrah.

Sparkling wine: Effervescent wine made according to the méthode champenoise; only wines made in France's Champagne region may bear the name "Champagne."

Steuben: A blue-black native American grape that is a cross between the Wayne and Sheridan grapes; first propagated by Cornell University's Geneva experiment station.

Super-Tuscan: Term used to describe wines made by blending Cabernet Sauvignon with Sangiovese, the traditional grape variety used in Chianti.

Symphony: An aromatic white grape that is a cross of Muscat of Alexandria and Grenache Gris, first propagated in California.

Syrah *(see-rah)*: One of the premier black grape varieties, thought to have originated in either Sicily or ancient Persia; widely grown in the Rhone region of France.

Tannat *(tah-nah)*: A black grape variety of Basque origin; noted for its deep color and high tannins.

Tannins: Chemical compounds from grape skins and pips that give wine an astringent taste.

Tempranillo *(tem-pra-NEE-yoh)*: A red grape variety from Spain that produces wines rich in color and often high in alcohol.

Terroir *(tehr-wahr)*: A French term that describes the totality of a vineyard's environment, particularly its climate and soil.

Tinta Cão *(TEEN-tah KAWM)*: A black grape once widely planted in Portugal's Douro region and one of the five varieties traditionally used to produce port; Portuguese for "red dog."

Touriga Nacional *(too-REE-gah nah-see-oh-NAL)*: A black grape that is generally considered the finest variety for port; also used to produce dry red wines.

Traminer Aromatico *(trah-mee-ner ah-roh-mah-tee-koh)*: A synonym for Gewurztraminer.

Traminette: An aromatic white grape that is a hybrid of Gewürztraminer and Riesling, first cultivated in 1968 at the University of Illinois.

Trebbiano *(treh-bee-AH-noh)*: A white grape variety, also called Ugni Blanc, that is the most widely planted white variety in Italy.

Varietal: A wine named for the dominant grape variety from which it is made; varietals may be pure (100%) or a blend consisting of at least 75% of the grape for which the wine is named.

Verdejo *(vehr-DAY-hoe)*: An aromatic white grape that is the primary variety in Spain's Rueda region.

Vermentino *(ver-men-TEE-noh)*: An aromatic white grape grown in Sardinia, Corsica, and the Languedoc-Roussillon region of France.

Vidal Blanc *(vee-dahl blahn)*: An aromatic white grape hybrid between Ugni Blanc and one of the parent grapes of Seyval Blanc that lends itself to sweet and late harvest wines; widely grown in Canada because of its hardiness.

Vignoles *(veen-yole)*: A French-American hybrid between the French-American Seibel 8665 grape and Pinot de Corton, a Pinot Noir clone; originally propagated in France in 1922 and named after the French town of Vignoles, the grape is now more commonly planted in the United States.

Villard Blanc: A white grape Seyve-Villard hybrid.

Vin de Paille *(van duh pie)*: French term designating a sweet white wine, traditionally made by drying grapes on mats of straw (*paille* in French).

Vin Gris *(van gree)*: A pale pink wine made from dark-skinned grapes, characterized by little skin contact with the juice.

Vinho Verde *(vee-nyo ver-day)*: A Portuguese wine that is light, acidic, and traditionally sold soon after fermenting; the term means "green wine" in English.

Viognier *(vee-oh-nyee-eh)*: An aromatic white grape variety from the Rhone region in France and increasingly planted in California and Virginia.

Virginia Green: A state-wide program whose aim is to preserve and protect the environment by promoting eco-friendly practices in Virginia's tourism industry.

Viticulture: The science and practice of growing grapes.

Yeast: A single-celled agent whose key role in fermenting grape juice into wine was first described by Louis Pasteur; yeast strains may be cultivated or naturally occurring.

White Moore's Diamond: A white native American cross between the Concord and the Iona; grown primarily in New York and Pennsylvania for juice and dry white wine.

Wine: Any fermented fruit juice, most often associated with grapes; in the United States, table wines are between 7% and 14% alcohol strength.

Zinfandel: A black grape variety widely planted in California; determined by DNA analysis to be closely related to the Italian Primitivo variety.

ALPHABETICAL INDEX OF WINERIES

GENERAL INDEX

ABOUT THE AUTHOR

Donna R. Gough has enjoyed learning about and appreciating wines since first discovering them during a year in France. Since then, she has visited vineyards in the United States, Canada, Germany, and Chile. A geographer and linguist, she lives in Northern Virginia with her family. She blogs about wine and shares photos from her visits to Virginia wineries at www.facebook.com/goughpubs and about cooking, wine pairings, and Virginia travel in general at goughpubs.wordpress.com.

Back cover photos: Cabernet Franc grapes at Sunset Hills Vineyard (top), vineyards at Chateau O'Brien at Northpoint (bottom)